ANSELM OF CANTERBURY
VOLUME TWO

ANSELM
OF CANTERBURY

VOLUME TWO

PHILOSOPHICAL FRAGMENTS
DE GRAMMATICO
ON TRUTH
FREEDOM OF CHOICE
THE FALL OF THE DEVIL
THE HARMONY OF THE FOREKNOWLEDGE, THE
PREDESTINATION, AND THE GRACE OF GOD
WITH FREE CHOICE

Edited and Translated by
Jasper Hopkins and Herbert Richardson

THE EDWIN MELLEN PRESS
Toronto and New York

Library of Congress Catalog Card Number 74-19840
ISBN 0-88946-250-x (Vol. II)
0-88946-977-6 (Set of 4 vols.)

First Edition by The Edwin Mellen Press 1976
© 1976 The Edwin Mellen Press
Toronto and New York

CONTENTS

Translators' Preface	vii
Philosophical Fragments	1
De Grammatico	37
On Truth	75
Freedom of Choice	103
The Fall of the Devil	127
The Harmony of the Foreknowledge, the Predestination, and the Grace of God with Free Choice	179
Abbreviations	225
Notes	226

TRANSLATORS' PREFACE

The dialogues and fragments contained in this volume attest amply to St. Anselm's philosophical genius. In them he raises important questions about both the relation of logic to language and the relation of language to reality. He distinguishes (1) *dicere secundum formam* from *dicere secundum rem*, (2) *significatio per se* from *significatio per aliud*, and (3) *dicere proprie* from *dicere improprie*. Moreover, he sketches a theory of paronymy which helps to settle various puzzles arising in connection with names (e.g., "illiterate") that derive from other names (e.g., "illiteracy") and that function as both nouns and adjectives. In the process he commits himself to the Aristotelian distinction between substance and accident, makes an exegetical comment on Aristotle's *Categories*, and appropriates from *De Interpretatione* (as mediated through Boethius) Aristotle's definitions of ὄνομα (*"nomen"*), ῥῆμα (*"verbum"*), and λόγος (*"oratio"*). Indeed, by way of Boethius, Anselm is familiar with, and appeals to, Aristotle's rules governing the validity of syllogisms. And he illustrates how, in some cases, the premises of invalid syllogisms can be reformulated so as to entail a different conclusion from the one which does not follow validly.

In a different vein, Anselm's thinking is unified around a notion of *rectitudo* which serves as the basis for his respective definitions of "truth" ("rightness perceptible only to the mind"), "justice" ("uprightness-of-will kept for its own sake"), and "freedom" ("the ability to keep uprightness-of-will for its own sake"). In the case of truth he distinguishes two truths which a statement, a thought, an action, or a volition may have. And he argues that just as time exists independently of any given temporal object, so truth exists independently of any given thing which is true. As for justice, he regards its absence from the will as an unqualified evil which conduces to moral unbridledness in much the way that the absence of reins conduces to a horse's running wild. Here Anselm has recourse to Augustine's teaching that evil is not a substance but is a privation. Finally, in the case of freedom Anselm considers free choice to be an inalienable human possession. But he qualifies his theory in such a way that he stands with Augustine over against Pelagius.

The subtle richness of Anselm's ideas can only be hinted at in this brief preface. But, at the outset, nothing more is needed. For Anselm himself is a superb pedagogue. His philosophical dialogues make their points without sophistry, without dramatization, without dogmatism. Thereby they coax the gratified reader into examining the entire corpus of treatises so that he may observe for himself their coherent unfolding. For only then can he make his own peace with their claims — perhaps by instigating his own quarrel with their arguments.

. . . .

The present translations of *De Veritate, De Libertate Arbitrii,* and *De Casu Diaboli* are more literal than those published earlier in *Truth, Freedom, and Evil: Three Philosophical Dialogues* (Harper & Row, 1967), now out of print. Likewise, the translation of the *Philosophical Fragments* is somewhat more literal than the one which appears in *A Companion to the Study of St. Anselm* (Minneapolis: University of Minnesota Press, 1972).

Since the present rendering of *De Concordia* is based upon the one which appeared in *Trinity, Incarnation, and Redemption: Theological Treatises* (Harper & Row, 1970), we acknowledge G. Stanley Kane and Charles Waldrop, who collaborated with us on the earlier version.

Jasper Hopkins
Philosophy Department, University of Minnesota

Herbert Richardson
St. Michael's College, University of Toronto

NOTE: Where, for clarification, words from the Latin text have been inserted into the translations, the following rule has been employed: When the Latin term is noted exactly as it appears in the Latin text, parentheses are used; when the case-endings of nouns have been transformed to the nominative, brackets are used.

The numbering of the Psalms accords with the Douay Version and, in parentheses, with the King James (Authorized) Version.

The symbol ∼ indicates negation.

PHILOSOPHICAL FRAGMENTS

PHILOSOPHICAL FRAGMENTS[1]

EXORDIUM[2]

23:1 *Student.* There are many [notions] which I have long been wanting you to clarify. Among these are [the notions of] ability and inability, possibility and impossibility, freedom and necessity.[3] I list these together in my inquiry because knowledge about them seems to me to be interconnected. Let me disclose in part what disturbs me with regard to them, so that after you have given me a satisfactory analysis of them, I may go on more easily to other matters, at which I am aiming.

We sometimes speak of there being an ability in a thing in which there is no ability. For everyone acknowledges that whatever can, can by virtue of an ability. Therefore, when we say "What does not exist can exist," we are saying that there is an ability in that which does not exist — for example, when we say that a house which does not yet exist can exist. But I cannot comprehend this. For in that which does not exist, there is no ability.

Moreover, let me say: That which does not in any respect exist has no ability. Therefore, it does not have either the ability to exist or the ability not to exist. Hence, it follows that what does not exist both cannot exist and cannot not exist. Indeed, from the one negation — viz., that what does not exist cannot exist — it follows that what does not exist is not possible to be and is impossible to be and is necessary not to be. But if we accept the other negation — by which we say that what does not exist cannot not exist — we find that what does not exist is not possible not to be and is impossible not to be and is necessary to be. Therefore, from the fact that what does not in any respect exist cannot exist, it is impossible to be and is necessary not to be. But from the fact that it cannot not exist, there follows that it is impossible not to be and is necessary to be.

23:25 Furthermore, what cannot exist is not able to be; and what is not able to be is unable to be. Similarly, what cannot not exist is not able not to be; and what is not able not to be is unable not to be. Therefore, what does not exist both cannot exist and cannot not exist: it is unable to be and is unable not to be. But "What is unable to be is able not to be" and "What is unable not to be is able to be" are in equal measure true. Therefore, what does not exist is able and unable to be; and, similarly, it is able [and unable] not to be. Hence, it has in equal measure both an ability and an inability to be and not to be.

24:8 But all these [results] are very absurd. For "It is impossible to be" and "It is impossible not to be" are never true [of something] at the same time; nor are, "It is necessary to be" and "It is necessary not to be"; nor, "[There is in it] an ability to be (or not to be)" and "[There is in it] an inability to be (or not to be)." Hence, if these [pairs of statements] are inconsistent, then the premise from which they follow is also inconsistent: viz., "What does not in any respect exist both cannot exist and cannot not exist, since it has no ability." But I cannot at all discern that this premise is false.

24:16 Concerning impossibility and necessity, I am also troubled by the fact that we say that something (e.g., to lie) is impossible for God or that God is something (e.g., that He is just) of necessity.[4] For *impossibility* suggests powerlessness, and *necessity* suggests compulsion; but in God there is neither powerlessness nor compulsion. For if God keeps to the truth because of a powerlessness to lie or if He is just because of compulsion, then He is not freely truthful or just.[5] But if you answer that in the case of God this *impossibility* and this *necessity* signify an insuperable strength,[6] then I ask: why is this strength indicated by names signifying weakness?

These [problems], and perhaps others as well, cast me into a quandary about [the notions of] ability and possibility and their opposites, and about [the notions of] freedom and necessity. Although these questions of mine are puerile, nevertheless I ask you to teach me — for I admit I do not know — what to answer if someone else asks them of me.[7]

25:1 *Teacher.* Even if your questions seem to you to be puerile, nevertheless the answers to them are not so easy for me that these answers seem to me to be anile. For, indeed, I already see from a distance that when I begin to reply, you will summon me to greater matters. Nevertheless, even if I am not able to do all that you have asked, I ought not to turn away from what I am able to do with the help of God.

PRAENOTANDA

T. In order to examine the questions which you pose, I deem it necessary to set forth something about the verb "to do" ("*facere*") and to explain what is properly called one's own possession, [or one's prerogative].[8] Otherwise, when we come to need these [analyses] we shall have to make a digression because of them. Only, keep your questions well in mind.

S. If only you return to what has been asked, whatever you place first will not displease me.

FACERE[9]

T. We have the practice of using the verb "to do" in place of every other verb, whether finite or infinite,[10] and regardless of its signification.[11] (We even use "to do" in place of "not to do.") For when we ask about someone "What (How) is he doing?": if we consider the matter carefully, [we see that] here "doing" is used in place of any verb that can be given in reply; and every verb given in reply is used in place of "doing." For to one asking "What (How) is he doing?" there is not rightly given in reply any verb in which there is not understood the doing which is being asked about. For example, when we reply "He is reading" or "He is writing," it is the same as saying "He is doing this, viz., reading" or "He is doing this, viz., writing."

25:23   However, any verb can be given in answer to one asking the foregoing question. In many cases this point is evident — as, for example, "He is singing," "He is composing." But in other cases it may be less evident — as are the following: viz., "He is," "He lives," "He is powerful" (*potest*), "He owes" (*debet*), "He is named" (*nominatur*), "He is summoned" (*vocatur*). But no one would reproach us if to someone who asked "What (How) is he doing?" we were to reply: "He is in church," or "He is living as a good man [lives]," or "He is powerful over the whole domain in which he lives," or "He owes much money," or "He is named [i.e., is renowned] above all his neighbors," or "Wherever he is, he is summoned before all others." Therefore, if there is someone who knows how to do it appropriately, any verb can at times be given in answer to one who asks "What (How) is he doing?" Thus, whatever verbs are used in reply to one who asks "What (How) is he doing?" are (as I said) used in the answer in place of "doing"; and in the question "doing" is used in place of these verbs. For the question answered is the question asked, and the question asked is the question answered.

26:5   In fact, everything of which a verb is predicated is a cause of there being what is signified by this verb. And in common parlance every cause is said to do that of which it is a cause.[12] Therefore, everything of which a verb is predicated does (causes) what is signified by that verb. For — not to discuss those verbs which properly signify a doing (e.g., the verb "to run," and other verbs of this kind) — the point I am making is evidenced even in the case of other verbs, which seem far removed from properly signifying a doing. For example, in the foregoing way, whoever is sitting is doing (causing) sitting, and whoever is enduring is doing (causing) enduring — because if there were not one who was enduring, there would not be enduring.[13] And there would not be any naming unless there were that which is named. Nor would anything in any respect be said *to be* unless what is said to be were first conceived. So of whatever thing (*re*) a verb is predicated, in the foregoing manner a doing (causing) is signified — viz., the doing (causing) which is indicated by this verb. Therefore, with good reason the verb "to do" is in everyday discourse at times used in place of every other verb.

26:20 *S.* To one who is willing to understand, what you are saying is clear. Still, I do not yet understand for what purpose you are saying these things.

T. You will understand in what follows.[14]

. . . .

27:26 For when we say "A man is" or "A man is not," what is signified by the name "man" is conceived before it is said to be or not to be. And so, what is conceived is a cause of the fact that "to be" is predicated of it. Also, if we say "A man is an animal," *man* is a cause of there being, and being said to be, an animal. I do not mean that *man* is a cause of the existence of *animal*; rather, I mean that *man* is a cause of man's being, and being said to be, an animal. For by the name "man" we signify and conceive of man in his totality (*totus homo*); and in this totality *animal* is contained as a part.[15] In this way, then, the part here follows from the whole, because it is necessary that the part be where the whole is. Therefore, because in the name "man" we conceive of the whole man, *man* is a cause of man's being, and being said to be, an animal. For the conception of the whole is a cause of the part's being conceived in it and being predicated of it. In this way, then, of whatever thing "to be" is predicated — whether it is predicated simply (e.g., "A man is"), or whether it is predicated with an addition (e.g., "A man is an animal" or "A man is healthy"[16]) — the conception of this thing precedes and is a cause of this thing's being said to be (or not to be), and is a cause of the intelligibility of what is said. So of whatever thing (*re*) a verb is predicated, in the foregoing manner a doing (causing) is signified — viz., the doing (causing) which is indicated by this verb. Therefore, with good reason the verb "to do" is in everyday discourse at times used in place of every other verb, and every verb is said to be a doing.

28:13   For, indeed, even the Lord in the Gospel uses *"facere,"* (or *"agere,"* which means the same thing) in place of every other verb when He says: "Whoever does (*agit*) evil hates the light"[17] and "Whoever does (*facit*) the truth comes to the light."[18] Now, assuredly, he who does what he ought not or who does not do what he ought does evil. This point is understood to hold true, in a similar way, for every verb. For example, he does evil who is present where or when he ought not to be, or who is sitting or is standing where or when he ought not to be. And he does evil who is not present, not sitting, or not standing where and when he ought to be. But he does the truth who does what he ought and who does not do what he ought not. Likewise, he does the truth who is present or is sitting or is standing where and when he ought to be, and who is not present, not sitting, and not standing where and when he ought not to be.[19] In this way the Lord reduces every verb, whether positive or negative, to a doing.

28:26   There is a further consideration about the verb *"facere"*: viz., in how many modes common discourse uses it. Although this classification [of modes] is especially complex and very complicated, let me nevertheless say about it something which I think bears upon what we shall be saying later and which can be of some help to someone who wants to pursue this classification more carefully.

Some causes are called efficient causes (e.g., someone who composes a literary work); in comparison with these, others are not called efficient (e.g., the matter from which something is made).[20] Nevertheless, (as I said), every cause is said to do, and everything which is said to do is called a cause. Now, whatever is said to do (*facere*) either causes (*facit*) something to be or causes something not to be. Therefore, every doing can be said either (A) to cause to be or (B) to cause not to be. These two are contrary affirmations whose negations are (C) "not to cause to be" and (D) "not to cause not to be." Now, the affirmation (A) "to cause to be" is sometimes used in place of the negation (D) "not to cause not to be"; and, conversely, "not to cause not to be" is sometimes used in place of "to cause to be." Likewise, (B) "to cause not to be" and (C) "not to cause to be" are used in place of each other. For example, sometimes the reason someone is said to *cause* evil things *to be* is that he does *not cause* them *not to be*; and sometimes the reason he is said not to cause evil things not to be is that he causes them to be. Likewise, sometimes the reason someone is said to *cause* good things *not to be* is that he does *not cause* them *to be*; and sometimes the reason he is said not to cause good things to be is that he causes them not to be.

29:20 Let us now understand *doing* (*causing*) in terms of a classification. Since a doing (causing) is always either in relation to being or in relation to not-being, (as has been said), we will be obliged to add "to be" or "not to be" to the distinct modes of doing (causing) in order for them to be clearly distinguished. Accordingly, we speak in six modes[21] about causing [to be]: in two modes when a cause (A.1) causes to be, or (A.2) does not cause not to be, that very thing which it is said to cause [to be]; and in four modes when it (A.3 – A.6) either does or does not cause something else to be or not to be. For, indeed, we say of any given thing "It causes something to be" either because it (1) causes-to-be the very thing which it is said to cause [to be], or because it (2) does not cause this very thing not to be, or because it (3) causes something else to be, or because it (4) does not cause something else to be, or because it (5) causes something else not to be, or because it (6) does not cause something else not to be.[22]

29:31 When someone who kills a man with a sword is said to cause him to be dead, [it is said] in the first mode. For he directly (*per se*)[23] causes the very thing which he is said to cause.

Regarding to-cause-to-be-dead I do not have an example of the second mode unless I posit the case of someone who can restore a dead man to life but who is unwilling to.[24] If this were the case in the present context, then he would in the second mode be said to cause the other to be dead, because he would *not cause* him *not to be dead*. In other matters examples are abundant — as, for instance, when we say that someone causes-to-be the evil things which he does not cause not to be, although he is able to [do so].

30:3 It is in terms of the third mode when we say of any given person "He has killed another" (i.e., "He has caused him to be dead") because he ordered that the other be killed, or because he caused the killer to have a sword, or because he brought an accusation against the man who was killed,[25] or [it is an instance of the third mode] even in the case where we say of the man who was killed "He killed himself" because he did something on account of which he was killed.[26] For, indeed, these persons did not themselves directly (*per se*) cause that very thing which they are said to cause — i.e., they did not directly kill or directly cause to be dead or to be killed. Rather, by *causing* something else, they indirectly (*per medium*) caused what they are said to cause.

It is in the fourth mode when we say that someone who did not give weapons to the slain man before he was killed — or who did not restrain the killer, or who did not do something which, had he done, the other would not have been killed — has killed him.[27] These men too did not kill the other directly (*per se*); rather, by *not causing* something else *to be* they have caused what they are said to cause.

30:16 It is the fifth mode when we say of someone "He has killed another" because by removing his weapons he caused the intended victim not to be armed, or by opening a door he caused the killer not to be confined where he was being detained. In this instance as well, the one who is said to have killed the other did not kill him directly (*per se*); rather he killed him indirectly (*per aliud*), by *causing* something else *not to be*.

It accords with the sixth mode when the one who did not cause the killer not to be armed, by removing his weapons, is accused of having killed the victim — or when the man who did not lead the intended victim away so that he would not be in the presence of the killer is so accused. These individuals too did not kill directly.

Rather, they killed indirectly — viz., by *not causing* something else *not to be*.

30:26 To-cause-not-to-be receives the same classification. For whatever is said to cause something not to be is said [to do so] either because it (1) causes that very thing not to be, or because it (2) does not cause that very thing to be, or because it (3) causes something else to be, or because it (4) does not cause something else to be, or because it (5) causes something else not to be, or because it (6) does not cause something else not to be.

Examples of these modes can be found in the case of killing a man, just as I have cited for to-cause-to-be.[28]

Just as in the first mode of causing-to-be the one who kills causes to be dead, so in the first mode of causing-not-to-be he *causes not to be living*.

But in the second mode I do not have an example of causing-not-to-be-living unless (as I did earlier) I posit the case of someone who can restore a dead man to life. For if he were unwilling to do this, we would say (in the second mode) "He causes not to be living" because he does *not cause to be living*. For even though to be dead is not the same thing as not to be living (for only what is deprived of life is dead, but many things which are not deprived of life are not living — e.g., a stone), nevertheless just as to kill is nothing other than to cause to be dead (and to cause not to be living) so to restore to life is the same as to cause to be living (and to cause not to be dead). In other matters there are many examples of this second mode. Indeed, he is said to cause goods not to be who does not cause them to be, although able to do so.

31:13 In the four remaining modes (viz., causing or not causing something else to be or not to be) the examples which have been cited for (A) to-cause-to-be are sufficient.

Let us now[29] speak about to-cause-not-to-be, which I have said also to consist of six modes. These modes are in every respect the same as those found in to-cause-to-be, except that here they are in to-cause-not-to-be and there they are in to-cause-to-be.

For here the first mode is when we say of a thing "It

causes not to be'' because the very thing which it is said to cause not to be it does cause not to be. For example, we say of someone who kills a man "He *causes* him *not to be living*" because he causes the very thing which he is said to cause.

The second mode is when we say of [a thing] "It causes not to be" because the thing which it is said to cause not to be it *does not cause to be*. In regard to causing a man to be living (or not to be living), I cannot give an example of this [second] mode unless I posit the case of someone who can cause a dead man to be living. In the present context, if he were not to do this, we would say "He causes the dead man not to be living" because he would *not cause* him *to be living*. In other matters examples are abundant. For instance, if someone whose job it is to cause a house to be lit up at night does not do what he ought to, we say "He causes the house not to be lit" because he does not cause it to be lit.

31:33 The third mode is when we say of [a thing] "It causes not to be" because it *causes* something else (i.e., something other than what it is said to cause not to be) *to be* — as, for example, when we say of someone "He caused the victim not to be living" because he caused the killer to have a sword.

The fourth mode is when we say of [a thing] "It causes not to be" because it *does not cause* something else *to be* — as, for example, when we say of someone "He caused the victim not to be living" because he did not cause him to be armed prior to his having been killed.

The fifth mode is when we say of a thing "It causes not to be" because it *causes* something else *not to be* — as, for example, when we say of someone "He caused another not to be living" because he caused him not to be armed prior to his having been killed.

The sixth mode is when a thing causes not-to-be because it *does not cause* something else *not to be* — as, for example, when someone (although he is able to do so) does not cause the killer not to be armed, by removing his weapons.

32:6 Note 1. Moreover, notice that although "to cause to

be" and "not to cause not to be" are used for each other, nevertheless they are different from each other. For, indeed, properly speaking, he causes to be who causes there to be what previously was not. But not only he who causes something to be but also he who does not cause anything either to be or not to be are, in equal measure, said not to cause not to be.

Likewise, to-cause-not-to-be and not-to-cause-to-be differ from each other. For, properly speaking, he causes not to be who causes there not to be what previously was. But not only he who causes there not to be what previously was but also he who does not cause either to be or not to be are, in equal measure, said not to cause to be.

Note 2. Indeed, I have taken these examples (which I have given of causing-to-be and of causing-not-to-be) from [the class of] efficient causes, since what I wanted to show appears more clearly in these causes. But just as the aforementioned six modes are discerned in efficient causes, so also they are found in nonefficient causes, if anyone cares to investigate them carefully.

S. I see this clearly.

T. Indeed,[30] I have taken these examples from [the class of] efficient causes, since what I want to show appears more clearly in these causes. Now, in the five modes after the first mode efficient causes do not cause what they are said to cause. Nevertheless — since the second mode does not cause not to be what the first mode causes to be, and since the third mode causes something else to be, and the fourth mode causes something else not to be, and the fifth mode does not cause something else to be, and the sixth mode does not cause something else not to be — efficient causes are said to cause what the first mode causes (as I have exemplified in every mode). Similarly, nonefficient causes are said to cause in accordance with the same modes.

For there are nonefficient proximate causes of the existence of what they are said to cause; and there are [nonefficient] remote causes of the existence of something else rather than of the existence of what [they are said to cause]. For example, a window which causes a house to be lighted is not an efficient cause but is only that through which light-rays [efficiently] cause [the house to be lighted]. Nevertheless, the window is a proximate cause of the existence of what it is said to cause; for through itself (*per se*) rather than through an intermediary (*per aliud*) it is a cause of there being what [it is said to cause]. This [cause] belongs to the first mode of causing, since what the window is said to cause to be it does (in its own way) cause to be. But if when the window is missing or when it is shuttered it is said to cause the house to be dark, this [cause] belongs to the second mode; for we say of the window "It causes the house to be dark" because it does not cause this very state of affairs [viz., the house's darkness] not to be. But if he who has made a window is said to cause a house to be lighted, or if he who has not made a window is said to cause a house to be dark, or if someone says that his own land nourishes him, then these are remote causes. For they do not cause through themselves (*per se*). Rather, the man [causes] by means of the window which he has made, or which (when he ought to have) he has not made; and the land [causes nourishment] by means of the produce which it has yielded.

Thus, those causes — whether they be efficient or nonefficient — which are in the first or the second mode can be called proximate causes; but the other causes [i.e., in modes 3 – 6] are remote causes.

33:9   The negations (C) "not to cause to be" and (D) "not to cause not to be" are divided into just as many modes [as the affirmations (A) and (B)]. This fact is recognizable in the examples which have been given for the modes of (A) causing-to-be and of (B) causing-not-to-be, if [in these tables] the affirmative modes are changed into negations and the negative modes are changed into affirmations. [This contradicting of each of the modes in the two affirmative tables transforms them into two corresponding negative tables.] However, for the four modes subsequent to the second mode [i.e., for modes 3 – 6], if anyone wants to keep here [i.e., in the negative tables] the same [lexical] order as I set forth above [i.e., in the affirmative tables], then let him state affirmatively in the third mode [of the negative tables] what I have stated negatively in the fourth mode [of the affirmative tables]; and let him state negatively in the fourth mode [of the negative tables] what was stated affirmatively in the third mode [of the affirmative tables]. And likewise let him do a similar thing with the fifth mode [of the negative tables] and the sixth mode [of the affirmative tables], and with the sixth mode [of the negative tables] and the fifth mode [of the affirmative tables].

33:17   Moreover, we must note that in the modes of the negative tables the first mode simply denies, without suggesting anything else. But the five subsequent modes [in the negative tables] have [this] negation in place of the contrary of its [i.e., the first mode's] affirmation.[31] For example,[32] he who revives someone is said, in the second mode, not-to-cause-him-to-be-dead in place of to-cause-him-not-to-be-dead; and he is said not-to-cause-him-not-to-be-living in place of to-cause-him-to-be-living. But he who (in the third mode) *causes* the intended victim *to be* armed, by giving him weapons, or who (in the sixth mode) *does not cause* him *not to be* armed, although able to remove his weapons, or who (in the fifth mode) *causes* the intending killer *not to be* armed, by removing his weapons, or who (in the fourth mode) by not giving weapons to the intending killer *does not cause* him *to be* armed: if he is said not to cause to be dead (or not to cause not to be living), he is understood to cause, as far as he can do so, not to be dead (and to cause to be living).

33:30   The same principle of classification which I cited for to-cause-to-be and to-cause-not-to-be obtains for whatever verb "to cause" is similarly conjoined with — as, for example, when I say "I cause you to do something" or "I cause you to write something," or "I cause something to be done" or "I cause something to be written." These modes which I have cited for "to cause" ("*facere*") are in a certain respect found in other verbs too. Although not every mode is found in every verb, nevertheless one or more are found in each verb — and especially in those verbs (such as "ought to" and "is able to") which are transitive to verbs. Indeed, when we say "I am able to read" or "I am able to be read [through my writings]," or "I ought to love" or "I ought to be loved," then "able to" and "ought to" are transitive to verbs.

33:40 There are also verbs which are transitive not to verbs but to some thing (*rem*) — as, for example, [when we say] "to eat bread" and "to cut wood." There are also verbs which are intransitive — as, for example, "to recline," "to sleep." Nonetheless, some of these intransitive verbs appear to be transitive to a verb — as, for example, when we say "The people sat down to eat and to drink, and they rose up to play."[33] But it is not so. [That is, it is not the case that such verbs (e.g., "to sit," "to arise") are transitive to a verb.] For it is not the case that just as we say "The people want to eat and to drink and to play" so we say "The people sat down to eat and to drink, and they rose up to play." For the latter is analyzed as "The people sat down in order to eat and drink, and they rose up in order to play."

Some modes, from the aforementioned ones, are also found in the verb "to be." Indeed, the first two modes are easily recognized; but the four subsequent ones — which cause or do not cause something else to be or not to be — are more difficult to detect, because there are many ways in which these modes cause and do not cause something else to be or not to be. Nevertheless, I shall say a few things about this matter. And by comparison with these statements [of mine] you will be able to notice in Scripture and in common discourse other points which I shall not mention.

34:16 The verb "to be" also imitates the verb "*facere*." For something is said to be what it is not — not because this something is what it is said to be but because it is something else which is the reason (*causa*) for what is said. For, indeed, someone is said[34] to be a foot for the lame and an eye for the blind — not because he is what he is said to be [viz., a foot, an eye], but because he is something else which serves the lame man in place of a foot and serves the blind man in place of an eye. Also, the lives of just individuals who are living amidst many toils because of their desire for eternal life are called happy — not

Philosophical Fragments

because their lives are in fact happy but because their present lives are a cause of their some day being happy.

A resemblance with the verb *"facere"* is also found in the verb "to have." For example, someone bereft of eyes is said to have eyes — not because he really has eyes but because he has someone else who does for him what eyes do. And he who does not have feet is said to have feet simply because he has something else which serves him in place of feet.

34:29 We often attribute a name or a verb *improperly* to some object [and do so] because that object to which the name or the verb is improperly attributed [stands in one of the following relations] to the object to which the name or the verb is *properly* attributed:

It is similar to it.
It is its cause, effect, genus, species, whole, or part.
It has the same capability.
It is its external form [i.e., shape][35] or a thing shaped according to that form (True, every external form is similar to the thing shaped according to it, but not every similarity is an external form or a thing shaped according to that form.)
In some other way (as I began to say) than through external form it signifies, or is signified by, that whose name or verb it [improperly] receives.
It is its content or container,

or they are related as the one who uses some thing and the thing which he uses. It seems to me that as often as this [kind of attribution occurs, it is] this [improperly spoken of object] which is said to do [what the other object really does].

34:40 All the modes which I have cited for the verb *"facere"* are sometimes found in other verbs as well; although not all of the modes are found in every particular verb, one or more are present. For example, every verb which is properly predicated of a thing (so that the thing does what it is said to do) is predicated according to the first mode. Some examples of this are: "He reclines," "He sits," "He runs" (when he does so with his own feet), "He builds a house" (when he does so with his own hands), "It is day," "The sun shines," or something else. But if it is not the case that the thing does that which it is said to do, then we are predicating in accordance with some mode other than the first. Some examples of this are: when someone who orders [a house to be built] but does not do the actual work is said to build a house; or when we say that a horseman runs, although he himself does not run but causes his horse to run. Therefore, as often as we hear a verb being predicated of some object which is not doing what it is being said [to do], then a careful observer will find [that this is being said] in one of the five modes (which I have cited) subsequent to the first mode.

35:14 For, indeed, when someone says to me "I ought to be loved by you," he is speaking improperly.[36] For if he *ought*, then he has an obligation to be loved by me. And so he ought to demand from himself that he be loved by me, for he is [the one who is] under obligation. (Moreover, if he does not discharge his obligation, he sins.) But even though this is the way he is saying it, this is not the way he means it. Accordingly, "He ought to be loved by me" is said because he is a cause of my obligation to love him. For if he deserved [my love], he was a cause of my obligation to love him; and if it is not the case that because of his action he deserved [my love], then by the mere fact that he is a man, he has within himself a reason (*causa*) for my obligation to love him. Therefore, just as we say "He causes it" of someone who does not [directly] cause a thing but who is in one of the aforesaid modes a cause of someone else's [directly] causing this thing (as I have shown above), so we say "He is under this obligation" of him who is not under an obligation but who in some way causes someone else to be under that obligation; for he is a cause of the other's being obliged. After the same fashion, we say "The poor ought to receive from the wealthy," even though the poor are not under obligation;[37] rather, they are something else, viz., in need; and this [condition] is the reason (*causa*) why they cause the wealthy to be obliged to expend money.[38]

36:3 We also say that we are not-obliged-to-sin in place of saying that we are obliged-not-to-sin. Yet if the matter is properly considered [we see that] not everyone who does what he is not obliged to do sins. For, indeed, just as to-be-obliged is the same as to-be-under-obligation, so not-to-be-obliged is nothing other than not-to-be-under-obligation. Now, it is not always the case that a man sins when he does what he is not under obligation to do. For, indeed, a man is not under obligation to marry, for he is permitted to maintain his virginity.[39] It follows, then, that he is not obliged to marry. And yet, if he does marry he does not sin. Therefore, it is not always the case — provided "not obliged to" is properly understood — that a man sins when he does what he is not obliged to do. Nevertheless, no one denies that a man ought to marry. Therefore, he is both obliged and not obliged. Now, if you recall what has already been said, then [you will see that] just as we say "not to cause to be" in place of "to cause not to be," so we say "not to be obliged to do" in place of "to be obliged not to do." And so, where "to be obliged not to sin" is found, "not to be obliged to sin" is said in place of it. Our custom [of speaking] has adopted this latter expression to such an extent that nothing else is understood by it than "to be obliged not to sin."

36:18 But as for our saying that if a man wants to marry, then he ought to marry: "ought to marry" is said in place of "is not obliged not to marry," just as earlier I showed that "to cause to be" is said in place of "not to cause not to be." Similarly, then, just as we say "not to be obliged to do" in place of "to be obliged not to do," so we say "to be obliged to do" in place of "not to be obliged not to do." However, the expression "to be obliged to do" [i.e., "ought to do"] can be understood in the sense in which we say that God ought to rule over everything.[40] For it is not the case that God is obliged with respect to anything; rather, all other things ought to be subject to Him. Therefore, we say that God ought to rule over all other things because He is the cause that all other things ought to be subject to Him — even as I said that the poor *ought* to receive from the wealthy because within them is the reason (*causa*) why the wealthy ought to contribute to them. In this sense, then, we can say that a man ought to marry. For everything which is someone's possession, [or prerogative], ought to be subject to his will. Now, each man who has not vowed chastity has the prerogative either to marry or not to marry. Accordingly, since to marry or not to marry ought to be in accordance with his wishes, we say that if he wants to he ought to marry, and if he does not want to he ought not to marry.[41]

37:6   Now, when we ask God to forgive us our sins, it is not to our advantage for God to do for us precisely what our words say. For if He forgives us our sins, He neither blots them out nor removes them from us. But when we pray that [our] sins be forgiven us, what we are asking is not that they themselves be forgiven us but that the debts which we owe for our sins be forgiven us. For, indeed, since [our] sins are the cause of (and do cause) our owing the debts which we need to have forgiven us, we pray that the sins be forgiven, although we ought to pray that the debts be forgiven. In this case, what we desire is not that the sins be forgiven us but that the debts which the sins have caused be forgiven us. This fact is evident in the Lord's Prayer, where we pray "Forgive us our debts."[42]

Thus it happens that a man typically says to someone who burns down his house or causes him some other detriment: "Restore to me the damage you have caused." And the one who has burned down the house says: "Forgive me the damage I have caused you." [But we do] not [take these statements to mean] that the damage must be restored or forgiven. Rather, [we take them to mean that] what has been removed because of the damage must be restored, and that what must be paid because of the damage must be forgiven.

For the same reason, the Lord says that those whom we mercifully forgive and to whom we mercifully give "will give into your bosom a good measure, pressed down, shaken together, and running over."[43] For since those to whom mercy is shown are a cause of mercy being returned to men who show it, the former are said to return mercy to the latter.

VELLE, VOLUNTAS

37:29   We say "to will to be" in the same six modes as we say "to cause to be."[44] Likewise, we say "to will not to be" in just as many different modes as we say "to cause not to be."

It is noteworthy that sometimes we so will [something] that, if we can, we cause the occurrence of what we will — as, for example, when a sick man wills health. For if he can, he causes himself to be healthy; and if he cannot, nevertheless he would cause it if he could. This willing can be called an *efficient* will, since insofar as it can it effects the existence of what it wills.

Sometimes, however, we will that which we are able to cause and yet do not cause. Still, if it does occur we are pleased by its occurrence and approve of it.[45] For example, if a poor, naked man whom I am unwilling to clothe were to tell me that he is naked because I want him to be naked or because I do not want him to be clothed, I might answer that I want him to be clothed and not to be naked. Moreover, I approve of his being clothed rather than being naked, even though I do not cause him to be clothed. The will by which I thus want the man to be clothed can be called an *approving* will.

38:14   We also will in another way — as, for example, if a creditor wills, as a concession, to accept from a debtor barley in place of the wheat which the debtor cannot pay. We can call this will merely a *conceding* will, for the creditor prefers wheat but concedes the debtor's paying with barley because of the latter's indigence.

Moreover, it is customary to say that someone wills a thing which he neither approves nor concedes but only permits (although able to prevent it).[46] For example, when a ruler does not will to restrain robbers and plunderers in his dominion, we say that he wills the evils which they do (even though these evils displease him), since he wills to permit them.

38:24   Now, it seems to me that every kind of willing is contained within this fourfold classification. Of these four different kinds of will, that which I have called the efficient will causes (insofar as it can) what it wills; and it also approves, concedes, and permits. But the approving will does not cause what it wills; it only approves, concedes, and permits. And (except for the sake of something else) the conceding will neither causes nor approves what it wills; it only concedes and permits. And the permissive will neither causes nor approves nor concedes what it wills; it only permits this thing — though disapproving it.

Divine Scripture makes reference to all four kinds of willing. Let me give a few examples of this. For instance, when Scripture says of God "He has done whatsoever He has willed to do"[47] and "He is merciful to whom He wills to be,"[48] this will is an efficient will; and it belongs to the first mode of willing-to-be (after the fashion of causing-to-be), because it wills the very thing it is said to will.

But when Scripture says "He hardens whom He wills to,"[49] this will is a permissive will and belongs to the second mode of willing-to-be, since the reason He is said to will-to-be-hard is that He does not will (by means of an efficient will) not-to-be-hard (i.e., He does not will to cause not to be hard). On the other hand, if the reason we say "He wills to harden" is that He does not will to soften, the meaning is the same, and this will is likewise a permissive will. But it belongs to the fourth mode of willing-to-be. For the reason God is being said to will to harden is that He does not will something else to be, viz., [He does not will] to be softened.[50] For He who softens causes to be softened and causes not to be hardened.

39:21 Now, when we hear that "God wills for every man to be saved,"[51] this will is an approving will. Like to-will-to-harden, it belongs to the second mode of willing-to-be, since it does not will to cause not to be saved; and it belongs to the fourth mode because it does not will for something else to be (i.e., it does not will, by an efficient will, for a man to be condemned — i.e., it does not will to cause something on the basis of which he would be condemned). This verse is directed against those who say that the will of God is the cause of their being unjust (rather than just) and of their not being saved — although the injustice for which they are condemned comes from themselves and does not come from the will of God.

If we say "God wills for virginity to be kept," in the case of those whom He causes to keep it, then His will is an efficient will in the first mode of willing-to-be. But in the case of other men this will is an approving will, because God does not will (with an efficient will) for their virginity not to be kept (second mode), or does not will for their virginity to be violated (fourth mode).

CAUSAE

40:1 Some causes are called efficient causes — for instance, a craftsman (for he produces his own work) and wisdom (which makes someone wise). By comparison with these, other causes are not called efficient causes (e.g., the matter from which something is made, and the place and time in which spatial and temporal things occur). Nonetheless, every cause — each in its own way — is said to do, and everything which is said to do is called a cause.

Every cause does (*facit*) something. One [kind of] cause causes (*facit*) — and is a cause of — the existence of what it is said to cause either to be or not to be; another [kind of] cause does not cause the existence of what it is said [to cause], but is only a cause of what is said. For example, both a guard and Herod are, in equal measure, said to have killed John [the Baptist], since both caused (and were causes of) the occurrence of that which they are said to have caused. And a resemblance — viz., that the Lord Jesus during infancy and childhood dwelt with Joseph as if He were his son — caused (and was a cause of) His being called (but not of His actually being) the son of Joseph. God granting, I shall first say something about the cause which causes the existence of what it is said to cause; and afterwards[52] I shall speak about the other [kind of] cause.

40:18 Some causes of this kind are proximate causes. They do through themselves (*per se*) that which they are said to do, with no other cause intervening between them and the effect which they cause. And there are remote causes, which do what they are said to do, but do so not through themselves but only through one or more intermediary causes. For example, the man who orders that a fire be set, and the man who sets the fire, and the fire itself — all cause burning. However, through itself and without any

Anselm of Canterbury

intermediate cause between itself and its effect, the fire causes [burning]. But he who sets-on-fire causes burning by the sole intermediary of fire. And he who orders that the fire be set causes burning by means of two other intermediate causes, viz., a fire and the man who sets the fire. Thus, some causes do through themselves that which they are said to do, whereas others — because they are remote causes — do something else which, nonetheless, produces the same effect. Nevertheless, it sometimes happens that an effect is attributed to a cause which causes something else rather than to a cause which through itself causes the same [effect] — as, for example, when we impute to a magistrate what is done by his command and authority, and when we say that the man who does something because of which he is killed, is killed by himself rather than by someone else.

41:3 Now, just as some efficient causes cause proximately and through themselves the very thing which they are said to cause, whereas others cause remotely and by means of intermediaries [what they are said to cause] — so it is in the case of nonefficient causes. For example, iron is a proximate [material] cause of a sword; in its own way and through itself (*per se*) it causes the sword, and does so without the presence of any intermediate cause. And the earth of which the iron is made is a remote cause of the sword, and causes it through something else (*per aliud*), i.e., through an intermediary (*per medium*), viz., iron. For every cause has other causes of itself. [This chain of causation continues] until [it reaches] the Supreme Cause of all things, viz., God, who, although He is the cause of everything that is something, has no cause. Moreover, every effect has a plurality of causes of different kinds — except for the first effect [which has only one cause], since only the Supreme Cause created everything else. In fact, in the killing of one man there are several causes: he who does the killing, he who orders the killing, the reason for which the victim is killed, and also (as necessary conditions) the place and the time [of the killing], and several other causes as well.

Moreover, some causes are said to cause by doing

[something], others by not doing [anything] — and sometimes not only by not doing [anything] but also by not even existing. For he who does not prevent evil things is said to cause them to be, and he who does not cause good things is said to cause them not to be. Similarly, just as when learning is present it causes good things to be and evil things not to be, so when learning is not present, it is said to cause, by its absence, evil things to be and good things not to be. However, causes of this last kind are included among those which are said to cause by not doing [anything].

41:25 Although quite frequently causes are said to cause through something else (rather than through themselves), i.e., through an intermediary (and thus in this case they can be called remote causes), nevertheless every cause has its own proximate effect, which it causes through itself and for which it is a proximate cause. For example, he who kindles a flame is a proximate cause of the flame; and through the medium of the flame he sets a fire, of which he is a remote cause. Therefore, when a cause is proximate, it is properly said to cause, since it causes through itself; but when it is remote, the reason it is said to cause [what it is said to cause] is that it causes something else.

Every cause is either a being or a not-being. And, likewise, every effect is either a being or a not-being; for every cause either causes to be or causes not to be. Now, by "a (state of) being" I mean anything, [or any state of affairs], which is spoken of without negation — whether it is spoken of with one word or with more than one word. And by "a (state of) not-being" I mean what is spoken of by way of denial. When the sun is spoken of, a being is spoken of, but it is not yet signified to be a cause. Likewise, when I say "shines," I speak of something, but I do not yet signify that it is the effect of anything. But when I say "The sun shines," [I signify that] the sun is a cause and shining is an effect; and each is something and an existent, because the sun has its own being and causes light to be. Therefore, in this example, the cause is a being, and the effect is a being. However, if I say "The
42:2 sun causes night not to be," here the cause is a being but

the effect is a (state of) not-being. In a similar way, I speak of a (state of) being by means of more than one word. For example, the sun's being above the horizon (*terram*) is something and causes day to be and night not to be. In this example being causes both being and not-being. Moreover, the sun's not being above the horizon causes night to be and day not to be. In this example (*prolatione*) not-being causes both being and not-being. Just as what is said to cause is obviously a cause, so what in some respect or other is signified to be a cause causes that of which it is said to be a cause. For example, to say "Because of the sun's presence it is day and not night" or "Because of the sun's absence it is night and not day" is tantamount to saying "The sun's presence causes it to be day and not to be night" and "The sun's absence causes it to be night and not to be day."[53] Thus, he who says "My knees are weak from fasting, and my flesh is changed because of oil,"[54] is saying the same thing as: "Fasting has weakened my knees; oil has changed my flesh." But fasting [has caused weakness] because it was present; and oil [has caused a change] because it was absent, i.e., because it was not present. For often we say that a cause causes to be and not to be through its presence and absence — even though we do not explicitly append the words "presence" and "absence." For example, we might say that the sun causes day to be and night not to be, and causes day not to be and night to be. But it causes the one state of affairs by its presence, the other by its absence.

ALIQUID

42:22   We speak of something (*aliquid*) in four modes.

1. For we properly label as something that which is spoken of by a name of its own and is conceived by the mind and exists in reality — as is true of a stone or a tree. For these latter have their own names and are conceived by the mind and exist in reality.

2. We also speak of as something that which has a name and is conceived by the mind, but does not exist in reality — as, for example, a chimera. For by the name

"chimera" there is signified a mental concept of a kind of animal; nevertheless a chimera does not exist in reality.

3. It is also our custom to speak of as something that which has only a name (without there being in our minds any concept corresponding to this name) and which altogether lacks existence — as, for example, injustice and nothing.[55] For we call injustice something when we state that someone who is punished on account of injustice is punished on account of something. And we call nothing something[56] if we say either "Something is nothing" or "Something is not nothing." For whether [either] statement is true or whether it is false, we say that something is affirmed of something or that something is denied of something. Nevertheless, in our minds there is no concept of injustice and of nothing, even though they signify, even as do infinite names. For, indeed, to signify[57] is not the same as to form something in the understanding. For, in fact, "not-man" signifies, because it causes the hearer to understand that *man* is not contained in (but is removed from) its signification. Nevertheless, *not-man* does not form in the understanding something which is signified by this utterance — as *man* does form a concept, which the name "man" signifies. Thus, "injustice" signifies the removal of required justice and does not posit anything else in the understanding; and "nothing" signifies the removal of something and does not posit anything in the understanding.

4. We also speak of as something that which does not have a name of its own and does not have a concept and does not have any existence — as, for example, when we call not-being something and say that not-being is. For instance, when we say that the sun's not being above the horizon (*terram*) causes it not to be day: if every cause is called something and if every effect is called something, then we shall not deny that its not being day and the sun's not being above the horizon are something, since the one is a cause and the other an effect. And [in the following case] we say that not-being *is*: when someone says that something is not the case and we reply by stating that the matter is as he says it is. Yet, if we were to speak prop-

erly, we ought rather to say that the matter is not, even as he says it is not.

Therefore, although we speak of something in four modes, one thing is properly called something, whereas it is not the case that the others are [properly called] something. Instead, they are as-if something, because we speak of them as if they were something.

DE POTESTATE

44:1 Ability is an aptitude-for-doing. I use "doing" here in place of every verb, finite or infinite, which occurs in ordinary discourse. For example, he does rightly who speaks or sits or stands when he ought to, and who wills or endures what he ought to, and who is where and when he ought to be. But he does wrongly who does not speak or sit or stand when he ought to, and who does not will or endure what he ought to, and who is not where or when he ought to be. Moreover, he does wrongly who does not do what he ought to; and he does rightly who does not do what he ought not to do. Therefore, it is evident that "to do" is used in place of every verb, finite or infinite– and even in place of "not to do."

So ability is an aptitude-for-doing; and every aptitude-for-doing is an ability. But here we must be careful not to take aptitude-for-doing (*aptitudo ad faciendum*) and aptitude-to-do (*aptitudo faciendi*) as exact equivalents. For every aptitude-for-doing is also an aptitude-to-do; but not every aptitude-to-do is also an aptitude-for-doing. For example, that aptitude-to-write (*aptitudo scribendi*) which is also an aptitude-for-writing (*aptitudo ad scribendum*) exists even before anything is written, and it is called the ability-to-write. But that aptitude-to-write which is also an aptitude-at-writing (*aptitudo in scribendo*), and in accordance with which we say [of someone that] he writes aptly, does not precede the writing and is not an ability to write; rather, it is the effect of the ability to write. For someone writes aptly because he has a prior ability to write aptly. It is not the case that the writing *can* be done aptly because it *is* done aptly.[58]

44:21 However, we have said "aptitude for doing" and not simply "aptitude for something," because there is an aptitude-for-something (e.g., the aptitude of clothing for the body) which is not an aptitude-for-doing, and this [aptitude-for-something] is not an ability. For although clothing is called apt for the body, it is not for that reason said to be able. Therefore, it was right to say that ability is an aptitude-for-doing. For in that it is called an aptitude, it is distinguished from everything which is not an aptitude. And in that it is specified to be an aptitude *for doing*, it is distinguished from every other [kind of] aptitude — whether from that aptitude which is not an aptitude for something (as, for example, is aptitude at writing) or from that aptitude which is an aptitude for something but not for doing (as, for example, the aptitude which clothing has for the body — an aptitude which can better be called [in Latin] "*aptitudo corpori*" [than "*aptitudo ad corpus*"], for clothing is said to be *apta corpori*). Hence, this definition of "ability" contains neither more nor less than it ought to. (However, this definition of "ability" is constructed in accordance with our way of speaking and not in accordance with the proper signification of the word "ability.") For this definition of "ability" accounts for whatever in any respect is able. For example, wood is able to be cut; and a man is able to cut. Wood is able to be cut because it has an aptitude for being cut; and a man is able to cut because he has an aptitude for cutting.

TRANSLATORS' APPENDIX
TO THE
PHILOSOPHICAL FRAGMENTS

Diagram I: "To Cause Someone to Be Dead"

Affirmative Tables

Table A: "To Cause to Be Dead"
1. A directly causes C to be dead.
2. A directly causes C to be dead, because A does not cause C not to be dead.
3. A causes C to be dead, because A causes B to be armed.
4. A causes C to be dead, because A does not cause C to be armed.
5. A causes C to be dead, because A causes C not to be armed.
6. A causes C to be dead, because A does not cause B not to be armed.

Table B: "To Cause Not to Be Living"
1. A directly causes C not to be living.
2. A directly causes C not to be living, because A does not cause C to be living.
3. A causes C not to be living, because A causes B to be armed.
4. A causes C not to be living, because A does not cause C to be armed.
5. A causes C not to be living, because A causes C not to be armed.
6. A causes C not to be living, because A does not cause B not to be armed.

Negative Tables

Table C: "Not to Cause to Be Living"
1. A does not directly cause C to be living.
2. A does not directly cause C to be living, because A directly causes C not to be living.
3. A does not cause C to be living, because A causes B to be armed.

Anselm of Canterbury

4. A does not cause C to be living, because A does not cause C to be armed.
5. A does not cause C to be living, because A causes C not to be armed.
6. A does not cause C to be living, because A does not cause B not to be armed.

Table D: "Not to Cause Not to Be Dead"
1. A does not directly cause C not to be dead.
2. A does not directly cause C not to be dead, because A directly causes C to be dead.
3. A does not cause C not to be dead, because A causes B to be armed.
4. A does not cause C not to be dead, because A does not cause C to be armed.
5. A does not cause C not to be dead, because A causes C not to be armed.
6. A does not cause C not to be dead, because A does not cause B not to be armed.

Diagram II: "To Cause Someone to Be Living"

Affirmative Tables

Table A: "To Cause to Be Living"
1. A directly causes C to be living.
2. A directly causes C to be living, because A does not cause C not to be living.
3. A causes C to be living, because A causes C to be armed.
4. A causes C to be living, because A does not cause B to be armed.
5. A causes C to be living, because A causes B not to be armed.
6. A causes C to be living, because A does not cause C not to be armed.

Table B: "To Cause Not to Be Dead"
1. A directly causes C not to be dead.
2. A directly causes C not to be dead, because A does not directly cause C to be dead.

Philosophical Fragments

3. A causes C not to be dead, because A causes C to be armed.
4. A causes C not to be dead, because A does not cause B to be armed.
5. A causes C not to be dead, because A causes B not to be armed.
6. A causes C not to be dead, because A does not cause C not to be armed.

Negative Tables

Table C: "Not to Cause to Be Dead"
1. A does not directly cause C to be dead.
2. A does not directly cause C to be dead, because A directly causes C not to be dead.
3. A does not cause C to be dead, because A causes C to be armed.
4. A does not cause C to be dead, because A does not cause B to be armed.
5. A does not cause C to be dead, because A causes B not to be armed.
6. A does not cause C to be dead, because A does not cause C not to be armed.

Table D: "Not to Cause Not to Be Living"
1. A does not directly cause C not to be living.
2. A does not directly cause C not to be living, because A directly causes C to be living.
3. A does not cause C not to be living, because A causes C to be armed.
4. A does not cause C not to be living, because A does not cause B to be armed.
5. A does not cause C not to be living, because A causes B not to be armed.
6. A does not cause C not to be living, because A does not cause C not to be armed.

Diagram III. Relationship between Tables

A: To cause to be.
B: To cause not to be.
C: Not to cause to be.
D: Not to cause not to be.

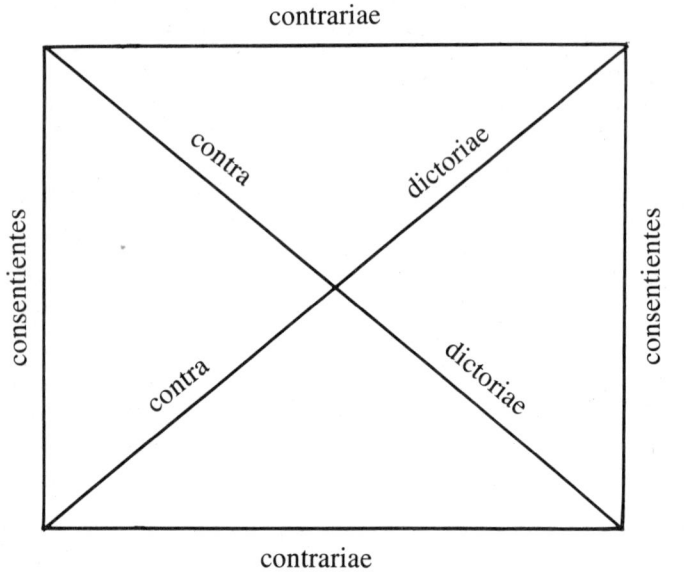

DE GRAMMATICO

HOW (AN) EXPERT-IN-GRAMMAR IS BOTH A SUBSTANCE AND A QUALITY
(Quomodo grammaticus sit substantia et qualitas)

How (an) Expert-In-Grammar[1] Is Both a Substance and a Quality.[2]

I

Student. Concerning (an) expert-in-grammar I ask that you make me certain whether it is a substance or a quality, so that once I know this I will know what I ought to think about other things which in a similar way are spoken of paronymously.[3]

Teacher. First tell me why you are in doubt.

S. Because, apparently, both alternatives — viz., that it is and is not [the one or the other] — can be proved by compelling reasons.

T. Prove them, then.

S. Do not be quick to contradict what I am going to say; but allow me to bring my speech to its conclusion, and then either approve it or improve it.

T. As you wish.

S. The premises

(i) Every/Everything expert-in-grammar is a man,
(ii) Every man is a substance,[4]

suffice to prove that (an) expert-in-grammar is a substance. For whatever (an) expert-in-grammar possesses that results in substantiality is possessed only by virtue of the fact that (an) expert-in-grammar is a man. Therefore, once it is conceded that (an) expert-in-grammar is a man, then whatever is a consequence of being a man is a consequence of being (an) expert-in-grammar. On the other hand, the philosophers[5] who have dealt with this topic maintain clearly that expert-in-grammar is a quality. And it is impudent to reject their authority on these matters.

Furthermore, it is necessary that (an) expert-in-grammar be either a substance or a quality. Thus, whichever one of these it is, it is not the other; and whichever one it is not, it has to be the other.

Accordingly, whatever suffices to prove the one alternative disproves the other; and whatever counts against the one counts for the other. Therefore, since one of these disjuncts is true and the other false, I ask that by detecting the falsity you show me the truth.

2

T. The arguments which you have invoked in support of both disjuncts are compelling — except for your saying that if the one disjunct is true, then the other cannot be true. Hence, you ought not to require me to show that the one disjunct is false (something which no one can do), but to require me to disclose (if I can) how these alternatives are not inconsistent with each other.

But first I would like to hear from you what objections you think can be raised against these arguments of yours.

S. I was eagerly waiting to hear from you the very thing which you are now demanding of me. But since you maintain that these proofs are irreproachable, it is up to me, who am in doubt, to disclose what troubles me, and it is up to you to show the tenability of each disjunct and the compatibility of both.

T. Tell me, then, what you think; and I shall try to do what you are requesting.

S. The proposition which says that (an) expert-in-grammar is a man can, it seems to me, be contested in the following way:

> (i) No/Nothing expert-in-grammar can be conceived without conceiving of expertise-in-grammar.
> (ii) Any man can be conceived without conceiving of expertise-in-grammar.

Moreover,

> (iii) Every/Everything expert-in-grammar admits of more and less.
> (iv) No man admits of more and less.

From each of these sets of two premises one and the same conclusion follows: viz., that

> (v) No/Nothing expert-in-grammar is a man.[6]

3

T. This conclusion does not follow.
S. Why not?

De Grammatico

T. Well, do you think that the name "animal" signifies something other than living-substance-capable-of-perception?

S. Assuredly, an animal is nothing other than a living-substance-capable-of-perception, and a living-substance-capable-of-perception is nothing other than an animal.

T. This is true. But tell me, as well, whether whatever is nothing other than a living-substance-capable-of-perception can be conceived without conceiving of rationality, and whether it need not be rational.

S. I cannot deny it.

T. Therefore, any animal can be conceived without conceiving of rationality, and no animal is necessarily rational.

S. I cannot say that it does not follow from the premises I have conceded — although I especially dread what I suspect you are aiming at.

T. Now, no man can be conceived without conceiving of rationality; and it is necessary that every man be rational.

S. I am hemmed in on both sides.[7] For if I agree, then you will conclude that no man is an animal; and if I disagree, then you will say that not only can I be conceived without conceiving of rationality but also that I really am without rationality.

T. Do not be alarmed. For there does not follow what you think [follows].

S. If [the outcome] is as you promise, then I willingly grant all that you have premised; but if [the outcome is] not [as you promise, then] I am unwilling [to grant your premises].

T. Well, then, formulate into two syllogisms the four last statements which I made.

S. Surely they can be arranged in the following order:

> (i) Any animal can be conceived without conceiving of rationality.
> (ii) No man can be conceived without conceiving of rationality.

Moreover,

> (iii) No animal is necessarily rational.
> (iv) Every man is, necessarily, rational.

From each of these arrangements of two propositions there is seen to follow:

> (v) No man is an animal.

But nothing is more false than this conclusion. Yet, I do not see that the foregoing premises are in any respect untenable. For the two premises which have "man" as their subject-term are so self-evident that it would be impudent to prove them; and the two premises which have "animal" as their subject-term seem to be so well-established that it would be impudent to deny them. Now, I see that the structure of these two syllogisms is in every respect similar to the two syllogisms which I set forth a little earlier.[8] Therefore, I suspect that you have introduced them only for the following reason: viz., that when I would recognize their obviously false conclusion, I would recognize the same thing about the similar syllogisms which I had constructed.

T. This is true.

S. Therefore, show in what respect there is — both in the present case and in the preceding one — so much deception that although the premises are seen to be true and to be conjoined according to the rules for syllogisms, nevertheless truth does not support their conclusions.

4

T. Let me do this in the case of your syllogisms. And, if you like, you examine mine by yourself.

S. Let it be done in accordance with your judgment.

T. Iterate and construct, once more, the syllogisms which you made.

S. "Any man can be conceived without conceiving of expertise-in-grammar."

T. What do you say that a man can be conceived *as* without conceiving of expertise-in-grammar?

S. [He can be conceived as] a man.

T. Therefore, in this premise, say what you mean.

S. Any man can be conceived as a man without conceiving of expertise-in-grammar.

T. I grant it. Add the minor premise.

S. "No expert-in-grammar can be conceived without conceiving of expertise-in-grammar."

T. What is (an) expert-in-grammar unable to be conceived *as* without conceiving of expertise-in-grammar?

S. (An) expert-in-grammar.

T. Therefore, say what you mean.

De Grammatico

S. No expert-in-grammar can be conceived as (an) expert-in-grammar without conceiving of expertise-in-grammar.

T. Conjoin these two propositions — thus expanded, as you have just now presented them.

S.
> (i) Any man can be conceived as a man without conceiving of expertise-in-grammar.
> (ii) No/Nothing expert-in-grammar can be conceived as (an) expert-in-grammar without conceiving of expertise-in-grammar.

T. See, then, whether they have a common term, without which they do not entail any conclusion.

S. I see that they do not have a common term and, hence, that no conclusion follows from them.

T. Construct the other syllogism.

S. It is no longer necessary for you to take pains to lay out this syllogism, because I already detect its fallacy. For I was construing its propositions to mean:

> (iii) No man is more or less a man.
> (iv) Every/Everything expert-in-grammar is more or less (an) expert-in-grammar.

And since these two propositions have no common term, they entail no conclusion.

T. Does it seem to you, then, that in the case of these conjoined premises of yours no conclusion at all can be inferred?

S. I certainly thought so. But your question makes me suspect that perhaps some logical power lies hidden in them. Yet, without a common term how can they entail any conclusion?

T. The common term of a syllogism must be common not so much in verbal form as in meaning. For just as no conclusion follows if it is common in verbal form but not in meaning, so no harm is done if it is common in meaning but not in verbal form. Indeed, the meaning — rather than the words — determines a syllogism.

5

S. I await your drawing an inference from my premises.

T. Assuredly, they entail something, but not what you expect.

S. Whatever it is, I accept it gratefully.

T. Does not someone who says

Anselm of Canterbury

> (i) Any man can be conceived as a man without conceiving of expertise-in-grammar,
>
> and (ii) No/Nothing expert-in-grammar can be conceived as (an) expert-in-grammar without conceiving of expertise-in-grammar,

signify the fact that?:

> (iii) Being (a) man does not require expertise-in-grammar,
>
> and (iv) Being (an) expert-in-grammar does require expertise-in-grammar.

S. Nothing is more true.

T. Do these two propositions — which I have just now said to be signified in those other[9] two propositions — have a common term?

S. They do.

T. Therefore, it follows that

> (v) Being (an) expert-in-grammar is not identical with being (a) man. (That is, there is not the same definition of each.)

S. Assuredly, I see that this follows and is the case.

T. Nevertheless, it does not hereby follow that (an) expert-in-grammar is not a man — in the sense in which you were construing [this proposition]. However, if you construe "(An) expert-in-grammar is not (a) man" to mean

> (vi) (An) expert-in-grammar is not the same as (a) man (i.e., they do not have the same definition),

then this conclusion is true.

6

S. I understand what you mean.

T. Well, then, if you correctly understand what I have said, tell me how you would refute the following syllogism if someone constructed it like this:

> (i) Every/Everything expert-in-grammar is spoken of as a quality.
> (ii) No man is spoken of as a quality.
> So: (iii) No man is (an) expert-in-grammar.

S. This seems to me to be like saying:

> (iv) Everything rational is spoken of as a quality.
> (v) No man is spoken of as a quality.
> So: (vi) No man is rational.

De Grammatico

But no proof can make it true that "rational" is not predicable of any man. Similarly, the syllogism which you have just now set forth does not conclude with logical necessity that "expert-in-grammar" is not predicable of any man. For if we understand them in accordance with their truth, the premises of your syllogism signify as if the following were being said:

> (vii) Every/Everything expert-in-grammar is spoken of as (an) expert-in-grammar, in terms of quality.
> (viii) No man is spoken of as a man, in terms of quality.

But from these two premises it does not at all follow that

> (ix) "Expert-in-grammar" is not predicable of any man,[10]

because [in them] the term affirmed of expert-in-grammar and denied of man is not the same. However, there would be a common term in these premises, and they would necessitate a conclusion, if, given the major premise as it has been stated, the following minor premise were true:

> (x) No man is spoken of as (an) expert-in-grammar, in terms of quality,

or else if, given the minor premise, the following major premise were true:

> (xi) Every/Everything expert-in-grammar is spoken of as a man, in terms of quality.

For from each of these conjunctions[11] there follows that

> (xii) "Expert-in-grammar" is not predicable of any man.

However, suppose someone wants to construe the proposition

> (xiii) (A) man is not (an) expert-in-grammar[12]

to mean

> (xiv) (A) man is not the same as (an) expert-in-grammar,

(as if I were to say "Lightning is a brilliant-flash" or "Lightning is not a brilliant-flash" — i.e., that lightning is (or that it is not) the very same as a brilliant-flash). If someone thus construes

> (xv) (A) man is not (an) expert-in-grammar,

then in accordance with this construal it follows from those[13] premises — if their import is rightly examined — that

> (xvi) No man is (an) expert-in-grammar.

For, indeed, the meaning of those propositions does have a common term which serves to prove that

> (xvii) Being (a) man is not identical with being (an) expert-in-grammar.

7

T. You have correctly understood what I have said. But perhaps you have not paid careful attention to what I have said.

S. In what way have I correctly understood it and yet not paid it careful attention?

T. Tell me what would follow if someone were to set forth the following premises:

> (i) No man can be conceived without conceiving of rationality.
> (ii) Any stone can be conceived without conceiving of rationality.

S. What would follow except?:

> (iii) No stone is a man.

T. How do you construe this conclusion? [Do you take it to mean] that

> (iv) A stone is in no respect a man

or [to mean] that

> (v) (A) stone is not the same as (a) man [i.e., that the two do not have the same definition].

S. [To mean] that a stone is in no respect a man.

T. Tell me, then, how this syllogism differs from that syllogism of yours[14] in which you say:

> (vi) (An) expert-in-grammar cannot be conceived without conceiving of expertise-in-grammar.
> (vii) A man can be [conceived without conceiving of expertise-in-grammar].
> So: (viii) (An) expert-in-grammar is not a man.

S. As far as concerns the cogency of the reasoning, I see that your syllogism does not differ from mine. For just as in mine we must understand that

> (ix) (An) expert-in-grammar cannot be conceived as (an) expert-in-grammar without conceiving of expertise-in-grammar,
> and (x) A man can be conceived as a man without conceiving of expertise-in-grammar,

De Grammatico

so in yours we must understand that

> (xi) A man cannot be conceived as a man without conceiving of rationality,
>
> and (xii) A stone can be conceived as a stone without conceiving of rationality.

And so — since the conclusion of your syllogism (viz., that a stone is in no respect a man) is certain — you seem to me earlier to have obscured by your clever explanations the conclusion of my syllogism (a syllogism which is in every respect similar to yours).[15] Hence, I now understand why you said that I have correctly understood but have not paid careful attention. For I correctly understood what you meant when you spoke to me, but I did not pay careful attention to the point you were making, because I did not realize how [what you said] was misleading me.

T. On the contrary! Your analysis was incorrect in that you did not realize how [what I said] was leading you.

S. In what way [was that]?

T. Surely, if the syllogism which I have just set forth were interpreted (as I interpreted yours) in such way as to say

> (xiii) No man can be conceived as a man without conceiving of rationality,
>
> but (xiv) Any stone can be conceived as a stone without conceiving of rationality,

it would have no other deductive power than I said[16] that yours has. But since my syllogism can be construed in another way — a way in which yours cannot be construed — it has the conclusion

> (xv) A stone can in no respect be a man.

For when I say that

> (xvi) No man can be conceived without conceiving of rationality,
>
> and (xvii) Any stone can be conceived without conceiving of rationality,

these propositions can — indeed, they ought to — be interpreted as if to say:

> (xviii) No man can in any respect be conceived without conceiving of rationality.
>
> (xix) Any stone can, in whatever respect, be conceived without conceiving of rationality.

And from these there follows that

> (xx) No stone is in any respect a man.

But in your premises the truth does not at all allow for a similar construal. For, indeed, we cannot say either that

> (xxi) No/Nothing expert-in-grammar can in any respect be conceived without conceiving of expertise-in-grammar,

or that

> (xxii) Any man can, in whatever respect, be conceived without conceiving of expertise-in-grammar.

For, on the one hand, every man who is (an) expert-in-grammar can be conceived as a man without conceiving of expertise-in-grammar. And, on the other hand, no man can be conceived as (an) expert-in-grammar without conceiving of expertise-in-grammar. Therefore, your premises cannot entail that

> (xxiii) (An) expert-in-grammar is in no respect a man.

8

S. I do not have anything to say against this verdict of yours. But since you have tacitly admonished me not to be content merely to understand what you mean but to pay attention to the point you are making, I think we must pay attention to the conclusion which you showed[17] to be derivable from my syllogism: viz., that

> (i) Being (an) expert-in-grammar is not identical with being a man.

For if this conclusion is true, then it is not necessarily the case that what is (an) expert-in-grammar is thereby a man. Now,

> (ii) If *man* follows from *expert-in-grammar*, then being a man follows from being (an) expert-in-grammar.

But,

> (iii) Being a man does not follow from being (an) expert-in-grammar.

Therefore,

> (iv) *Man* does not follow from *expert-in-grammar*.

Therefore,

> (v) It is not the case that every/everything expert-in-grammar is a man.

But since for every/everything expert-in-grammar there is one and the same reason why they are all men: assuredly,

De Grammatico

(vi) Either every/everything expert-in-grammar is a man or else no/nothing [expert-in-grammar is a man].

Now, it has been shown[18] that

(vii) Not every/everything [expert-in-grammar is a man].

Therefore,

(viii) No/Nothing [expert-in-grammar is a man].

Thus, it seems that you have conceded — by obtaining it more skillfully — the very conclusion which you have skillfully eliminated[19] from my syllogism.

T. Although I tactily admonished you to pay attention to what you hear, nevertheless I did not, it appears, do so in vain. For although you prove sophistically that no/nothing expert-in-grammar is a man — doing so by means of the consideration that being (an) expert-in-grammar is not identical with being a man — nevertheless this proof will be profitable to you when you will behold exposed in its fallaciousness the sophism which is deceiving you under the guise of correct reasoning.

S. Show, then, that this proof which I have just constructed concerning expert-in-grammar is misleading me; and show at what point it is misleading me.

T. Let's go back to the case of *animal* and *man*. In the case of these we so "feel" (so to speak) the truth that no sophism can persuade us — even though it enjoins us — to believe a falsity. Tell me, then, whether the [fact of] being such-and-such a thing is captured by that thing's definition.

S. This is true.

T. Is the definition of "man" identical with the definition of "animal"?

S. By no means. For if "rational, mortal animal" (which is the definition of "man") were the definition of "animal," then whatever "animal" applied to, "rational and mortal" would apply to — something which is false.

T. Therefore, it is not the case that being a man is identical with being an animal.

S. This follows.

T. Therefore, from this proposition[20] you can prove that no man is an animal — doing so by means of the same argument by which you have just proved that no/nothing expert-in-grammar is a man. Hence, if you see to be obvious falsity that which your line of reasoning entails in this case, do not believe to be assured truth that which deludes you in that other case.

S. You have now showed that my reasoning misleads me. Show, as well, at what point it misleads me.

T. Do you not remember what I said and you agreed to a short while ago,[21] viz., that "being (an) expert-in-grammar is not identical with being a man" amounts to saying "the definition of 'expert-in-grammar' is not identical with the definition of 'man'" (i.e., it is not the case that (an) expert-in-grammar and a man are in every respect the same)? For just as "man" ought not to be defined in terms of expertise-in-grammar, so "expert-in-grammar" cannot be defined except in terms of expertise-in-grammar. Therefore, your argument ought to be construed in the following way:

> If (ix) Being (an) expert-in-grammar is not identical with being a man in an unqualified sense of "being a man,"
> then (x) If anything is (an) expert-in-grammar, there does not thereby follow that it is a man in an unqualified sense of "being a man."

Similarly, we must understand that *man*, in an unqualified sense of "man," does not follow from *expert-in-grammar*. That is, if something is (an) expert-in-grammar, there does not follow that it is a man in an unqualified sense of "man." Thus, no other conclusion follows except that

> (xi) No/Nothing expert-in-grammar is a man in an unqualified sense of "man."

S. Nothing is more clear.

9

T. Now, it seems to me that we can easily prove that being (an) expert-in-grammar is not identical with being a man (just as being white is not identical with being a man; for a man can exist without the color white, and the color white can exist without the man). And if this proof were carried out, then it would indeed follow that some/something expert-in-grammar is able to be not-a-man.

S. Why, then, are we going to all this trouble, if this conclusion can be proven? Prove it, and let our inquiry be finished.

T. You ought not to demand this of me here. For in our inquiry we are not discussing whether some/something expert-in-grammar is able to be not-a-man; rather, we are discussing whether some/something expert-in-grammar is not-a-man. But you see that it cannot be proven [that some/something expert-in-grammar is not-a-man].

S. I do not yet see [the truth of this point], because I still have an objection to raise against it.

T. State it.

S. Aristotle declared[22] that

> (i) Expert-in-grammar belongs to the class of items which are present in a subject,
> and (ii) No man is present in a subject.

Therefore,

> (iii) No/Nothing expert-in-grammar is a man.

T. Aristotle did not intend for this conclusion to be drawn from his statements. For Aristotle himself says[23] that a man and *man* and *animal* are expert[s]-in-grammar.

S. How, then, is this syllogism refuted?

T. Answer the following question for me. When you speak to me of (an) *expert-in-grammar*, of what shall I understand you to be speaking?: of this name or of the things which this name signifies?

S. Of the things.

T. What things, then, does it signify?

S. Man and expertise-in-grammar.

T. Therefore, upon hearing "expert-in-grammar," I shall construe it [to signify] (a) man or expertise-in-grammar; and when I speak of (an) expert-in-grammar, I shall be speaking of (a) man or of expertise-in-grammar.

S. This is the way it ought to be.

T. Tell me, then: Is (a) man a substance, or is (a) man present in a subject?

S. (A) man is not present in a subject but is a substance.

T. Is expertise-in-grammar a quality, and is it present in a subject?

S. It is both of these.

T. Therefore, it is not strange for someone to say that with respect to being a man (an) expert-in-grammar is a substance and is not present in a subject, but with respect to expertise-in-grammar expert-in-grammar is a quality and is present in a subject.

10

S. I cannot deny it. But let me state one more argument for why expert-in-grammar is not a substance: viz., because
> (i) Every substance is either primary or secondary substance,
> but (ii) Expert-in-grammar is neither primary nor secondary substance.

T. Remember the statement of Aristotle which I cited a moment ago, in which he says (an) expert-in-grammar is both primary and secondary substance, in that he says a man and *man* and *animal* are called expert[s]-in-grammar. But, nevertheless, how do you prove that (an) expert-in-grammar is neither a primary nor a secondary substance?

S. Well, because it is present in a subject, whereas no substance is [present in a subject].[24] Moreover, it is predicated of more than one thing — a fact which is not true of primary substance. And, on the other hand, it is not genus or species, and is not predicated as something essential — both of which features are true of secondary substance.

T. If you correctly remember what we have already said, [you will realize that] none of these [reasons] prevents (an) expert-in-grammar from being a substance. For in a certain respect (an) *expert-in-grammar* is not present in a subject, and is genus and species, and is predicated as something essential. For (an) expert-in-grammar is man (*Man* is species) and is animal (*Animal* is genus); and "man" and "animal" are predicated as something essential. Furthermore, (an) expert-in-grammar is an individual, even as it is man and animal; for even as a man and an animal [are individuals], so an expert-in-grammar is an individual. For instance, Socrates is an animal and a man and an expert-in-grammar.

S. I cannot deny what you say.

11

T. If you do not have any other premises from which you can prove that (an) expert-in-grammar is not a man, then prove now that (an) expert-in-grammar is not expertise-in-grammar.

De Grammatico

S. I can do this more easily by pointing than by arguing. For, indeed, you crushed all my arguments when[25] you disclosed that different things are signified by "expert-in-grammar" and that we ought to understand and to speak about (an) expert-in-grammar in accordance with these things. And although I cannot deny this, nevertheless it does not satisfy my mind in such way that my mind rests tranquil, as if what it was seeking had been found. For you seem to me as if you did not care about teaching me, but to care only about impeding my arguments. But just as it was up to me to state what forces me to doubt both alternatives,[26] so it was up to you either to eliminate one alternative or to show how the two alternatives are not inconsistent with each other.

T. It has been shown[27] that the statement "(An) expert-in-grammar is a substance" and the statement "Expert-in-grammar is a quality" are not at all inconsistent with each other, inasmuch as it is proper to understand and to speak about (an) expert-in-grammar at times with respect to being a man, at times with respect to expertise-in-grammar. Why do you think that this proof is unsatisfactory?

S. Because anyone who understands the name "expert-in-grammar" knows that "expert-in-grammar" signifies man and expertise-in-grammar. And yet, if with this assurance I were to speak in public and to say

(i) (A) useful expertise is expert-in-grammar,

or

(ii) This man has expert-in-grammar,[28]

then not only would the experts-in-grammar be furious but even the unlearned would jeer. Therefore, I shall not at all believe that the expositors of dialectic did not have some other reason for having so often and so studiously written in their books what they themselves would have been ashamed to say in their conversations. For, indeed, very often when they want to exhibit a quality or an accident, they add the comment: "For example, expert-in-grammar and the like," although the customary usage of all speakers attests that (an) expert-in-grammar is a substance rather than a quality or an accident. On the other hand, when [these expositors of dialectic] want to teach something about substance, they nowhere say: "For example, expert-in-grammar or the like." Add to this point the following one: if (an) expert-in-grammar is to be called both a substance and a quality simply because [its name] signifies both man and expertise-in-grammar, then why is not man likewise both a substance and a quality? For, in fact, "man" signifies a substance together with all the differentia which are in (a) man — for example, mortality and capability-of-perception. But in none of the places where something has been written about some quality or other has the phrase "as is (a) man" been offered by way of example.

12

T. As for your repudiating — simply because it does not apply in the case of the name "man" — the explanation I gave of why expert-in-grammar is indeed both a substance and a quality: you do so, it seems to me, because you do not consider how dissimilarly the name "man" signifies the things of which a man consists and the name "expert-in-grammar" signifies man and expertise-in-grammar. Assuredly, of and by itself[29] the name "man" signifies as a single thing[30] those things of which the whole of (a) man consists. Among these things substance holds the principal place, since it is the cause of the others and since it possesses them (not as itself needing them but) as things needing itself. (For there is no differentia of a substance without which this substance could not exist; yet none of its differentia can exist without it.) Therefore, although all the things at once, and as a single whole, and in a single signification, and with a single name, are called man, nevertheless the name "man" so principally signifies, and is appellative of, the substance that although it is correct to say

> (i) (The) substance is a man, and (the) man is a substance,

nevertheless no one would say

> (ii) (The) rationality is a man,

or

> (iii) (The) man is rationality.

Rather, [everyone would say]

> (iv) (The) man is someone who has rationality.

However, it is not the case that the name "expert-in-grammar" signifies as a single thing man and expertise-in-grammar; rather,

De Grammatico

of and by itself it signifies expertise-in-grammar, and on the basis of something else it signifies man. Moreover, although the name "expert-in-grammar" is appellative of (a) man, nevertheless it is not proper[31] to say that it signifies man; and although "expert-in-grammar" signifies expertise-in-grammar, nevertheless it is not appellative of expertise-in-grammar. Now, I term the name of any given thing appellative of it if this thing is called by this name in the customary course of speaking. For example, it does not accord with the customary way of speaking to say "Expertise-in-grammar is (an) expert-in-grammar" or "(An) expert-in-grammar is expertise-in-grammar." But [it does accord with the customary way of speaking to say] "A man is (an) expert-in-grammar" and "An expert-in-grammar is a man."

13

S. I do not see why you say that of and by itself "expert-in-grammar" signifies expertise-in-grammar and that on the basis of something else it signifies man. [And I do not see] in what sense "expert-in-grammar" signifies only expertise-in-grammar. For just as (a) man consists of animal and rationality and mortality, and thus "man" signifies these three things, so (an) expert-in-grammar consists of man and expertise-in-grammar, and thus the name "expert-in-grammar" signifies both of these. For in the absence of expertise-in-grammar a man is never called (an) expert-in-grammar; and in the absence of a man expertise-in-grammar is never called (an) expert-in-grammar.

T. Well, then, if the facts of the matter are as you claim, being (an) expert-in-grammar and the definition of "expert-in-grammar" would be: *man who has expertise-in-grammar*.

S. They cannot be anything else.

T. Therefore, since expertise-in-grammar would distinguish (a) man who is (an) expert-in-grammar from (a) man who is not (an) expert-in-grammar, expertise-in-grammar would conduce to the existence of (an) expert-in-grammar, and would be a part of its being,[32] and could not be first present in and then absent from (an) expert-in-grammar without resulting in the destruction of this very subject.[33]

S. What follows from this?

T. Therefore, expertise-in-grammar would not be an accident

Anselm of Canterbury

but would be a substantial differentia; and *man* would be the genus, and *expert-in-grammar* would be the species. And there would be a similar argument concerning the color white and other accidents of this kind. But an exposition of the complete art [of dialectic] would show this outcome to be false.

S. Although I cannot deny what you say, nevertheless I am not yet convinced that "expert-in-grammar" does not signify man.

T. Let us suppose there is some rational animal — other than man — which has expertise-in-grammar, even as does a man.

S. It is easy to suppose this.

T. Therefore, there is something which is not a man but which has expertise-in-grammar.

S. This follows.

T. But anything that has expertise-in-grammar is (an) expert-in-grammar.

S. I grant it.

T. Therefore, there is something which is not a man but is (an) expert-in-grammar.

S. It follows.

T. Now, you say that "expert-in-grammar" signifies man.

S. I do.

T. Therefore, something which is not a man is a man — a conclusion which is false.

S. [I agree that] the argument is brought to this conclusion.

T. Therefore, do you not see that the only reason "expert-in-grammar" seems to signify man more than does "white" is that expertise-in-grammar is an accident only of man, whereas whiteness is not an accident only of man?

S. This follows from what we have supposed. But I want you to prove this without a supposition which is contrary to fact.

T. If man were signified by "expert-in-grammar," then "man" would not be predicated of anything at the same time as "expert-in-grammar" — just as because animal is signified by "man," "animal" is not predicated [of anything] at the same time as "man." For example, it is not appropriate to say that

   (i) Socrates is a man who is an animal.[34]

S. This cannot be contradicted.

T. But it is appropriate to say that

   (ii) Socrates is a man who is (an) expert-in-grammar.

De Grammatico

S. [Yes, it is] appropriately [said].

T. Therefore, it is not the case that "expert-in-grammar" signifies man.

S. I see that this follows.

T. Likewise, if (an) expert-in-grammar were (a) man-who-has-expertise-in-grammar, then wherever "expert-in-grammar" would be put, it would be appropriate to put "man who has expertise-in-grammar."

S. This is true.

T. Therefore, if it is appropriate to say

> (iii) Socrates is a man who is (an) expert-in-grammar,

then it would also be appropriate to say

> (iv) Socrates is a man who is a man who has expertise-in-grammar.

S. It follows.

T. Now, every man who has expertise-in-grammar is a man who is (an) expert-in-grammar.

S. This is true.

T. Therefore, Socrates — who is a man who is a man who has expertise-in-grammar — is a man who is a man who is (an) expert-in-grammar. And since (an) expert-in-grammar is a man who has expertise-in-grammar, it follows that Socrates is a man who is a man who is a man who has expertise-in-grammar — and so on, to infinity.

S. I cannot resist this obvious inference.

T. Moreover, if we must take "expert-in-grammar" to signify both man and expertise-in-grammar, then we must likewise take any other paronymous name of this kind to signify both that which is named paronymously and that from which the paronymous name is derived.

S. This is what I was thinking.

T. Therefore, "today's" would signify both today and that which is called today's.

S. What follows next?

T. Thus, "today's" would signify something along with signifying a time.

S. This would have to be the case.

T. Therefore, "today's" would be a verb[35] and not a name;[36]

for it would be a [simple] utterance — and not a phrase[37] — signifying something along with signifying a time.

14

S. You have satisfactorily proven to me that "expert-in-grammar" does not signify man.

T. So you realize why I said that "expert-in-grammar" does not signify man?

S. I do, and I am waiting for you to show that "expert-in-grammar" signifies expertise-in-grammar.

T. Did not say a moment ago[38] that "expert-in-grammar" signifies man-who-has-expertise-in-grammar?

S. Yes, and I believed it.

T. But now it has been satisfactorily proven that "expert-in-grammar" does not signify man.

S. Yes, satisfactorily.

T. What, then, remains?

S. That "expert-in-grammar" does not signify anything other than having-expertise-in-grammar.

T. So it signifies expertise-in-grammar?

S. It has been satisfactorily proven that "expert-in-grammar" is appellative of man but not of expertise-in-grammar, and signifies expertise-in-grammar but not man. But since you have said that of and by itself "expert-in-grammar" signifies expertise-in-grammar and that on the basis of something else it signifies man, I ask you to distinguish clearly for me these two significations, so that I may understand in what sense "expert-in-grammar" does not signify that which in some sense it does signify, and [may understand] in what sense it is appellative of that which it does not signify.

T. Suppose that without your knowing about it a white horse has been shut up in a building. And suppose someone says to you: "In this building there is whiteness" (or "In this building there is white"). Would you thereby know that a horse is in that building?

S. No. For whether he said "white" or "whiteness" or "that in which there is whiteness" I would not conceive of the being of any definite thing except of this color.

De Grammatico

T. Even if you did conceive of something other than this color, it is certain that you would not — on the basis of the name "white" — conceive of the being of the thing in which this color is present.

S. This is certain. For even if [the thought of] a material object or [of] a surface came to mind (something which happens only because I have experience of the fact that whiteness is usually present in these things), still the name "white" would not itself signify any of these things (even as has been proven about "expert-in-grammar"). However, I am still waiting for you to show that it *does* signify [such things].

T. What if you saw a white horse and a black ox standing beside each other, and someone said to you with regard to the horse, "Poke it," but did not indicate by a gesture which one he was speaking of. Would you know that he was speaking of the horse?

S. No.

T. But if in reply to you — who do not know, and who have asked "Which one?" — he were to say "The white one," would you discern which one he was talking about?

S. On the basis of the name "white" I would understand that the horse was meant.

T. Therefore, the name "white" would signify to you the horse.

S. Yes, it certainly would.

T. Do you not see that [the name "white" would signify the horse] in a way other than does the name "horse"?

S. I see it. Surely, even before I would know that the horse is white, the name "horse" — of and by itself, and not on the basis of anything else — would signify to me the substance of the horse. But the name "white" would not of and by itself signify [to me] the substance of the horse, but would signify it on the basis of something else, viz., on the basis of the fact that I know the horse to be white. For since the name "white" would signify nothing other than does the phrase "having whiteness": just as by itself this phrase would signify to me whiteness but not the thing which has whiteness, so also the name "white" [would by itself signify to me whiteness but not the thing which has whiteness]. But I would know that whiteness is in the horse, and [I would know] this on some basis other than on the basis of the name "white" (viz., [I would know it] on the basis of sight). Therefore, having understood on the basis of the name "white" that whiteness is meant, I would — on the basis of the fact that I know the whiteness to be in the horse — understand that the horse was meant. That is, on some basis other than on the basis of the name "white," which is, however, appellative of the horse, [I would understand that the horse was meant].

15

T. Do you see, then, in what sense "white" does not signify that which in some sense it does signify? [And do you see] in what sense it is appellative of that which it does not signify?

S. Yes, I also see these points. For "white" does and does not signify the horse, since of and by itself it does not signify the horse, but on the basis of something else it does signify the horse. And, nevertheless, "white" is an appellative of the horse. And what I see to be the case with the word "white" I recognize to be the case with "expert-in-grammar" and with other paronyms of this kind. Therefore, I think that the signification of names and verbs can be divided in such way that there is (1) signification of and by itself, and there is (2) signification on the basis of something else.

T. Consider also that of these two significations the one which exists of and by itself belongs to significant utterances substantially; but the other signification belongs to them accidentally. For example, when in the definition of "name" or of "verb" it is said that a name or a verb is a significant utterance, we must interpret "significant" to mean only the signification which exists of and by itself. For if that signification which exists on the basis of something else had to be included in the definition of a name or of a verb, then "today's" would no longer be a name but would be a verb. For in terms of this [accidental] signification "today's" would upon occasion signify something together with signifying a time (as I said earlier).[39] And this is the characteristic of a verb rather than of a name.

16

S. What you say is clear. But it is not without qualms that my mind accepts the view (1) that *expert-in-grammar* is a quality

De Grammatico

(even though it does signify expertise-in-grammar) or (2) that (a) man by himself — i.e., apart from expertise-in-grammar — is (an) expert-in-grammar (even though we have proven[40] that (a) man and expertise-in-grammar are not together (an) expert-in-grammar — from which proof it follows that (a) man by himself is (an) expert-in-grammar, since he cannot be (an) expert-in-grammar except either by himself or together with expertise-in-grammar). For although the name "expert-in-grammar" signifies expertise-in-grammar, nevertheless to one who asks what (an) expert-in-grammar is it would not be appropriate to answer: "expertise-in-grammar" or "quality." And if no one/nothing is (an) expert-in-grammar except by participating in expertise-in-grammar, then it follows that (a) man is not (an) expert-in-grammar except together with expertise-in-grammar.

T. As for the claim that (a) man by himself — i.e., apart from expertise-in-grammar — is (an) expert-in-grammar: this claim can be construed in two ways, in one of which it is true and in the other of which it is false. And this distinction suffices to clear up your perplexity. By himself and apart from expertise-in-grammar (a) man is, in fact, (an) expert-in-grammar, because he is the only one who has expertise-in-grammar. For, indeed, expertise-in-grammar does not — either by itself or together with (a) man — have expertise-in-grammar. On the other hand, by himself — i.e., in the absence of expertise-in-grammar — (a) man is not (an) expert-in-grammar, because in the absence of expertise-in-grammar no one/nothing can be (an) expert-in-grammar. The case is comparable to someone's leading another by going before him. By himself the leader is ahead; for the one who is behind is not ahead — either by himself or in such way that the two of them together constitute a single leader who is ahead. On the other hand, it is not the case that by himself the leader is ahead, because if there is not one who is behind there cannot be one who is ahead.

Now, when it is said that expert-in-grammar is a quality, this is correctly said only in the sense which accords with Aristotle's treatise *On the Categories*.

17

S. Does that treatise contain anything other than?:

> (i) Everything which exists is either a substance or a quantity or a quality, (etc.).

So if (a) man by himself is (an) expert-in-grammar, (a) substance by itself is (an) expert-in-grammar. In what sense, then, according to that treatise, is (an) expert-in-grammar a quality rather than a substance?

T. Although what you have just said is a correct interpretation of that text (because everything which exists is some one of these things), nevertheless it was not Aristotle's primary aim to show this fact in his book; instead [his aim was to show] that every name and verb signifies some of these things. For he did not intend to show what each thing, individually, is or to show of what things each word, individually, is appellative; instead [he intended to show] of what things [each word, individually,] is significative. But since words signify only things:[41] in saying what it is that words signify, he had to say what it is that things are. To mention only one [evidence of Aristotle's intention]: the classification which he makes at the beginning of his treatise *On the Categories* amply bears out what I am saying. For he does not say

> (ii) Each of those things which exist is either a substance or a quantity, (etc.).

Nor does he say

> (iii) Each of those things which are spoken of in accordance with no complexity is called either a substance or a quantity, [(etc.)].

Rather, he says

> (iv) Each of those things which are spoken of in accordance with no complexity [is spoken of by a word which] signifies either a substance or a quantity, [(etc.)].[42] [43]

S. This argument convinces me of the point you are making.

T. Therefore, when Aristotle says "Each of those things which are spoken of in accordance with no complexity [is spoken of by a word which] signifies either a substance or a quantity," (and so forth), which signification does he seem to you to be speaking about?: about the signification by which these words signify of and by themselves (and which belongs substantially to these words) or about the other signification, which exists on the basis of something else (and [which belongs to these words] accidentally)?

S. Only about that signification by which these words signify of and by themselves — which signification he himself (in defining "name" and "verb") affirmed to be present in these words.

T. Do you think that in his treatise he proceeded otherwise than he proposed to in his classification? Or [do you think] that any of those who succeeded him and who wrote about dialectic wanted to entertain a different view on this matter than he held?

S. Their writings do not at all allow anyone to think this, because nowhere is any one of these writers found to have set forth some word in order to show something which it signifies on the basis of something else; rather they always [do so] in order to [show] that which it signifies of and by itself. For no one who wants to indicate a substance sets forth the word "white" or "expert-in-grammar"; rather, one who teaches about a quality sets forth the words "white," "expert-in-grammar," and other words of this kind.

18

T. Therefore, if having proposed the aforementioned classification I were to ask you "What is *expert-in-grammar* according to this classification and according to those who adhere to it in writing about dialectic?" then about what would I be asking, or about what would you be answering me?

S. Surely, one can here be asking only about either the word or the thing which the word signifies. Therefore, because it is evident that in accordance with this classification "expert-in-grammar" signifies expertise-in-grammar and not man: if you were asking about the word "expert-in-grammar," I would unhesitatingly answer that it is a word which signifies a quality; but if you were asking about the thing, [I would answer] that the thing is a quality.

T. You are aware, are you not, that in his book Aristotle himself calls words by the name of the things they signify and not by the name of the things of which they are merely appellatives?

For example, he says that
> (i) Every substance seems to signify something particular.⁴⁴

That is,
> (ii) Every word which signifies a substance [seems to signify something particular].

Likewise, he names — or rather "shows" (as you put it a moment ago)⁴⁵ — things by the words which merely signify them but which in many cases are not appellative of them.

S. I cannot fail to be aware of this. Therefore, whether one asks about the word or about the thing: when one asks "What is (an) expert-in-grammar according to Aristotle's treatise and according to Aristotle's successors?" the correct answer is: "A quality." And yet with respect to appellation, (an) expert-in-grammar is really a substance.

T. This is true. For if even the experts-in-grammar say one thing in accordance with the form of words and another thing in accordance with the nature of things,⁴⁶ then it ought not to disquiet us that the dialecticians write in one way about words with respect to the fact that they signify, and in conversation use them in another way with respect to the fact that they are appellatives. For, in fact, the experts-in-grammar say that *"lapis"* is masculine in gender, *"petra"* feminine, but *"mancipium"* neuter; and that *"timere"* is active, but *"timeri"* passive. And yet no one says that a stone [*lapis*] is masculine or a rock [*petra*] feminine, or that a servant (*mancipium*) is neither masculine nor feminine, or that to fear (*timere*) is to do something, whereas to be afraid (*timeri*) is to undergo something.

19

S. Your clear explanation does not allow me to doubt any of the things you have said. But regarding the topic at hand there is still something that I want to learn. If *expert-in-grammar* is a quality because it signifies a quality, then I do not see why it is not the case that *armed* is a substance because it signifies a substance. And if the reason *armed* is a having⁴⁷ is that it signifies a having, then I do not know why it is not the case that *expert-in-grammar* is a having because it signifies a having. For [the following comparison holds] in every respect: Just as "expert-in-grammar" is proved to signify a quality because it signifies the having of a quality, so "armed" signifies a substance because it signifies the having of a substance, viz., the having of weapons. And just as "armed" is proven to signify a having because it signifies the having of weapons, so "expert-in-grammar" signifies a having because it signifies the having of learning.

T. Given this reasoning, I cannot at all deny either that armed is a substance or that expert-in-grammar is a having.

S. Well, then, I would like to learn from you whether a single thing can belong to different categories.

T. I do not think that one and the same thing can be fitted under different categories, even though in some cases my verdict can be doubted. This issue, it seems to me, needs fuller and deeper examination than we have undertaken in our present short discussion. However, I do not see what prevents a single utterance which signifies more than one thing (but without signifying them as a single thing) from being placed, at times, under more than one category — as, for example, if *white* is said to be both a quality and a having. For it is not the case that as "man" signifies as one thing both the substance and the qualities of which a man consists, so "white" signifies as a single thing both a quality and a having. For the thing of which "man" is appellative is some one thing which consists of the things I have mentioned.[48] But the thing of which "white" is appellative is not some one thing which consists of a having and a quality. For "white" is appellative only of a thing which has whiteness; and this thing does not at all consist of a having and a quality. Therefore, if it were said that

(i) Man is a substance and man is a quality,

then one and the same thing — which is signified by the name "man," and of which the name "man" is appellative — would be stated to be both a substance and a quality. But this statement seems inconsistent. However, when we say that white is both a quality and a having, we are not stating that the thing of which "white" is appellative is both a quality and a having but are stating that these two things [viz., a quality and a having] are signified by the name "white." And from this statement nothing inconsistent results.

S. But why is it not the case that in accordance with Aristotle's classification *man* is both a substance and a quality because it signifies both a substance and a quality — just as *white* is both a quality and a having because it signifies both a quality and a having?

T. One who asks this question can, I think, be satisfactorily answered by what I said earlier:[49] viz., that "man" principally signifies a substance and that the one thing which "man" principally signifies is a substance; i.e., this thing is not a quality but is something qualified. By contrast, "white" does not principally signify anything, but instead equally signifies both a quality and a having; and it is not the case that from these [viz., from this quality and this having] there results a single thing which would be more a quality [than a having] or more a having [than a quality] — which predominant thing "white" would signify [the more].

20

S. I would like to have explained to me more clearly why it is not the case that a single thing results from the [two] things which "white" signifies.

T. If something consisted of these [two] things, then either it would be a substance or else it would be something belonging to one of the other categories.

S. It could not be anything else.

T. But nothing belonging to any of the categories results from a having and a whiteness.

S. I cannot contradict this.

T. Likewise, a single thing is produced from more than one thing only [in one of the following ways]: (1) by means of a composition of parts which belong to the same category (as, for example, an animal consists of a body and a soul); or (2) by means of the harmonious union of a genus and one or more differentia (as, for example, *material object* or *man*); or (3) by means of a species and a collection of distinguishing properties[50] (as, for example, Plato). However, the [two] things which "white" signifies do not belong to a single category; nor is either one of them related to the other as its genus or its differentia or its species or its collection of individuating properties; nor is either one a differentia of a single genus. Rather, both are accidents of the same subject; but "white" does not signify this subject,

De Grammatico

because "white" does not at all signify anything other than a having and a quality. Therefore, a single thing does not result from those things which "white" signifies.

S. Although the argument seems to prove to me the point you are making, nevertheless I would like to hear what answer you would give if, to your claim that in no respect does "white" signify anything other than a having and a quality, someone raised the following objection:

> (i) Since *white* is the same as having-whiteness, it does not determinately signify this or that thing (e.g., a material object) having whiteness, but indeterminately signifies something-having-whiteness.
>
> (ii) For [in support of the conclusion of (*i*)] white is either what-has-whiteness or else what-does-not-have-whiteness. Now, it is not the case that white is what-does-not-have-whiteness. Therefore, white is what-has-whiteness. Thus, since whatever has whiteness can only be something, it is necessary that white be something-which-has-whiteness, or something-having-whiteness. Finally, either "white" signifies something-having-whiteness or else it signifies nothing-having-whiteness. Now, "white" cannot signify nothing-having-whiteness.
>
> (iii) Therefore, it is necessary that "white" signify something-having-whiteness.

21

T. The point we are discussing is not whether whatever-is-white is something-[having-whiteness], or is what-has-[whiteness]. Instead, we are discussing whether the signification of the name "white" includes (as the signification of "man" includes *animal*) the expression "something," or "what has" — with the consequence that just as a man is a rational mortal animal, so white is something-having-whiteness, or what-has-whiteness.[51] For, indeed, it is necessary for any given thing to be a multiplicity of features which, nevertheless, are not signified by its name. For example, it is necessary for any animal to be colored and to be either rational or nonrational. Nevertheless, the name "animal" does not signify any of these. Therefore, although white is only something-having-whiteness, or what-has-whiteness, nevertheless it is not necessarily the case that "white" signifies this. For let us suppose that "white" or "whiteness" signifies something-having-whiteness. Now, something-having-whiteness is nothing other than something-white.

S. It cannot be anything else.

T. Therefore, "white" or "whiteness" would always signify something-white.

S. This is true.

T. Therefore, where "white" or "whiteness" would be put, it would always be right to substitute "something white."

S. This follows.

T. Therefore, where "something white" would be said, it would also be correct to say redundantly: "Something something white." And where this would be said redundantly, it would be correct to say it a third time, and so on to infinity.

S. This follows and is absurd.

T. Let it also be the case that white is the same as what-has-whiteness. Now, *has* is nothing other than *is having*.

S. It cannot be [anything else].

T. Therefore, white would be nothing other than what-is-having-whiteness.

S. Nothing else.

T. But when "having whiteness" is said, this phrase signifies nothing other than white.

S. This is true.

T. Therefore, white would be the same as what-is-white.

S. This follows.

T. Thus, wherever "white" would be put, it would be correct to substitute "what is white."

S. I cannot deny it.

T. Therefore, if white were what-is-white, it would also be what-is-what-is-white. And if it were this, it would also be what-is-what-is-what-is-white, and so on to infinity.

S. This inference follows no less logically and is no less absurd than the inference that oftentimes white is something something.

T. However, if someone says that "white" either signifies something-having-whiteness or signifies nothing-having-whiteness, [then this statement can be interpreted in two ways]. If it is interpreted as saying "'White' either signifies something-having-[whiteness] or signifies not-something-having-[whiteness]" (so that "not-something" is an infinite name), then the disjunction is neither exhaustive nor correct; and so it proves nothing. (It would be like someone's saying "A blind-being either sees something or sees not-something.) But if the statement is interpreted [as saying] "['White'] either signifies something-having-[whiteness] or does not signify [something-having-whiteness], then the disjunction is exhaustive and correct; and this construal is not opposed to the points previously made.

S. It is sufficiently clear that "white" does not signify something-having-whiteness nor what-has-whiteness but signifies only having-whiteness, i.e., only a quality and a having. And from these [two] alone there is not produced some one thing. And so *white* is both of these, because it signifies both of them equally. And I see that this reasoning holds for all things that are spoken of by a noncomplex expression which similarly signifies howsoever many things from which, nevertheless, a single thing does not result. And I do not think that any objection can rightly be raised against the things which you have maintained in this disputation.

T. Right now I do not think so either. However, since you know how vigorously the dialecticians contend, in our day, with the problem you have proposed, I do not want you to cling so tightly to the points we have made that you would hold to them with stubborn persistence even if by weightier arguments someone else could destroy them and could prove something different. But should this destruction occur, you would not deny that at least our discussion has benefited us in the practice of argumentation.

THREE DIALOGUES

Preface

At different times in the past I wrote three treatises pertaining to the study of Sacred Scripture. They are similar in having been written in dialogue form; the person inquiring is designated "the Student," and the person answering, "the Teacher." Because a fourth [treatise] — which begins with the words "*De Grammatico*," and which I also published in dialogue form and regard as not without use to those who need to be introduced to dialectic — pertains to a different study[1] from these three, I do not wish to number it with them.

One of the three is *On Truth*: [it asks] what truth is, in what things truth is usually said to be, and what justice is. A second treatise is on *Freedom of Choice*: [it asks] what freedom of choice is, whether a man always has it, and how many distinctions of freedom there are with respect to having or not having uprightness-of-will. (Freedom of choice was given to rational creatures in order that they might keep uprightness-of-will.)[2] In this treatise I show only the natural strength of the will for keeping the uprightness which it has received; I do not show how in order to keep uprightness the will needs the accompaniment of grace.[3] But the third treatise deals with the question of how, since God did not give the Devil the perseverance which he was not able to have without God's giving, it could have been sin for the Devil not to stand steadfast in the truth. For if God had given him perseverance, he would have had it — just as the good angels had it because God gave it to them. And although in this work I spoke about the confirmation of the good angels, I entitled the treatise *The Fall of the Devil*; for what I said about the good angels was incidental, but what I wrote about the evil angels was essential to the theme.

Although these three treatises are not connected through any continuation of text, their subject-matter and similarity of discussion require that they be placed together in the order in which I have mentioned them. Thus, although certain rash individuals have transcribed them in another order before they were completed, I want them ordered as I have listed them here.

— [Anselm]

ON TRUTH
(De Veritate)

CHAPTER TITLES

1. Truth has no beginning or end.
2. The truth of signification and the two truths of a statement.
3. The truth of thought.
4. The truth of the will.
5. The truth of natural action and nonnatural action.
6. The truth of the senses.
7. The truth in the being of things.
8. The various meanings of "ought" and "ought not," "able" and "unable."
9. Every action signifies either what is true or what is false.
10. The Supreme Truth.
11. The definition of "truth."
12. The definition of "justice."
13. Truth is one in all true things.

ON TRUTH[1]
(De Veritate)

Chapter One: Truth has no beginning or end.

Student. Since we believe that God is truth,[2] and since we say that truth is in many other things, I would like to know whether in whatever things it is said to be we ought to believe that truth is God. For in your *Monologion*, by appealing to the truth of a statement, you too demonstrate[3] that the Supreme Truth has no beginning and no end:

> Let anyone who can, try to conceive of when it began to be true, or was ever not true, that something was going to exist. Or [let him try to conceive of] when it will cease being true and will not be true that something has existed in the past. Now, if neither of these things can be conceived, and if both statements can be true only if there is truth, then it is impossible even to think that truth has a beginning or an end. Indeed, suppose that truth had had a beginning, or suppose that it would at some time come to an end: then even before truth had begun to be, it would have been true that there was no truth; and even after truth had come to an end, it would still be true that there would be no truth. But it could not be true without truth. Hence, there would have been truth before truth came to be, and there would still be truth after truth had ceased to be. But these conclusions are self-contradictory. Therefore, whether truth is said to have a beginning or an end, or whether it is understood not to have a beginning or an end, truth cannot be confined by any beginning or end.

You make this argument in your *Monologion*. Therefore, I hope to learn from you the definition of "truth."

Teacher. I do not recall having arrived at a definition of "truth"; but if you wish, let us inquire as to what truth is by [examining] the various things in which we say there is truth.

S. If I cannot do anything else, I will at least help by being a good listener.

Chapter Two: The truth of signification and the two truths of a statement.

T. Then, let us first ask what truth in a statement is since most frequently we call a statement true or false.

S. You conduct the investigation, and I will heed whatever you find out.

T. When is a statement true?

S. When what it states, whether affirmatively or negatively, is the case. I mean what it states even when it denies that what-is-not is; for even then it expresses what is the case (*quemadmodum res est*).

T. Then, does it seem to you that the thing stated is the truth of the statement?

S. No.

T. Why not?

S. Because nothing is true except by participating in truth; and so the truth of something true is in that true thing. But the thing stated is not in the true statement, and thus must not be called its truth; rather, it must be called the *cause* of the statement's truth. Therefore, it seems to me that the truth of the statement must be sought only in the statement itself.

T. Consider, then, whether the truth you are looking for is either the statement itself or its signification or something in its definition.

S. I do not think it is.

T. What is your reason?

S. Because if the truth of the statement were any of these, then the statement would always be true. For the statement's definition remains the same irrespective of whether what it states is or is not the case. In fact, the statement, its signification, and the other things remain the same.

T. Then, as you see it, what is truth in the statement?

S. All I know is that when the statement signifies that what is is, then it is true and truth is in it.

T. What is an affirmation designed to do?[4]

S. To signify that what is is.

T. Then, this is what an affirmation ought to do?

S. Certainly.

De Veritate

T. So when an affirmative statement signifies that what is is, it signifies what it ought to.

S. Obviously.

T. But when it signifies what it ought to, it signifies rightly, or correctly.

S. That's right.

T. And when it signifies correctly, its signification is correct.

S. No doubt about it.

T. Therefore, when it signifies that what is is, its signification is correct.

S. This follows.

T. Moreover, when it signifies that what is is, its signification is true.

S. Yes, its signification is both correct and true when it signifies that what is is.

T. So for an affirmation to be correct is the same as for it to be true, namely, for it to signify that what is is.

S. Yes, these are the same.

T. Therefore, the affirmation's truth is simply its rightness, or correctness (*rectitudo*).[5]

S. I now see clearly that truth is this rightness.

T. This conclusion also applies when the statement signifies that what-is-not is not.

S. I understand what you mean. But teach me how to reply, if someone should maintain that even when a statement signifies that what-is-not is, it signifies what it ought to. For the statement has received the capability of signifying both that what is is and that what-is-not is. For if it had not received the capability of signifying that what-is-not is, then it would not signify this. Hence, even when it signifies that what-is-not is, it signifies what it ought to. But if by signifying what it ought to the statement is correct and true, as you have argued, then it is true even when it states that what-is-not is.

T. Admittedly, we are not accustomed to call the statement true when it signifies that what-is-not is; nevertheless it has a truth and a correctness because it does what it ought. But when it signifies that what is is, it does what it ought in two respects: for it signifies (1) what it has received the capability of signifying and (2) what it is designed to signify. Now, a statement is usually said to be correct and true in accordance with the latter correctness and truth, by which it signifies that what is is; and we do not ordinarily call a statement correct and true in accordance with the former correctness and truth, by which it signifies that what-is-not is. For the statement [does what it] ought more with respect to what it is designed to signify than with respect to what it is not designed to signify. Indeed, it has received the capability of signifying that a thing is, when it is not, or is not, when it is, only because it was not able to be restricted to signifying that this thing is, when it is, or that it is not, when it is not. Therefore, a statement has one correctness and truth because it signifies what it is designed to signify; and it has another correctness and truth because it signifies what it has received the capability of signifying. The first of these correctnesses, or truths, belongs variably to the statement; but the second belongs to it invariably. The statement does not always have the first kind of truth; but it always possesses the second. The first kind of truth belongs to the statement accidentally and depends upon its usage, whereas the second kind of truth belongs to it naturally. For example, when I say "It is day" in order to signify that what is is, I use the signification of this statement correctly because the statement is designed for this [viz., for signifying that what is is]; and so it is said to signify correctly on this occasion. But when by means of the same statement I signify that what-is-not is, I do not use the signification of the statement correctly, because the statement is not designed for signifying this; and so its signification is said not to be correct on this occasion.

Now, in some statements these two truths, or correctnesses, are inseparable, as when we say "A man is an animal" or "A man is not a stone." For the affirmative statement always signifies that what is is, and the negative statement always signifies that what-is-not is not. Moreover, we cannot use the affirmation to signify that what-is-not is (for a man is always an animal); nor can we use the negation to signify that what is is not (because a man is never a stone).

Since our common way of speaking judges a statement to be true in accordance with that truth which a statement has by virtue of someone's using it correctly, we began by inquiring about that truth. We shall speak later[6] about that truth which a statement cannot fail to have.

S. Return, then, to the issue with which you began. For you

De Veritate

have distinguished to my satisfaction the two truths of a statement — provided you will show that a statement has a kind of truth when it lies, as you maintain.

T. For the time being let these things suffice regarding the truth of signification, with which we have begun. For the same notion of truth which we have examined in spoken statements must be examined in all the signs which are formed in order to signify that something is or is not — for example, in written characters or in sign-language with the fingers.

S. Proceed, then, to these other topics.

Chapter Three: The truth of thought.

T. We call a thought true when there is what we — either by reason or in some other[7] way — suppose there to be. And [we call a thought] false when there is not [what we suppose there to be].

S. This is our custom.

T. Then, what does truth in a thought seem to you to be?

S. According to the reasoning evidenced in the case of statements, the truth of thought is best called its rightness, or correctness (*rectitudo*). For to the end that we might think that what is is and that what-is-not is not, we have been given the capability of thinking that something is or is not. Thus, whoever thinks that what is is thinks what he ought to; and so his thinking is correct. Accordingly, if our thought is correct and true simply because we think that what is is, or that what-is-not is not, then the truth of thought is simply its rightness, or correctness.

T. Your thinking is correct.

Chapter Four: The truth of the will.

T. But when Truth itself [viz., God] says that the Devil "did not stand in the truth,"[8] He declares that truth is also in the will. For it was only with respect to his will that the Devil was in the truth and deserted the truth.

S. I believe this. For he deserted the truth only by sinning; and if he had always willed what he ought to have willed, then he never would have sinned.

T. Tell me, then, what you understand truth in his will to be.

S. It is only rightness, or uprightness [*rectitudo*]. For as long as the Devil willed what he ought to have willed — namely, the end for which he had received a will — he was in the truth and in uprightness; and when he willed what he ought not to have willed, he deserted truth and uprightness. So truth in his will can only be understood to be uprightness, since truth and uprightness in the Devil's will each consisted only in his willing what he ought to have willed.

T. You understand well.

Chapter Five: The truth of natural action and nonnatural action.

T. But we must no less believe that truth is also in actions — just as the Lord says, "He who does evil hates the light" and "He who does the truth comes to the light." [9]

S. I see what you mean.

T. Then, if you can, consider what truth in actions is.

S. Unless I am mistaken, truth in actions must be considered along the same lines as the truth we have already recognized in other things.

T. That's right. For if to do evil and to do the truth are opposites — as the Lord indicates when He says: "He who does evil hates the light" and "He who does the truth comes to the light" — then doing the truth is the same thing as doing good. For doing good and doing evil are opposites. Therefore, if doing the truth and doing good have the same opposite, their significations are not different. But everyone admits that whoever does what he ought does what is good and what is right. So it follows that to do what is right is to do the truth. For it is evident that to do the truth is to do what is good and that to do what is good is to do what is right. Therefore, nothing is clearer than that the truth of an action is its rightness [*rectitudo*].

S. I see no respect in which your reasoning is shaky.

T. Consider whether every action which does what it ought is appropriately said to do the truth. For there are rational actions,

De Veritate

such as giving alms, and there are nonrational actions — such as the action of fire, which heats. Now, is it appropriate to say that fire does the truth?

S. If fire has received the power to heat from Him from whom it has its being,[10] then when it heats it does what it ought. Therefore, I do not see anything inappropriate [in saying] that fire does what is true and what is right when it does what it ought.

T. That's the way it seems to me too. Hence, we can note that there is a necessary and a nonnecessary rightness, or truth, of action. For of necessity fire does what is right and true when it heats; but out of no necessity a man does what is right and true when he does what is good. However, when the Lord said, "He who does the truth comes to the light,"[11] He wanted us to understand the verb "to do" not only as standing for what is properly called a doing, but also as a substitute for every other verb.[12] For He excludes from this truth, or light, neither the man who *undergoes* persecution for the sake of justice[13] nor the man who *is* when and where he ought to be, nor the man who *is standing* or *sitting* when he ought to — and the like. For no one denies that such persons do what is good. And when the apostle says that each man shall receive [recompense] "in accordance with what he has done,"[14] we must understand this phrase to indicate all that we commonly call doing good and doing evil.

S. Even our ordinary way of speaking calls enduring and many other things doings which are not [properly] doings.[15] So unless I am wrong, we can also number among right actions the upright willing whose truth we discussed before dealing with the truth of action.

T. You are not mistaken. For he who wills what he ought is said to do what is right and good; and he is included among those who do the truth. But since we are speaking of truth by analyzing it, and since the Lord seems to be speaking especially of that truth which is in the will when He says that the Devil "did not stand in the truth,"[16] I wanted to examine separately what truth in the will is.

S. I am glad you did.

T. Since, then, it is evident that there is both a natural and a nonnatural truth of action, *that* truth of a statement which (as we have seen)[17] cannot be separated from it must be classified as natural. For just as when fire heats it does the truth because it has received [the power to heat] from Him from whom it has its being, so also the statement "It is day" does the truth when it signifies that it is day (whether it is daytime or not) since it has received the nature to do this.

S. Now for the first time I see the truth in a false statement.

Chapter Six: The truth of the senses.

T. Do you think that we have discovered all the abodes of truth, leaving aside consideration of the Supreme Truth?

S. I recall now a certain truth which I do not find among those you have dealt with.

T. What is it?

S. There is truth in the bodily senses — but not always, for at times they deceive us. For sometimes when I am looking at an object through a glass, my sight deceives me, because sometimes it reports to me that the object I see beyond the glass is the same color as the glass; yet it really is a different color. And sometimes my sight causes me to believe that the glass is the color of the object on the other side of it, even though it is not that color. And there are many other cases in which sight and the other senses deceive.

T. This truth or falsity, it seems to me, is not in the senses but in the judgment (*opinione*). For the outer sense does not lie to the inner sense, but the latter deceives itself. This fact is sometimes easy to recognize, at other times difficult. For when a boy is afraid of the statue of an open-mouthed dragon, we easily recognize that sight does not cause this fear (for sight reports to the boy nothing other than it reports to aged people); rather, the fear is caused by the childish inner sense, which does not yet know how to discern well between a real object and its likeness. The same thing happens when we see a person who resembles someone else and we mistake him for the one he resembles — or, again, when someone who hears what is not a man's voice thinks it to be a man's voice. The inner sense also causes these mistakes.

Now, what you say about glass happens the way it does because when sight passes through a body which has the color of air, it is no more prevented from receiving the likeness of the color it sees beyond the glass than when it passes through the air.

De Veritate

[And this is always the case] except insofar as the body it passes through is denser or darker than air. For example, [this is the case] when sight passes through glass of its own color — i.e., glass which has no color admixed to its own — or when it passes through very clear water or through a crystal or through something having a similar color. But when sight passes through some other color (for example, through tinted glass),[18] it receives the color which it first encounters. Thus, after sight has received one color, then depending upon the extent to which it has been modified by this color, it receives either partially or not at all whatever other color it encounters. Therefore, sight reports the color it has apprehended first, and reports it either by itself or in combination with the color it meets subsequently. For if sight is modified by the first color up to its full capacity for receiving color, then it cannot at the same time sense another color. But if sight is affected by the first color less than exhausts its capacity to sense color, then it can still sense another color.

For example, if sight passes through a certain body, say glass, which is so perfectly red that sight is fully modified by this redness, then it is unable to be modified by another color at the same time. But if sight finds and first encounters a lesser degree of redness than exhausts its capacity to sense color, then (being not yet full, so to speak) it will be able to receive an additional color, to the degree that its capacity has not been exhausted by the first color. Accordingly, someone who is unaware of this fact thinks that sight reports that all the things it perceives after receiving the first color are either partially or entirely the same color as the first. Thereby the inner sense imputes its own failure to the outer sense.

Similarly, when an unbroken stick, partly in water, partly not, is thought to be broken, or when we think that our sight sees our real faces in a mirror, and when sight and the other senses seem to report to us many things as being other than they really are — the fault is not with the senses, which report in accordance with their natural powers,[19] but must be attributed to the soul's judgment (*iudicio*), which does not clearly discern what the senses can and ought to do. I do not think that time need be spent in showing this [in any more detail], since for our purposes it would be more tedious than profitable. Let it suffice to say that whatever the senses are seen to report, whether as a result of their nature or of some other cause [for example, because of a tinted glass], they do what they ought. Therefore, they do what is right and true, and their truth falls within the classification of truth in actions.

S. Your answer has satisfied me. I do not wish for you to dwell longer on the topic of the senses.

Chapter Seven: The truth in the being of things.

T. Leaving out of consideration the Supreme Truth, consider now whether we must understand truth to be in anything other than the things we have already mentioned.

S. What could that be?

T. Do you think that there is anything, at any time or place, which is not in the Supreme Truth, or has not received from the Supreme Truth what it is, insofar as it is, or is able to be other than what it is in the Supreme Truth?

S. No, we must not think so.

T. Therefore, whatever is is truly — insofar as it is what it is in the Supreme Truth.

S. You can conclude unreservedly that everything which is is truly since it is nothing other than what it is there.

T. Thus, there is truth in the being[20] of all that exists, because all things are what they are in the Supreme Truth.

S. I see that in the being of things there is truth to such an extent that no falsehood can be there, since what falsely exists does not exist.

T. That's a good answer. But, tell me, ought anything to be different from what it is in the Supreme Truth?

S. No.

T. So if all things are what they are in the Supreme Truth, then without doubt they are what they ought to be.

S. Yes, all things are what they ought to be.

T. But whatever is what it ought to be, is rightly.

S. No other conclusion is possible.

T. Therefore, everything which is is rightly.

S. Nothing follows more consistently.

T. So if truth and rightness are in the being of things because these things are what they are in the Supreme Truth, then assuredly the truth of things is rightness [*rectitudo*].

S. Nothing is clearer with respect to the logic of the argument.

De Veritate

Chapter Eight: The various meanings of "ought" and "ought not," "able" and "unable."

S. But how can we say truthfully that whatever is ought to be, since there are many evil deeds which certainly ought not to be?
T. Why should it be strange that the same thing both ought to be and ought not to be?
S. How can this be so?
T. I know you believe that nothing at all *is* except by God's causing it or permitting it.
S. Nothing is more certain to me.
T. Would you dare to suggest that God unwisely or evilly causes or permits something?
S. I would say, rather, that [He causes or permits] something only wisely and well.
T. Would you say that what such great Goodness and Wisdom causes or permits ought not to be?
S. What intelligent person would dare to suppose this?
T. Therefore, both what happens by God's causing and what happens by His permitting ought equally to be.
S. What you say is evident.
T. Tell me also, do you think that the effect of an evil will ought to be?
S. This is the same as asking whether an evil deed ought to be; and no one with any sense would concede this.
T. Nevertheless, God permits some men to do evilly what they will evilly.
S. Would that He permitted it less often!
T. So the same thing both ought and ought not to be. It ought to be since it is permitted wisely and well by God, without whose permission it could not have happened. Yet, with respect to him by whose evil will it is committed (*concipitur*), it ought not to be. In this way, then, the Lord Jesus ought not to have undergone death because He alone [among men] was innocent; and no one ought to have inflicted death upon Him; nevertheless, He ought to have undergone death because He wisely and graciously and usefully willed to undergo it. For in many ways the same thing admits in different respects of opposites.[21] This is frequently the

case in regard to an action [*actio*] — for instance, a beating [*percussio*].²² For "beating" is predicable both of one who gives it [i.e., of an agent] and of one who gets it [i.e., of a patient]. Hence, [in different respects] it can be called both an action and a passion. Nevertheless, according to their grammatical form "*actio*" and "*percussio*" (and likewise any other words which have passive forms but active meanings) seem to pertain more to a patient than to an agent. Indeed, with reference to acting, it seems more proper to say "*agentia*" or "*percutientia*"; and with reference to undergoing, it seems more proper to say "*actio*" and "*percussio.*" For "*agentia*" and "*percutientia*" are derived from "*agens*" and "*percutiens,*" even as "*providentia*" is derived from "*providens,*" and as "*continentia*" from "*continens*"; all of these forms (viz., "*agens*," "*percutiens*," "*providens*," and "*continens*") are active. But "*actio*" and "*percussio*" are derived from "*actus*" and "*percussus,*" which are passives. Now — to take one example that holds true of the other terms as well — just as giving a beating (*percutiens*) always occurs in connection with getting a beating [*percussus*] and getting a beating always occurs in connection with giving a beating, so giving a beating and getting a beating cannot occur separately: one and the same thing is signified by different words in accordance with its different aspects. Hence, beating (*percussio*) is said to consist of both giving a beating [*percutiens*] and getting a beating [*percussus*].

Thus, depending upon whether agent and patient are subject to the same or to opposite judgments, the two aspects of the action will be judged to be alike or opposite. Therefore, (1) when the one who gives a beating does so rightly and the one who gets that beating does so rightly — for example, when a sinner is corrected by someone whose prerogative it is — both aspects of the action are right because in both respects a beating ought to be. And (2) when, on the contrary, a just man is beaten by an unjust man, neither aspect of the action is right because the just man ought not to get a beating nor ought the unjust man to give a beating, and so in neither respect ought a beating to occur. But (3) when a sinner is beaten by one whose prerogative it is not, then a beating both ought and ought not to be, since the sinner ought to get a beating but the other man ought not to give a beating; and so the action cannot be denied to be both right and not right. But if you

De Veritate

consider whether or not from the standpoint of Supernal Wisdom and Goodness there ought to be a beating in either or both of these respects (viz., with respect to the agent and with respect to the patient), would you or anyone else dare to deny that what such great Wisdom and Goodness permits ought to be?

S. Let him deny it who dares. I am not that bold.

T. If you also consider something from the standpoint of the nature of things — for example, the driving of iron nails into the body of the Lord — would you say that His frail flesh ought not to have been penetrated, or that, once penetrated by sharp iron, it ought not to have felt pain?

S. I would be speaking against nature.

T. Therefore, it is possible that with respect to nature there ought to be either an action or a passion which, with respect to the agent or the patient, ought not to be since neither the agent ought to do it nor the patient to undergo it.

S. I cannot deny any of this.

T. So you see that it very often can happen that the same action both ought and ought not to be, though in different respects.

S. You present this so clearly that I cannot help seeing it.

T. But I want you to be aware as well that "ought" and "ought not" are sometimes said improperly — as, for example, when I say that I ought to be loved by you.[23] For if I truly *ought*, then I am indebted to repay what I *owe*, and am at fault if I am not loved by you.

S. It follows.

T. But when I ought to be loved by you, then payment should be exacted not from me but from you.

S. I must concede it.

T. So when I say that I ought to be loved by you this means not that *I* owe something but that *you* owe me love. Likewise, when I say that I ought not to be loved by you, what is meant is only that you ought not to love me.

This same mode of speaking also occurs in conjunction with the notions of ability and inability.[24] We say, for instance, "Hector was able to be overpowered by Achilles" and "Achilles was not able to be overpowered by Hector." Yet, ability was not in the one who was able to be overpowered, but was in the one who was able to overpower; and inability was not in him who was not able to be overpowered, but was in him who was not able to overpower.

S. What you say pleases me. Indeed, I think it useful to know.

T. You think correctly.

Chapter Nine: Every action signifies either what is true or what is false.

T. But let us return to [the topic of] the truth of signification. I began with this topic in order to lead you from the more familiar to the less familiar. For everyone speaks about the truth of signification, but few consider the truth which is in the being of things.

S. I have been aided by your having led me in this sequence.

T. Let us see, then, how extensive the truth of signification is. For there is a true or a false signification not only in those things which we ordinarily call signs, but also in all the other things which we have discussed. For since someone should do only what he ought to do, then by the very fact that someone does something, he says and signifies that he ought to do it. Now, if [morally speaking] he ought to do what he does, he speaks the truth. But if [morally speaking] he ought not [to do what he does], he speaks a lie.

S. Although I seem to understand, show me more clearly what you mean, because I have not heard this before.

T. Suppose you were in a place where you knew there to be edible herbs and poisonous ones, but you did not know how to tell them apart; suppose too that with you was another person, whose ability to discriminate between the two you trusted. Now, suppose that you asked him which ones were edible and which were poisonous, and that he told you that the one kind was edible but himself ate the other kind. Which would you believe the more: his word or his deed?

S. I would believe his deed more than his word.

T. Therefore, by his action more than by his word he would be telling you about which herbs were edible.

S. Yes, that's right.

T. So, then, if you did not know that one should not lie, and if someone lied in your presence, then even were he to say that he

De Veritate

ought not to lie, his telling you by his deed that he ought to lie would outweigh his telling you by his word that he ought not to lie. Similarly, when someone thinks or wills something: if you did not know whether he ought to think or will it, then if you could see his thought and will, by his act of thinking and of willing he would signify to you that he ought to think and will this thing. Now if, [morally speaking], this person ought [to be thinking and willing this, then by his thinking and willing] he would be telling the truth; and if, [morally speaking], he ought not [to be thinking and willing this], then he would be lying.

There is also a similarly true or a false signification in the existence of things, since by the very fact that they are, they declare that they ought to be.

S. I now see clearly what I had not noticed before.

T. Let us go on to the remaining topics.

S. Lead the way. I will follow.

Chapter Ten: The Supreme Truth.

T. You will not deny that the Supreme Truth is rightness [*rectitudo*], will you?

S. Indeed not. I cannot call it anything else.

T. Consider the following: Although all the different rightnesses which were mentioned earlier are rightnesses because the things they are in either are what they *ought* to be or else do what they *ought* to do, nevertheless it is not the case that the Supreme Truth is rightness because it is under any *indebtedness*. For all other things are indebted to it; it does not owe anything to anyone. It has no other reason for being what it is except that it is.

S. I understand.

T. Do you also see how this Rightness is the cause of all other truths and rightnesses, and how nothing is the cause of it?

S. Yes, I do. And I notice among these other truths and rightnesses that some are only effects, whereas some are both causes and effects. For example, although the truth which is in the existence of things is the effect of the Supreme Truth, it is the cause of the truth of thought and of the truth which is in statements; but these two truths[25] are not causes of any truth.

T. That's a keen observation. On the basis of it you can now understand how in my *Monologion* I proved by means of the truth of a statement that the Supreme Truth has neither beginning nor end.[26] For when I asked "When was it ever not true that something was going to exist?" I did not mean to suggest (1) that the statement which asserted that something was going to exist was itself without a beginning, or (2) that the truth of this statement was God. I meant to say only that, given the statement, we cannot understand there to be a time when truth would not have been in it — so that from the fact that we do not understand there to be a time when this truth could have failed to be in it (given the statement in which truth could be), we should understand that that other Truth, which is the first cause of the statement's truth, was without beginning. Indeed, the truth of the statement could not always be unless its cause always were. For the statement which says that something is going to exist is true only if something is, in fact, going to exist. And something is going to exist only if it exists in the Supreme Truth.

We must understand in a similar way the other statement, which says that something has existed in the past. For if truth could in no respect fail to be in this statement (given the statement), then it follows that that Truth which is the supreme cause of this statement's truth cannot be understood to have an end. For it is true to say that something has existed, because thus in fact it has; and something has existed because thus it exists in the Supreme Truth.

Therefore, if it was never able not to be true that something was going to exist, and never will be able not to be true that something has existed, then it is impossible that the Supreme Truth had a beginning or will have an end.

S. I do not see any possible objection to your reasoning.

Chapter Eleven: The definition of "truth."

T. Let us return to the investigation of truth which we began.

S. All that [we were just discussing] is pertinent to investigating truth. But nonetheless, return to whatever you wish.

T. Tell me, then, whether you think that there is still another rightness in addition to those rightnesses we have examined.

S. There are no other rightnesses than those — except for the

De Veritate

rightness which is in corporeal things, such as the rightness, or straightness, (*rectitudo*) of a stick. But this is quite different from the other kinds.

T. In what way does this rightness seem to you to differ from the others?

S. Because it can be apprehended by bodily sight, whereas rational reflection apprehends the others.

T. Cannot reason understand and apprehend the straightness of material objects separably from the objects? Or if there is doubt about whether the surface (*linea*) of an absent object is straight and it can be shown that no part of it is curved, then does not reason infer that the surface must be straight?

S. Yes. But the same rightness which is thus known by reason is perceived in the object by sight, whereas the other kinds of rightness can only be perceived by the mind.

T. Therefore, unless I am mistaken we can define "truth" as "rightness perceptible only to the mind."

S. I see that he who says this, is in no way mistaken. Without doubt, this definition of "truth" contains neither more nor less than is proper (*expediat*), since "rightness" distinguishes it from everything which is not called rightness, and "perceptible only to the mind" distinguishes it from visible rightness.

Chapter Twelve: The definition of "justice."

S. But since you have taught me that all truth is rightness and since rightness seems to me to be the same thing as justice, teach me also what I may understand justice to be. For it seems that whatever it is for a thing to be right is also what it is for that thing to be just, and that, conversely, whatever it is for a thing to be just is what it is for that thing to be right. For it seems to be both just and right for fire to be hot and for each person to reciprocate another's love. For if (as I believe) whatever ought to be, rightly and justly is, and if nothing else rightly and justly is except what ought to be, then justice can only be rightness. Indeed, although it is not the case that the Supreme and Simple Nature is just or right because it ought [to be or to do] anything, nevertheless rightness and justice are assuredly identical in it.

T. Therefore, if justice is nothing other than rightness, you have the definition of "justice." And since we are speaking about the rightness which is perceptible only to the mind — "truth," "rightness," and "justice" are definable in terms of one another. As a result, if someone knows what one of them is but does not know what the other two are, he can infer from his knowledge of one to a knowledge of the others. In fact, if anyone knows one of them, he cannot keep from knowing the other two.

S. What then? Shall we call a stone *just* because it does what it ought when it seeks to move downwards — even as we call a man just when he does what he ought?

T. No, we usually do not call anything just on the basis of this kind of justice.

S. Why, then, is a man any more just than is a stone, if both behave justly?

T. Don't you think that the activity of a man differs in some respect from the activity of a stone?

S. I know that a man acts freely but that a stone acts by nature and not freely.

T. This is why we do not call a stone just; for if a thing which does what it ought does not will what it does, then it is not just.

S. Shall we say, then, that a horse is just when it wills to eat, because it willingly does what it ought?

T. I did not say that something is just which willingly does what it ought; rather, I said that whatever does not do willingly what it ought is not just.

S. Tell me, then, who or what is just.

T. As I see it, you are asking for a definition of that justice which is praiseworthy, even as its opposite, viz., injustice, is blameworthy.

S. That's the justice I am seeking.

T. It is evident that this justice is not in any nature which does not know rightness. For whatever does not will rightness does not merit to be praised for having it, even if it does have it. But a nature which does not know rightness is not able to will it.

S. That's true.

T. Therefore, the rightness which brings praise to a thing which has rightness is present only in a rational nature, which alone perceives the rightness we are talking about.

S. It follows.

T. Therefore, since all justice is rightness, the justice which

De Veritate

makes the one who keeps it worthy of praise is present only in rational natures.

S. It cannot be otherwise.

T. Then where do you think this justice is to be found in man, who is rational?

S. It must be either in his will or his knowledge or his action.

T. What if someone understands rightly or acts rightly but does not will rightly: will anyone praise him on account of justice?

S. No.

T. Therefore, this justice is not rightness of knowledge or rightness of action but is rightness of will.

S. It shall be either this or nothing.

T. Do you think that the justice we are seeking has been adequately defined?

S. You decide.

T. Do you think that whoever wills what he ought wills rightly and has rightness, or uprightness, of will?

S. Not if he unknowingly wills what he ought. Take the case of a man who wills to lock out another without knowing that this other wants to kill a third person inside the house. Whether the one who locks the door does or does not have some kind of uprightness-of-will, he does not have that uprightness-of-will which we are seeking.

T. What do you say about a person who knows that he ought to will what he does will?

S. It can happen that he knowingly wills what he ought [to will] and yet does not want to be under the obligation [of so willing]. For example, when a robber is compelled to return the stolen money, then from the very fact that he is *compelled* to will (*velle*) to return it because he ought, it is evident that he does not want (*velle*) to be under the obligation [so to will]. He is not at all entitled to be praised on account of this rightness.

T. Anyone who feeds a poor hungry man on account of his own vainglory *does* want to be under the obligation to will what he wills. And indeed, he is praised because he wills to do what he ought [to will to do]. So what is your judgment about him?

S. His rightness must not be praised; and so it is not to be identified with the justice we are seeking. But identify for me now the justice we are in search of.

T. Even as every will wills something, so it also wills for the sake of something. And just as we must consider *what* it wills, so we must also notice *why* it wills. For a will ought to be upright in willing what it ought and, no less, in willing for the reason it ought. Therefore, every will has both a *what* and a *why*. Indeed, whatsoever we will, we will for a reason.

S. We all recognize this in ourselves.

T. But in order for a man's will to be praiseworthy, *for what reason* do you think he ought to will what he does will? *What* he must will is clear, since whoever does not will what he ought to will is not just.

S. And it seems no less clear to me that in order for a man's will to be just, he must will for the reason he ought, even as he must will what he ought.

T. You understand well that these two things are necessary for a will to be just: willing what it ought [to will] and willing for the reason it ought [to will]. But tell me whether these two things are sufficient [for the will's being just].

S. Why wouldn't they be?

T. When someone wills what he ought to will and does so because he is compelled [to will it], and is compelled [to will it] because he ought to will it, is he not in a certain sense willing what he ought [to will] for the reason he ought [to will]?

S. I cannot deny it. But whereas *he* wills in one manner, a just man wills in another manner.

T. Distinguish these two manners.

S. When a just man wills what he ought [to will], then — insofar as he is to be called just — he keeps uprightness-of-will only for its own sake. By contrast, someone who wills what he ought to will but does so only if compelled to or only if induced by external rewards, does not keep uprightness-of-will for its own sake, but keeps it for the sake of something else — if he should at all be said to keep it.

T. Then, that will is just which keeps its uprightness on account of that uprightness itself.

S. Either that will is just or no will is.

T. Therefore, justice is uprightness (*rectitudo*)-of-will kept for its own sake.

S. Yes, this is the definition of "justice" I was seeking.

De Veritate

T. See whether something in this definition ought perhaps to be amended.

S. I do not see anything in it to be improved.

T. Nor do I. For there is no justice which is not rightness (*rectitudo*); and no rightness other than uprightness (*rectitudo*)-of-will is called, in and of itself, justice. For rightness-of-action is called justice, but only when that action is performed by means of a just will. However, uprightness-of-will does not at all lose the name "justice" — not even when it is impossible to do what we rightly will.

Now, as regards the word "kept," someone will perhaps say: "If uprightness-of-will is to be called justice only when it is kept, then uprightness-of-will is not justice from the moment this uprightness is possessed; and we do not receive justice when we receive uprightness-of-will, but we make this uprightness become justice by keeping it. For we receive and have uprightness-of-will before we keep it. We do not receive it and have it for the first time because we keep it, but we begin to keep it because we have received it and already have it."

But to these inferences we can reply that at one and the same time we receive the willing it and the having it. For we have uprightness only by willing it; and by the very act of willing it we have it. However, just as we simultaneously have it and will it, so we simultaneously will it and keep it; for just as we do not keep it except when we will it, so there is no time when we will it and do not keep it. Now, as long as we will it we keep it; and as long as we keep it we will it. Therefore, since our willing it and having it occur at the same time, and since our willing it and keeping it do not occur at different times, then it necessarily follows that we receive simultaneously the having of it and the keeping of it. And just as we have it as long as we keep it, so we keep it as long as we have it. These assertions involve no contradiction.

Of course, the receiving of this uprightness is by nature prior to having it or willing it (since having it or willing it is not the cause of receiving it, but receiving it makes possible both the having and the willing it); and yet receiving, having, and willing occur simultaneously (for we begin to receive and to have and to will this uprightness at the same time; and as soon as uprightness is received, it is both had and willed). Similarly, having uprightness and willing it occur simultaneously with keeping it, even though they are by nature prior to keeping. Therefore, we receive justice through receiving simultaneously the having, the willing, and the keeping of uprightness-of-will. And as soon as we have and will this uprightness-of-will, this uprightness is to be called justice.

The phrase "for its own sake," which we included [in our definition of "justice,"] is so essential that this very uprightness is in no respect justice unless it is kept for its own sake.

S. I can think of no objections to this.

T. Do you think that this definition can be applied to the Supreme Justice — insofar, that is, as we are able to speak about a thing of which nothing, or almost nothing, can properly be said?

S. Since in God's divinity, power is not other than the divinity itself, we speak of the power of His divinity or of His divine power or of His powerful divinity. Similarly, although God's will is not one thing and His uprightness another, nevertheless it is not unsuitable for us to speak of His uprightness of will or of His voluntary uprightness or of His right will. But if we say that God's uprightness is kept for its own sake, then we seem not to be able to say this as suitably about anyone else's uprightness. For just as nothing else keeps God's uprightness, but it keeps itself, and just as it keeps itself through nothing other than through itself, so it keeps itself for the sake of nothing but itself.

T. Then, we can say with certainty that justice is uprightness-of-will which is being kept for its own sake.

Now, since [in Latin] we do not have a present passive participle of the verb "*servatur*" ("is being kept"), we can use the perfect passive participle of this verb in order to express present time.

S. We have the well-known practice of using perfect passive participles as substitutes for present passive participles, which Latin does not have. Similarly, Latin lacks perfect participles of active and neuter verbs; and for these past participles which are lacking we use present participles. For example, I might say about someone, "Only compelled (*coactus*) does he teach what he learned studying and reading (*studens et legens*)"; that is, "Only when he is compelled does he teach what he learned while he studied and read."

T. Then we did well to say that justice is uprightness-of-will kept (*servatam*) for its own sake, i.e., which is being kept (*ser-*

De Veritate

vatur) for its own sake. Accordingly, men who are just are sometimes called upright in heart (i.e., upright in will); and sometimes they are simply called upright, without the qualifying phrase "in heart," since no one is understood to be upright except one whose will is upright. Thus, Scripture says: "Glory, all of you who are upright in heart,"[27] and also "The upright shall see and shall rejoice."[28]

S. With your definition of "justice" you have satisfied even children. Let us go on to other matters.

Chapter Thirteen: Truth is one in all true things.

T. Let us go back to [the notion of] rightness, or truth. Since we are talking about rightness perceptible only to the mind, "rightness," or "truth," signifies a single thing which is the genus of justice. Let us ask whether there is only one truth in all the things in which we say there is truth, or whether there is more than one truth, even as there is more than one thing in which we know truth to be.

S. I very much desire to know the answer to this.

T. It is evident that regardless of what thing truth is in, truth is nothing other than rightness (*rectitudo*).

S. I do not doubt this.

T. Then, if in accordance with the many things there were many truths, there would also be many rightnesses.

S. This is equally certain.

T. And if there had to be as many different rightnesses as there are different kinds of things, then surely these rightnesses would exist in accordance with these various things; and just as the things in which there is rightness vary, so there would have to be a variety of rightnesses.

S. By taking as an example one thing in which we say that there is rightness, show me what I may understand about other things [in which we also say that there is rightness].

T. I mean that if the rightness of signification [i.e., correctness] were different from the rightness of the will [i.e., uprightness] simply because the former rightness is in the signification and the latter in the will, then the former rightness would exist on account of signification and would be changed in accordance with it.

S. But isn't this the case? For when what is is signified to be, or when what-is-not is signified not to be, then the signification is correct, or right, and (assuredly) rightness exists, without which the signification could not be right. But if what-is-not is signified to be, or if what is is signified not to be, or if nothing at all is signified, then there will be no rightness of signification since this rightness can exist only in the signification. Hence, this rightness has its existence through the signification and is changed with the signification — just as color has its existence and nonexistence through a material object. For as long as the material object exists it is necessary that its color exist; but when the material object perishes, it is impossible for its color to remain.

T. No. Rightness does not belong to signification as color belongs to a material object.

S. Show me the difference.

T. If no one wishes to signify by means of a given sign what should be signified,[29] then will there be any signification by means of signs?

S. No.

T. And so, it will not be right for what-ought-to-be-signified to be signified?

S. On the contrary, it will be no less right,[30] and rightness will no less demand this.[31]

T. Therefore, when the signification does not exist, that rightness does not perish by which it is right that there be signified what should be signified, and by which it is demanded that there be signified what should be signified.

S. If that rightness had perished, then it would not have been right [for what-ought-to-be-signified to be signified], and rightness would not have demanded this.

T. Don't you think that when what ought to be signified is signified, the signification is right on account of and in accordance with this very rightness?

S. Indeed, I cannot think differently. For if the signification were right by virtue of some other rightness, then were the above-mentioned rightness to perish, nothing would prevent the signification from being right. But no signification is right which

De Veritate

signifies what is not right to be signified, or which signifies what rightness does not demand that it signify.

T. Therefore, no signification is right by virtue of any other rightness than that which remains when the signification perishes.

S. Clearly not.

T. Therefore, don't you see that rightness is in the signification not because rightness begins to be when what is is signified to be or when what-is-not is signified not to be, but because the signification is made in accordance with a rightness which always exists? Don't you see too that rightness is absent from signification not because rightness perishes when the signification is not as it ought to be or when there is no signification, but because the signification lacks this rightness which never perishes?

S. I see this so clearly that I cannot fail to see it.

T. Then, the rightness in terms of which the signification is called correct, or right, neither exists through nor changes with the signification, regardless of how the signification changes.

S. Nothing is now clearer to me.

T. Can you prove that rightness belongs to a signification in a way similar to the way that color belongs to a material object?

S. I am now more prepared to prove that the two ways are very dissimilar.

T. I think you now know what must be thought about the will and its rightness, and about the other things which ought to have rightness.

S. I see perfectly that your reasoning proves that rightness remains unchangeable, regardless of how these other things are.

T. So what conclusion do you think follows regarding these rightnesses? Are they different from one another, or is there one and the same rightness of all things?

S. I conceded previously that if there is more than one rightness simply because there is more than one thing in which rightness is seen to be, then it necessarily follows that these rightnesses exist and change in accordance with those things. But you have proven that this does not at all happen. Therefore, it is not the case that there is more than one rightness simply because there is more than one thing in which there is rightness.

T. Do you have any other reason for supposing that there is a plurality of rightnesses except that there is a plurality of things?

S. Just as I recognize that the argument from a plurality of things is faulty, so I see that no other argument can be found.

T. Therefore, the rightness of all things is one and the same.

S. Yes, I have to agree.

T. Moreover, if it is only when things are in accordance with what they ought to be that rightness is in those things which ought to have it, and if for them to be right is only [for them to be in accordance with what they ought to be], then it is evident that the rightness of all these things is only one.

S. It cannot be denied.

T. Therefore, truth is one in all these things.

S. This is also impossible to be denied. But nevertheless, if truth assumes no plurality as a result of the plurality of things, show me why we say "the truth of this thing" or "the truth of that thing," as if we were distinguishing different truths. For many persons will be quite reluctant to concede that there is no difference between the truth of the will and what we call the truth of, say, action, or [the truth of] one of the other things.

T. We speak improperly when we say "the truth of this thing" or "the truth of that thing." For truth does not have its being *in* or *from* or *through* the things in which it is said to be. But when these things are in accordance with truth, which is always present to things which are as they ought to be, then we say "the truth of this thing" or "the truth of that thing" (for example, "the truth of the will" or "the truth of action"). Similarly, we say "the time of this thing" or "the time of that thing," although there is one and the same time for all things which exist together at the same time. And if *this* thing did not exist or if *that* thing did not exist, time would nonetheless remain the same; for we say "the time of this thing" or "the time of that thing" not because time is in these things but because these things are in time. Now, when considered in itself, time is not called the time of anything; but when we consider things which are in time, we say "the time of this thing" or "the time of that thing." Similarly, Supreme Truth, existing in and of itself, is not the truth of anything; but when something accords with Supreme Truth, then we speak of the truth, or rightness, of that thing.

FREEDOM OF CHOICE
(De Libertate Arbitrii)

CHAPTER TITLES

1. The ability to sin does not pertain to freedom of choice.
2. Nevertheless, the angel and the man sinned by means of this ability and by free choice; and although they were able to serve sin, sin was not able to master them.
3. How after [Satan and Adam] had made themselves servants of sin, they still had free choice. What free choice is.
4. How [Satan and Adam] have the ability to keep uprightness, which they do not have.
5. No temptation compels one to sin against his will.
6. How our will is powerful against temptations although it appears powerless against them.
7. How [the will] is stronger than temptation even when it is overcome by temptation.
8. Even God is not able to remove uprightness-of-will.
9. Nothing is more free than an upright will.
10. How one who sins is a servant of sin. It is a greater miracle when God restores uprightness to a will which has deserted it than when He restores life to the dead.
11. This servitude does not remove freedom of choice.
12. Why when a man *does not* have uprightness it is better to call him free (on the ground that when he *does* have uprightness it cannot be taken away from him) than it is, when he *does* have uprightness, to call him a servant (on the ground that when he *does not* have uprightness he cannot recover it by himself).
13. "The ability to keep uprightness-of-will for the sake of this uprightness itself" is the complete definition of "freedom of choice."
14. The division of this same freedom.

FREEDOM OF CHOICE[1]
(*De Libertate Arbitrii*)

Chapter One: The ability to sin does not pertain to freedom of choice.

Student. Since free choice seems to be opposed to the grace, predestination, and foreknowledge of God, I desire to know what freedom of choice is and whether we always have it. For if freedom of choice consists in being able to sin and not to sin (as some persons are accustomed to say) and if we always have this ability, how is it that we sometimes need grace? But if we do not always have this ability, why is sin imputed to us when we sin without a free choice?

Teacher. I do not think that freedom of choice is the ability to sin and not to sin. Indeed, if this were its definition, then neither God nor the angels who are not able to sin would have free choice — a blasphemous thing to say.

S. What if we say that the free choice of God and of the good angels is different from ours?

T. Although the free choice of men differs from that of God and of the good angels, nevertheless the definition of this freedom ought to be the same in both cases, in accordance with the name "freedom." For example, although one animal differs from another either substantially or accidentally, the definition [of animal] is the same for all animals, in accordance with the name "animal."[2] Hence, it is necessary to give such a definition of "freedom of choice" — a definition which contains neither more nor less than freedom does. Therefore, since the free choice of God and of the good angels is not able to sin, "to be able to sin" does not pertain to the definition of "freedom of choice." In fact, the ability to sin does not constitute either freedom or a part of freedom. To understand this point clearly, pay attention to what I am going to say.

S. That's the reason I am here.

T. Which will seems the more free to you: the will which so wills and is so able not to sin that it cannot at all be turned away from the uprightness [*rectitudo*] of not sinning, or the will which in some way is able to be turned to sinning?

S. I do not see why a will which has both abilities [viz., to sin and not to sin] is not the more free.

T. Don't you see that someone who so possesses what is fitting and advantageous that he cannot lose it is more free than someone else who possesses the same thing in such a way that he can lose it and can be induced to what is unfitting and disadvantageous?

S. I think that no one doubts this.

T. Will you admit that it is equally certain that sinning is always unfitting and harmful?

S. No one of sound mind thinks otherwise.

T. Then, the will which is not able to turn away from the uprightness of not sinning is more free than the will which is able to desert uprightness.

S. Nothing can more reasonably be asserted, it seems to me.

T. Do you think that something which if added decreases freedom and if subtracted increases it is either freedom or a part of freedom?

S. I am not able to think this.

T. Then, the ability to sin, which if added to the will decreases the will's freedom and if subtracted from the will increases its freedom, is neither freedom nor a part of freedom.

S. Nothing follows more logically.

Chapter Two: Nevertheless, the angel and the man sinned by means of this ability and by free choice; and although they were able to serve sin, sin was not able to master them.

T. Therefore, that which[3] is so foreign to freedom does not pertain to freedom of choice.

S. I cannot at all contradict your reasoning. Yet, I am quite disturbed by the fact that in the beginning angelic nature and our nature had the ability to sin, without which neither would have sinned. If, then, each of these natures sinned by means of this

De Libertate Arbitrii

ability which is so foreign to free choice, how shall we say that it sinned by free choice? But if it did not sin by free choice, it is seen to have sinned of necessity. Surely [it sinned] either freely or of necessity. Now, if it sinned freely, how could it have failed to sin by free choice? Hence, if it did not sin by free choice, then surely it is seen to have sinned of necessity.

There is also something else which bothers me about this ability to sin. Someone who is able to sin is able to be the servant of sin since "He who does sin is the servant of sin."[4] But whoever is able to be the servant of sin is able to be mastered by sin. So how is it that either of these natures was created free if sin was able to master it, or of what kind was that free choice which sin could master?

T. It was by means of an ability to sin, as well as freely and by free choice and of no necessity, that in the beginning our nature and angelic nature sinned and were able to serve sin. Nevertheless, sin was not able to master either nature to the point that the nature or its choice could be called unfree.

S. I need to have you disclose what you mean, for it is concealed from me.

T. Because the apostate angel [Satan] and the first man [Adam] sinned by their own choice which was so free that it could not be compelled by any other thing to sin, each of them sinned by free choice. Therefore, each of them is justly blamed because in spite of having this freedom of choice, each sinned freely and out of no necessity and without being compelled by anything else. However, each sinned by his own choice, which was free; but neither sinned by means of that in virtue of which his choice was free. That is, neither sinned by means of the ability in virtue of which he was able not to sin and not to serve sin; but each sinned by means of his ability to sin, and this ability neither helped him towards the freedom not to sin nor compelled him into the service of sin.

But it does not follow [rationally], as you suppose it to, that if each of them [viz., Satan and Adam] was able to be a servant of sin, then sin was able to master him, with the result that neither he nor his choice was free. Consider someone who has it in his power[5] not to serve and whom no other power can force to serve, even though he can serve by his own power. As long as he uses his power-not-to-serve rather than using his power-to-serve, nothing can force him to serve. For example, even if a free rich man were able to make himself the servant of a poor man, nonetheless as long as he does not do this he is properly described as free, and the poor man is not said to be able to be his master (or if it is said, it is said improperly, because to master is not in the poor man's power but in the rich man's). Accordingly, nothing prevents the [apostate] angel and the [first] man from having been free before they sinned or from having had free choice before they sinned.

Chapter Three: How after [Satan and Adam] had made themselves servants of sin, they still had free choice. What free choice is.

S. You have convinced me that before [Satan and Adam] sinned nothing at all prevented [them from having had free choice]. But after they had made themselves servants of sin, how is it that they were able to keep free choice?

T. Although they had subjected themselves to sin, they were not able to destroy their natural freedom of choice. However, they were able to cause themselves no longer to be able to use this freedom without a grace different from the grace they had originally possessed.

S. I believe, but I desire to understand.[6]

T. Let us examine first the manner in which they had freedom of choice before they sinned, when certainly they did have free choice.

S. I welcome this [examination].

T. For what end do you think they had freedom of choice? Was it in order to obtain what they willed, or was it in order to will what they ought to will and what was advantageous for them to will?

S. To will what they ought to will and what was advantageous to will.

T. Therefore, the end for which they had freedom of choice is uprightness-of-will. For, surely, as long as they willed what they ought to have willed, they had uprightness-of-will.

S. That's right.

T. When we say that the end for which they had freedom is uprightness-of-will, we still have not completely settled the issue

De Libertate Arbitrii

unless we add a further point. So I ask: in what manner did they have this freedom whose end is uprightness-of-will? Did they have it (1) in order to acquire uprightness-of-will without anyone's giving it, since they did not yet have it, or (2) in order to receive the uprightness-of-will they did not yet have if it should be given to them to have, or (3) in order to desert the uprightness-of-will they had received, and to recover it by themselves after they had deserted it, or (4) in order always to keep the uprightness-of-will they had received?

S. (∼1) I do not think they had freedom in order to acquire uprightness-of-will without anyone's giving it, because they were not able to have anything which they did not receive. (∼2) But because we must not believe that they were created without upright wills, we must not say that they had freedom in order to receive from a giver the gift of the uprightness they did not yet have — although we must not deny that they had the freedom to receive this same uprightness again if they deserted it and if it were returned to them by the one who originally gave it. (We often see evidence of this in men who are led back to justice from injustice by heavenly grace.)

T. It is true, as you say, that [Satan and Adam] were able to receive back the lost uprightness if it were given to them again. But we are not asking about that freedom which someone would need only if he had deserted the truth; rather, we are asking about that freedom which [Satan and Adam] possessed before they sinned, when they undoubtedly did have free choice.

S. Well then, I shall proceed to reply to what remains of your question. (∼3) It is not true that they had freedom in order to desert this uprightness, for to desert uprightness-of-will is to sin, and you have already shown that the ability to sin is neither freedom nor a part of freedom. Nor did they receive freedom in order to recover, by their own efforts, the uprightness they had deserted; for this uprightness was given to the end that it never be deserted. For the ability to recover uprightness-once-deserted would beget a negligence in keeping uprightness-already-possessed. (4) Therefore, it follows that freedom of choice was given to rational nature in order to keep the uprightness-of-will which it had received.

T. You have given a good reply to my questions. But we must still examine that on account of which rational nature was under obligation to keep this uprightness: Was it for the sake of the uprightness itself or was it for the sake of something else?

S. If freedom-of-choice had not been given to rational nature in order for it to keep uprightness-of-will for the sake of this uprightness itself, then freedom would not have been conducive to justice, since it is evident that justice is uprightness-of-will kept for its own sake.[7] But we believe that freedom of choice is conducive to justice. Therefore, we must maintain incontrovertibly that rational nature did not receive freedom except in order to keep uprightness-of-will for the sake of this uprightness itself.[8]

T. Accordingly, since all freedom is ability, freedom of choice is the ability to keep uprightness-of-will for the sake of this uprightness itself.

S. It cannot be anything else.

T. So it is now clear that a free choice is nothing other than a choice which is able to keep uprightness-of-will for the sake of this uprightness itself.

S. This conclusion is certainly obvious. But as long as [choice] had this uprightness it was able to keep what it had. However, after it has deserted uprightness, how is it able to keep what it does not have? Therefore, in the absence of the uprightness which can be kept, the free choice which is able to keep uprightness is also absent; for a choice is not able to keep what it does not have.

T. Even if uprightness-of-will is absent, rational nature still has without diminution what belongs to it essentially.[9] For in my opinion we have no ability which by itself suffices to any actual deed; nevertheless, when those conditions are absent without which our abilities are not at all brought into operation, we are said to have these abilities in ourselves without diminution. Indeed, no instrument suffices by itself to accomplish anything; nevertheless, when those conditions are absent without which we cannot use the instrument, we say without falsity that we have the instrument for a given kind of work. I shall give you an example of this in one case so that you may notice it in many cases. No one who has sight is said to be altogether unable to see a mountain.

S. Surely, anyone who is unable to see a mountain has no sight.

T. So anyone who has sight has the ability and the instrument

De Libertate Arbitrii

for seeing a mountain. However, if there is no mountain present and you say to someone, "See the mountain," he will answer: "I cannot because there is no mountain here; but if there were a mountain here, I would be able to see it." Likewise, if there were a mountain but were no light, he would answer the one instructing him to see the mountain: "I cannot since there is no light here; but if there were light, I would be able [to see the mountain]." Or again, if a mountain and light are present to a man who has sight, but if something obstructs his sight — for example, if someone covers the man's eyes — then he will say that he is not able to see the mountain; but if nothing were blocking his sight, without doubt he would have the ability to see the mountain.

S. Everyone knows all this.

T. So don't you recognize that there are several different capabilities involved in seeing an object? There is a capability (1) in the one who sees, (2) in the thing to be seen, and (3) in the medium — i.e., neither in the one who sees nor in the object to be seen. Moreover, the capability which is in the medium is twofold: (3a) a capability in the case of a thing-which-aids, and (3b) a capability in the case of a thing-which-does-not-impede (i.e., in a case where what is able to impede does not impede).

S. I see this clearly.

T. Therefore, these capabilities are four in number. If any one of them is missing, the other three are not able to accomplish anything either singularly or collectively. Nevertheless, when other of the capabilities are absent, we do not deny that the man who has sight does have sight (i.e., the instrument or ability to see) or that the visible object is able to be seen or that light is able to aid sight.

Chapter Four: How [Satan and Adam] have the ability to keep uprightness, which they do not have.

T. However, the fourth power [viz., 3b] is called a power improperly. For when what is accustomed to obstruct sight does not obstruct sight, then it is said to *give* the capability to see only because it *does not remove* the capability to see.

However, in the case of seeing light there are only three different capabilities, for in this case what is seen and what aids sight are identical. Doesn't everyone know this?

S. Surely no one is ignorant of it.

T. Therefore, when there is no object nearby to be seen, and when we are placed in darkness, and have our eyes closed or covered, we still have within us the ability to see any visible thing whatsoever. What, then, prevents our having the ability to keep uprightness-of-will for the sake of this uprightness itself — even in the absence of this uprightness — as long as within us we have *reason*, by which to recognize it, and *will*, by which to hold it fast? For the previously mentioned freedom of choice consists of both of these.

S. You have convinced me that the ability to keep uprightness-of-will belongs always to rational nature, and that this ability was free in the choice of the first man and [in the choices] of the angels, from whom[10] uprightness-of-will was not able to be removed against their wills.

Chapter Five: No temptation compels one to sin against his will.

S. But in what way is the choice of the human will free by virtue of this ability, since oftentimes a man who has an upright will deserts this uprightness against his will because of the pressure of temptation?

T. No one deserts this uprightness except by willing to. So if "against one's will" means "unwillingly," then no one deserts uprightness against his will. For a man can be bound against his will, because he can be bound when he is unwilling to be bound; a man can be tortured against his will, because he can be tortured when he is unwilling to be tortured; a man can be killed against his will, because he can be killed when he is unwilling to be killed. But a man cannot will against his will, because he cannot will if he is unwilling to will. For everyone-who-wills wills that he will.

S. If someone who lies in order not to be killed does so only willingly, then how is it that he is said to lie against his will? For just as against his will he lies, so against his will he wills to lie. And someone who against his will wills to lie, unwillingly wills to lie.

De Libertate Arbitrii

T. Perhaps he is said to lie against his will because when he so wills the truth that he does not lie except for the sake of his life, then he both wills the lie for the sake of his life and does not will it for its own sake (since he wills the truth). Thus, he lies both willingly and unwillingly. For the will by which we will something for its own sake (as when we will health for its own sake) is different from the will by which we will a thing for the sake of something else (as when we will to drink absinthe for the sake of health). Therefore, perhaps it can be said that the man lies both against his will and not against his will, in accordance with these different wills.[11] Accordingly, when the man is said to lie against his will because insofar as he wills the truth he does not will to lie, this statement does not contradict my claim that no one deserts uprightness-of-will against his will. For in lying, the man wills to desert uprightness for the sake of his life; and in accordance with this will he deserts uprightness willingly rather than against his will. This is the will we are discussing, for we are speaking about the will by which a man wills to lie for the sake of his life rather than about the will by which he does not will the lie for its own sake. On the other hand, he surely does lie against his will, in that against his will he either-lies-or-is-killed (i.e., against his will he is in a predicament in which, necessarily, one or the other of these happens). For although it is necessary that he either-lie-or-be-killed, it is not necessary that he be killed, because he can avoid being killed if he lies. And it is not necessary that he lie, because he can avoid lying if he [lets himself] be killed. For neither alternative is determined necessarily, because both are in his power. Hence, although against his will he either-lies-or-is-killed, it does not follow that he lies-against-his-will or that he is-killed-against-his-will.

There is another reason — one contained in common usage — why someone who willingly does something is said to do it against his will and unwillingly and of necessity. For when we are able to do something only with difficulty and hence refrain from doing it, we say that we are not able to do it and that we give up of necessity and against our wills. And when we are not able to cease doing something without difficulty and hence continue to do it, we say that we are doing it against our wills and unwillingly and of necessity. In this manner, then, someone who lies in order not to die is said to lie against his will and unwillingly and of necessity, because he is not able to avoid the lie without incurring the hardship of death. Therefore, just as someone who lies for the sake of his life is improperly said to lie against his will (since he lies willingly), so he is improperly said to *will to lie* against his will (since only willingly does he will to lie). For just as when he lies he wills that he lie, so when he wills to lie he wills that he will.

S. I cannot deny what you are saying.

T. So how can the will, which without its own consent cannot be subjected by an alien power, fail to be free?

S. By like reasoning, can we not say that the will of a horse is free because it serves the appetite of the flesh only willingly?

T. No, the case of a horse is not similar. For in a horse the will does not subject itself but is naturally subjected and always serves the appetite of the flesh by necessity. However, in a man, as long as the will is upright it neither is subjected to nor serves what it ought not; and it is not turned aside from uprightness by any alien force unless it willingly consents to what it ought not. And the human will is clearly seen to have this consent from itself and not by nature or of necessity, as in the case of a horse.

S. You have satisfactorily met my objection regarding the will of a horse. Return to where we were.

T. Will you deny that any given thing is free from a second thing which cannot constrain or restrain this first thing without the first thing's consent?

S. I do not see how to deny this.

T. Tell me as well how an upright will overcomes and how it is overcome.

S. To overcome is for it to will uprightness perseveringly; to be overcome is for it to will what it ought not [to will].

T. I think that only with the will's own consent can temptation keep an upright will away from uprightness or force it to what it ought not, so that the will does not will uprightness but wills what it ought not [to will].

S. I don't see any respect in which this is false.

T. Then, if without the will's own consent no temptation can turn the will away from uprightness toward sin — i.e., toward willing what it ought not [to will] — who can deny that the will is free in order to keep uprightness and is free from temptation and

De Libertate Arbitrii

sin? Therefore, when the will is overcome, it is overcome not by another power, but by its own.

S. What has been said proves this conclusion.

T. Don't you see too that what has been said entails that no temptation is able to overcome an upright will? For if it were able, it would have the power to overcome and would overcome by its own power. But temptation cannot do this since the will is overcome only by *its* own power. Therefore, temptation is not at all able to overcome an upright will; and when we say [that it is able], we are speaking improperly,[12] for we mean only that the will is able to subject itself to temptation. Compare, conversely, the case in which a weak man is said to be able to be overcome by a strong man. He is said *to be able* not with respect to his own ability but with respect to another's ability, for what is meant is only that the strong man has the ability to overcome the weak man.

Chapter Six: How our will is powerful against temptations although it appears powerless against them.

S. You so subdue all assaults on our will and so forbid any temptation to master it that I am not at all able to resist your claims. Nevertheless, I cannot keep from mentioning that in our will there is a powerlessness which nearly all of us experience when we are overcome by "irresistible" temptation. Accordingly, unless you render consistent the power you prove and the powerlessness we feel, my mind cannot regard our discussion as settled.

T. In what do you think the aforementioned powerlessness of will consists?

S. In the will's not being able perseveringly to cling to uprightness.

T. If because of powerlessness the will does not cling to [uprightness], then it is turned away from uprightness by an alien force.

S. Admittedly.

T. What is this force?

S. The force of temptation.

Anselm of Canterbury

T. This force does not turn the will from uprightness unless the will wills what the temptation suggests.

S. That's right. But the temptation by its own force compels the will to will what it is suggesting.

T. How does temptation compel the will to will?: in such a way that the will is indeed able to keep from willing, though not without great difficulty (*molestia*), or in such way that the will is not at all able to keep from willing?

S. Although I must admit that sometimes we are so pressured by temptations that we cannot without difficulty (*difficultate*) keep from willing what they suggest, I cannot say that they ever pressure us to the point that we cannot at all keep from willing what they advise.[13]

T. Nor do I know how it can be said. For if a man wills to lie in order to avoid death and to save his life for a while, who will say that it is impossible for him to will not to lie in order to avoid eternal death and to live endlessly? Hence, you ought no longer to doubt that this powerlessness-to-keep-uprightness which you say is in our will when we consent to temptations is the result not of impossibility but of difficulty. We are accustomed to say that we cannot [do] a thing, not because the thing is impossible for us [to do], but because we cannot [do it] without difficulty. But this difficulty does not destroy freedom of will. For it is able to beset the will though the will dissent, but it is not able to vanquish the will unless the will consent. In this way, then, I think that you are able to see how the power of the will which true reasoning ascribes is consistent with the powerlessness which our human nature feels. For just as difficulty does not at all destroy freedom of will, so powerlessness (which we say to be in the will only because the will can keep its uprightness only with difficulty) does not remove from the will the ability to persevere in uprightness.

Chapter Seven: How [the will] is stronger than temptation even when it is overcome by temptation.

S. Just as I am not at all able to deny what you prove, so I am not at all able to affirm that the will is stronger than temptation when it is overcome by temptation. For if the will-to-keep-uprightness

De Libertate Arbitrii

were stronger than the force of temptation, then in willing what was in its possession the will would resist more strongly than temptation would insist. For I have no way of knowing that my will has more or less strength except that I will more or less strongly. Therefore, when I will less strongly what I ought than temptation suggests what I ought not, I do not see how temptation is not stronger than my will.

T. I see that an equivocal sense of the word "will" is deceiving you.

S. I would like to know about this equivocation.

T. Just as the word "sight" has equivocal senses, so does the word "will." For we mean by "sight" the *instrument*-for-seeing, i.e., the ray passing through the eyes, by which ray we perceive light and the objects which are in the light. And we also mean by "sight" the *activity* of the instrument as used by us, i.e., the act of seeing. In the same way, we mean by "will" the instrument-for-willing, which is in the soul and which we direct towards willing this or that thing, even as we direct sight towards seeing various objects. And we also mean by "will" the use of the instrument-for-willing, just as by "sight" we mean the use of the instrument-for-seeing. Now, even when we are not seeing, we have sight in the sense of the instrument-for-seeing; but only while we *are* seeing do we have sight in the sense of the activity of the instrument. Similarly, even when it is not willing anything (e.g., during sleep), the will in the sense of the instrument-for-willing is always in the soul; but only while we *are* willing something do we have will in the sense of the activity, or use, of the instrument. Hence, the will which I call the instrument-for-willing is always one and the same thing regardless of what we will; but the will which is the instrument's activity is as multiple as the number of things we will and the number of occasions upon which we will. Similarly, the sight which we have even in darkness or with our eyes closed is always the same regardless of what we see; but the sight which is called the act of seeing, viz., the activity of the instrument, is as multiple as the number of things we see and the number of occasions upon which we see.

S. I see this clearly, and I am delighted by this distinction [of meanings] of "will." And I now seem to see what deception I was experiencing because of ignorance of this distinction. But go on, nevertheless, with what you have begun.

T. Then, since you see that there are two wills (viz., the instrument-for-willing and its activity),[14] in which of these two does the strength-to-will reside, as you understand the matter?

S. In the will which is the instrument-for-willing.

T. Then, if you knew a man so strong that while he was holding a wild bull, the bull was unable to get away, and if you saw the same man so holding a ram that the ram shook itself loose from the man's hands, would you think that the man was less strong while holding the ram than while holding the bull?

S. I would judge him to be equally strong in each task, but would maintain that he did not use his strength equally, for to hold a bull takes more strength than to hold a ram. Now, the man is strong because he has strength; but his action is called strong because it is done strongly.

T. Know, then, that the will which I call the instrument-for-willing has an inalienable strength which cannot be overcome by any other force. And in willing, the will uses this strength now more, now less. Hence, when presented with that which it wills less strongly, the will does not at all desert what it wills more strongly; and when it is offered what it wills more strongly, it immediately abandons what it wills less strongly. Thus, the will which we can call the act of the instrument, since the instrument acts when it wills something — this act of willing is called more or less strong since it is done more or less strongly.

S. I must admit that your explanation is now clear to me.

T. You see, then, that when a man deserts — under an assault of temptation — the uprightness-of-will that he possesses, he is drawn away by no alien force, but he turns himself to something which he wills more strongly.

Chapter Eight: Even God is not able to remove uprightness-of-will.

S. Is God able to remove uprightness from the will?

T. See how He cannot. Indeed, although He can reduce to nothing an entire substance which He has created from nothing, He is not able to separate uprightness from a will which has it.

S. I eagerly await an argument for this claim of yours, which I have not heard before.

De Libertate Arbitrii

T. We are discussing that uprightness-of-will by virtue of which the will is called just, i.e., the uprightness which is kept for its own sake. However, no will is just except one which wills what God wills that it will.

S. The will which does not will this is obviously unjust.

T. Therefore, to keep uprightness-of-will for the sake of this uprightness itself is, for everyone keeping it, to will what God wills him to will.

S. Yes, I must agree.

T. If God were to separate this uprightness from someone's will, He would do it either willingly or unwillingly.

S. He cannot [do it] unwillingly.

T. Then, if He were to remove (the aforementioned) uprightness from someone's will, He would will what He did.

S. Yes, without doubt, He would will it.

T. Were He to will to separate this uprightness from someone's will, surely He would not will this person to keep uprightness-of-will for the sake of this uprightness itself.

S. This follows.

T. But we have already accepted as true that to keep uprightness-of-will for its own sake is, for everyone keeping it, to will what God wills him to will.

S. Even if we had not accepted it it would be true.

T. Hence, if God were to remove (the oft-mentioned) uprightness from someone, He would not will him to will what He wills him to will.

S. Nothing follows more logically, and nothing is more impossible.

T. Therefore, nothing is more impossible than for God to remove uprightness-of-will. Nevertheless, He is said to remove uprightness-of-will when He does not cause it not to be deserted. On the other hand, the Devil or temptation is also said to remove uprightness or to overcome the will and to separate it from the uprightness it is keeping. [This is said] because unless the Devil or temptation permitted to the will, or threatened to remove from it, something which it preferred to uprightness, the will would not at all turn itself aside from that uprightness which it was willing in some measure.

S. What you say seems so obvious to me that I think nothing can be said against it.

Chapter Nine: Nothing is more free than an upright will.

T. Thus, you understand that nothing is more free than an upright will, whose uprightness no alien force can remove. It is simply not true to say: "The will which wills to lie in order not to lose life or security [*salus*] is compelled to abandon the truth from fear of death or from torment." For the will is no more compelled to will life than to will truth. Rather, since it is prevented by an alien force from keeping both at the same time, it chooses the one it prefers. To be sure, it chooses freely and not unwillingly, although unwillingly and unfreely it has been placed under the necessity of abandoning either alternative. For it has no less strength for willing the truth than for willing security; but it wills security more strongly. For if it should have a vision both of the eternal glory which it would immediately attain[15] upon keeping the truth and of the torments of Hell to which it would immediately be delivered upon telling a lie, then without doubt it would readily be seen to have sufficient strength to keep the truth.

S. This seems clear since the will would display greater strength for willing eternal salvation [*salus*] for its own sake and truth for the sake of [this] reward than [it would display] for keeping temporal salvation [*salus*].

Chapter Ten: How one who sins is a servant of sin. It is a greater miracle when God restores uprightness to a will which has deserted it than when He restores life to the dead.

T. Therefore, a rational nature always has free choice since it always has the ability to keep uprightness-of-will for the sake of this uprightness itself, even though to do so is sometimes difficult. But when free will deserts uprightness because of the difficulty of keeping it, then, assuredly, free will subsequently serves sin because of the impossibility of recovering uprightness through its own efforts. So, then, it becomes "a wind that goes out and does not return,"[16] since "he who sins is the servant of sin."[17] Indeed, just as before having uprightness, no will was

De Libertate Arbitrii

able to take it without God's giving it, so upon deserting the uprightness which has been received, the will is unable to recover it unless God gives it again.

Moreover, I think it a greater miracle when God restores to the will the uprightness it has deserted than when He restores to a dead man the life he has lost. For in dying by necessity, the body does not sin, and does not as a consequence of sinning fail ever to receive life again; but in deserting uprightness by its own efforts, the will deserves always to lack uprightness. And if someone voluntarily takes his own life, he does not remove what was never going to be lost; but someone who deserts uprightness-of-will throws away that which was supposed to be kept always.

S. I regard as exceedingly true what you say about the servitude by which one who sins becomes a servant of sin and about the impossibility of recovering uprightness, once deserted, unless it is returned by the one who originally gave it. And all those to whom it is given are supposed to observe uprightness continually, so that they may keep it forever.

Chapter Eleven: This servitude does not remove freedom of choice.

S. Nonetheless, by this conclusion you have greatly curbed my joy because I was already supposing myself to be certain that a man always has freedom of choice. Therefore, I ask that this servitude be explained to me lest perchance it seem opposed to the freedom we were discussing. For both freedom and servitude are in the will; and in accordance with the will a man is either free or enslaved. If, then, he is a servant, how is he free? Or if he is free, how is he a servant?

T. If you distinguish clearly, [you will see how] a man is both servant and free, without contradiction, when he does not have the uprightness we have been discussing. For he never has the ability to acquire uprightness when he does not have uprightness; but he always has the ability to keep uprightness when he does have it. With respect to the fact that he cannot return from sin, he is a servant; with respect to the fact that he cannot [forcibly] be drawn away from uprightness, he is free. Now, he can be turned away from sin and from servitude to sin only by someone else;

and he can be turned away from uprightness only by himself; but he cannot be deprived of his freedom either by himself or by anyone else. For he is always naturally free in order to keep uprightness, whether he does or does not have any to keep.

S. This consistency which you have worked out between servitude and freedom convinces me that they both can be present in the same man at the same time.

Chapter Twelve: Why when a man *does not* have uprightness it is better to call him free (on the ground that when he *does* have uprightness it cannot be taken away from him) than it is, when he *does* have uprightness, to call him a servant (on the ground that when he *does not* have uprightness he cannot recover it by himself).

S. But I greatly desire to know why when a man *does not* have uprightness it is better to call him free (on the ground that when he *does* have uprightness it cannot be taken away from him by someone else) than it is, when he *does* have uprightness, to call him a servant (on the ground that when he *does not* have uprightness he cannot recover it by himself). For with respect to the fact that he cannot return from sin he is a servant; and with respect to the fact that he cannot [forcibly] be drawn away from uprightness he is free. And just as he can never [forcibly] be drawn away [from uprightness] if he has it, so if he does not have it he can never return [from sin]. Therefore, just as he always has this freedom, so he seems always to have this servitude.

T. This servitude consists in nothing other than an inability to avoid sinning. For whether we call this servitude the inability to return to uprightness or the inability to recover uprightness, or to have it again, a man is a servant of sin for no other reason than this: with respect to the fact that he is not able to return to uprightness or to recover it or to have it, he is unable to avoid sinning. However, when he has uprightness, he does not have an inability to avoid sinning. Therefore, when he has uprightness, he is not a servant of sin. However, he always has the ability to keep uprightness — both when he has uprightness and when he does not — and so he is always free.

De Libertate Arbitrii

However, you are asking the following question: Why when a man *does not* have uprightness is it better to call him free (on the ground that when he *does* have uprightness it cannot be taken away from him by someone else) than it is, when he *does* have uprightness, to call him a servant (on the ground that when he *does not* have uprightness he cannot recover it by himself)? It is as if you were asking: Why is it better to say, when the sun is absent, that a man has the ability to see the sun (because of the fact that he is able to see the sun when it is present) than it is to say, when the sun is present, that the man is unable to see it (because of the fact that when the sun is absent he is unable to make it present)? For even when the sun is absent we have in us sight, by which to see the sun when it is present; similarly, even when uprightness-of-will is lacking to us, we have in us the ability to understand and to will, by which ability we are able to keep uprightness for its own sake when we have it. Now, only when we lack nothing for seeing the sun except the sun's presence do we lack the capability which its presence produces in us. Similarly, only when we lack uprightness do we have the incapability which its absence produces in us. Therefore, a man always has freedom of choice; but he is not always a servant of sin. [He is a servant of sin only] when he does not have an upright will.

S. If I had thought carefully about what was said earlier, when you distinguished into four capabilities the capability to see, I would not have been puzzled here. Therefore, I acknowledge that my confusion was my own fault.

T. I won't hold it against you now, provided that henceforth you will keep our points so at hand when needed that we shall not have to repeat them.

S. Thank you for your indulgence. But do not be surprised if those points about which I am unaccustomed to think are not all continually present in my mind for viewing after only one hearing.

T. Tell me whether you have any further qualms about our definition of "freedom of choice."

Anselm of Canterbury

Chapter Thirteen: "The ability to keep uprightness-of-will for the sake of this uprightness itself" is the complete definition of "freedom of choice."

S. There is one thing which still disturbs me somewhat about this definition. For we often have an ability to keep something, and yet that ability is not free to the point that it cannot be impeded by an alien force. Hence, when you say that freedom of choice is the ability to keep uprightness-of-will for the sake of this uprightness itself, see whether perhaps a clause should be added which would indicate that this ability is so free that it cannot be overcome by any force.

T. If the ability to keep uprightness-of-will for the sake of this uprightness itself could ever be found to be present apart from the freedom which we have examined, then it would be useful to add the clause you mention. But since with respect to genus and differentia the proposed definition is so complete that it includes neither more nor less than the freedom we are examining, nothing can conceivably need to be added to it or subtracted from it. For *ability* is the genus of *freedom*. However, the addition of "to keep" distinguishes this ability from every ability which is not an ability to keep — as, for example, the ability to laugh or the ability to walk. But by adding "uprightness," we distinguish this ability from the ability to keep gold and whatever is not uprightness. The additional words "of will" separate this ability from the ability to keep uprightness [*rectitudo*] of other things — as, for example, the rightness, or straightness, [*rectitudo*] of a stick or the rightness, or correctness, [*rectitudo*] of an opinion. However, by the words "for the sake of this uprightness itself" this ability is distinguished from an ability to keep uprightness-of-will because of something else — as, for example, when uprightness is kept for the sake of money or because of natural inclination (*naturaliter*). For a dog keeps uprightness-of-will by natural inclination when it loves its puppies or the master who cares for it. Therefore, since in this definition there is nothing which is not necessary for encompassing the freedom of choice of a rational will and for excluding other things, and since freedom is adequately included and other things are adequately excluded,

De Libertate Arbitrii

then surely our definition is neither too broad nor too narrow. Doesn't this seem to you to be the case?

S. Yes, the definition seems to me to be complete.

T. Tell me, then, whether you wish [to know] anything more about the freedom in virtue of which we hold its possessor accountable for his good and evil deeds. For our present discourse deals only with this freedom.

Chapter Fourteen: The division of this same freedom.

S. What remains now is for you to divide this same freedom. For although in accordance with your definition, freedom is common to every rational nature, nevertheless God's freedom is quite different from the freedom possessed by rational creatures; and among rational creatures there are differences of freedom.

T. [Here are the distinctions appropriate to freedom:]

I. There is an unoriginated freedom of choice, which was neither created by nor received from anyone else; this freedom is characteristic only of God.

II. There is a freedom of choice which was both created by and received from God; this freedom is characteristic of men and angels. However, this created or received freedom of choice either (A) *does* have uprightness to keep or (B) *does not* have uprightness to keep.

II-A. The freedom of choice which has uprightness keeps it either (1) so as *to be able* to lose it or (2) so as *not to be able* to lose it.

> II-A-1. The freedom of choice which keeps uprightness so as to be able to lose it was characteristic of all angels before the good ones were confirmed and the evil ones fell; and it characterizes prior to death all those men who have this uprightness.
>
> II-A-2. But the freedom of choice which keeps uprightness so as not to be able to lose it is characteristic of elect angels and elect men — of elect angels after the fall of the reprobate angels, and of elect men after death.

II-B. However, the freedom of choice which does not have uprightness lacks it in such way as either (1) *to be able* to recover it or (2) *not to be able* to recover it.

II-B-1. The freedom of choice which does not have uprightness and yet is able to recover it characterizes only men who lack it during their lifetime — although many might never recover it.

II-B-2. However, the freedom of choice which does not have uprightness and is not able to recover it is characteristic of reprobate angels and men — of reprobate angels after their fall, and of reprobate men after their lifetime.

S. Through the favor of God your definition and division of *freedom of choice* have so satisfied me that I can find nothing which I must ask regarding them.

THE FALL OF THE DEVIL
(*De Casu Diaboli*)

CHAPTER TITLES

1. "What do you have that you have not received?" is addressed even to angels. From God comes only good and being; every good thing is a being, and every being is a good thing.
2. Why it seems that the Devil did not receive perseverance because God did not give it.
3. God did not give because [the Devil] did not receive.
4. How [the Devil] sinned and willed to be like God.
5. Before the fall of the evil angels, the good angels were able to sin.
6. How the good angels were confirmed in their standing and the evil angels in their fallenness.
7. Whether the will and its turning to what it ought not are the very evil which makes [men and angels] evil. Why a rational creature cannot turn himself from evil to good, as he can turn himself from good to evil.
8. Neither the will nor its turning is the very evil [which makes men and angels evil].
9. Injustice is this very evil and is nothing.
10. How evil seems to be something.
11. By means of their names, evil and nothing cannot be proved to be something but [can be proved to be] as-if-something.
12. The angel [Satan] was not able to have his first willing from himself. Many things are said "to be able" by reason of another's ability and "not to be able" by reason of another's inability.
13. If [Satan] received only the will-for-happiness, he was able to will only happiness and was not able to keep from willing it; and regardless of what he willed, his will was neither just nor unjust.
14. The case is similar if [Satan] received only the will-for-

De Casu Diaboli

uprightness. And so he received both wills at the same time in order to be both just and happy.

15. Justice is something.
16. Injustice is only the absence of required justice.
17. Why the renegade angel is unable to return to justice.
18. How the evil angel caused himself to be unjust and the good angel caused himself to be just. The evil angel owes gratitude to God for the goods which he received and deserved, even as the good angel, who kept the goods which he received, [owes gratitude].
19. Insofar as it is, the will is something good. No thing is an evil.
20. How God causes evil wills and evil actions; how they are received from Him.
21. The evil angel was not able to foreknow that he would fall.
22. [The evil angel] knew that he ought not to will that which he sinned in willing; and he knew that he ought to be punished if he sinned.
23. [The evil angel] ought not to have known that if he sinned he would be punished.
24. Even the good angel ought not to have known this [viz., that if he sinned he would be punished].
25. Even if the only reason the good angel is said to be now unable to sin were that he now has this knowledge from the Devil's fall, nevertheless [not to be able to sin] would be to his glory.
26. What we dread when we hear the name "evil"; and what causes the works which injustice is said to cause, since injustice and evil are nothing.
27. From where evil came to an angel who was good.
28. The ability to will what he ought not to have [willed] was always good; and this willing, with respect to its being, was good.

THE FALL OF THE DEVIL[1]
(De Casu Diaboli)

Chapter One: "What do you have that you have not received?" is addressed even to angels. From God comes only good and being; every good thing is a being, and every being is a good thing.

Student. When the apostle asks, "What do you have that you have not received?"[2] is he addressing men only or angels as well?

Teacher. No created being has anything from itself. For how could a thing which does not exist from itself have anything from itself? In fact, if there is not anything except the one who has created and the things created by Him, it is clear that nothing at all can exist (*haberi*) except the one who has created and what He has created.

S. Perfectly clear.

T. But neither the Creator nor what has been created can exist (*haberi*) except from the Creator Himself.

S. This is no less clear.

T. Therefore, only the Creator has from Himself whatever He has; and all other things have something only from Him. And just as they have from themselves only nothing, so they have from Him only something.

S. I do not see clearly why you say that creatures have from God only something. For who but God causes the many things which we see passing from being to not-being not to be what they were, even if they do not pass altogether into nothing? Or who causes-not-to-be whatever is not except Him who causes-to-be all that is. Likewise, if there is something only because God causes it, then it follows that what-is-not is not because He does not cause it. Therefore, just as those things which exist have from Him their being something, so those things which do not exist, or which pass from being to not-being, seem to have from Him their being nothing.

T. We say that one who causes-to-be what is not or causes-not-to-be what is causes something to be or something not to be. But we also say that one who is able to cause something not to be and does not do so causes it to be, and that one who is able to cause something to be and does not do so causes it not to be.[3] Indeed, both the man who despoils another and the man who, although able to, does not restrain the despoiler are said to cause the despoiled person to be naked or not to be clothed. But the former is properly said to cause this; the latter, improperly. For when the latter is said to have *caused* someone *to be naked* or not to be clothed what is meant is only that, although he was able, he did *not cause* the other to remain clothed or *not to be naked*. In this [improper] mode God is said to cause many things which He does not cause. For example, He is said to lead into temptation because He does not keep from temptation, although He is able [to keep from temptation]. And [He is said] to cause what-is-not not to be because He does not cause it to be, although He is able [to cause it to be].

But if you consider existing things: when they pass to not-being, God does not cause them not to be. For not only does no other being exist except by His creating, but also a being cannot at all remain what it was made except by His conserving. Therefore, when He ceases to conserve what He has created, it returns to its original state of not-being, not because He causes it not to be but because He ceases to cause it to be. For when as though angered, God removes being by destroying something, not-being is not from Him. But when He reclaims as His own what He had bestowed, then that thing which was created by Him, and by Him was being conserved in existence, returns into not-being, which it had not from Him but from itself before it was created. For if you reclaim a tunic which you willingly gave to a naked man for a while, he does not have his state of nakedness from you; but when you reclaim what was yours, the man returns into the state he was in before having been clothed by you.

Assuredly, just as from the Supreme Good comes only good, and just as every good is from the Supreme Good, so from the Supreme Being comes only being,[4] and every being is from the Supreme Being. Thus, since the Supreme Good is the Supreme

De Casu Diaboli

Being, it follows that every good thing is a being and every being a good thing. Therefore, nothing and not-being are not goods, even as they are not beings. And so nothing and not-being are not from Him from whom comes only good and being.

S. I now see clearly that just as good and being come only from God, so from God come only good and being.

T. Be careful not at all to think — when we read in Scripture, or when in accordance with Scripture[5] we say, that God causes evil or causes not-being — that I am denying the basis for what is said or am finding fault with its being said. But we ought not to cling to the verbal impropriety concealing the truth as much as we ought to attend to the true propriety hidden beneath the many types of expression.

S. You need say these things only to someone unintelligent or slanderous.

T. Return to the topic you have begun, and see whether to an angel as well as to a man it can be said that he does not have what he has not received.

S. It is sufficiently clear that [this statement] applies no less to an angel than to a man.

Chapter Two: Why it seems that the Devil did not receive perseverance because God did not give it.

S. Therefore, it is evident that just as the angel who stood in the truth persevered because he had perseverance, so he had perseverance because he received it, and he received it because God gave it. It follows, then, that just as the angel who did *not* stand in the truth[6] did not persevere because he did not have perseverance, so he did not have perseverance because he did not receive it, and he did not receive it because God did not give it. So if you can, I want you to show me how he was to blame when he did not persevere because God did not give, without whose giving [the angel] was able to have nothing. For I am certain, even if I do not see why, that this angel was damned only justly by the one who is supremely just, and that he could not have been justly damned apart from being at fault.

T. Why do you think it follows that if the good angel received perseverance because God gave it, then the evil angel did not receive it because God did not give it?

S. Because I think that if giving is the cause of the good angel's receiving, then not-giving is the cause of the evil angel's not-receiving; and if not-giving is postulated, I see it to be a cause from which not-receiving follows logically.[7] Moreover, we all know that when we do not receive what we want, it is not the case that this thing is not given because we do not receive it, but is rather the case that we do not receive it because it is not given. Finally, everyone whom I have read or heard dealing with this subject has (as best I can remember) put it in the form of the following argument: "If the good angel received because God gave, then the evil angel did not receive because God did not give." I do not recall ever having seen a refutation of this implication.

Chapter Three: God did not give because [the Devil] did not receive.

T. The above inference does not hold. For even if giving were always the cause of receiving, not-giving need not be the cause of not-receiving.

S. Then, if not-giving is postulated, not-receiving does not necessarily follow. Therefore, there can be receiving without their being giving.

T. No, this is wrong.

S. I want you to show me by an example what you mean.

T. If I offer you something and you accept it, it is not the case that I give it because you receive it, but is rather the case that you receive it because I give it. Giving is the cause of receiving.

S. That's right.

T. What if I offer this same thing to someone else and he does not accept it: Is it the case that he does not receive it because I do not give it?

S. It seems rather that you do not give it because he does not receive it.

T. In this case, then, not-giving is not the cause of not-receiving; and yet if I postulate that I have not given, my not-giving is the cause of inferring that he has not received. Indeed,

De Casu Diaboli

the fact that one thing is the cause of another thing is different from the fact that the positing of a thing is the cause of what follows logically from it. For example, although burning is not the cause of fire, but fire of burning, nevertheless the positing of burning is always a cause from which the existence of fire follows logically. For if there is burning, there must be fire.

S. I must admit that this is right.

T. So I think you see that if you have received because I have given, it does not follow that someone who has not received has not received because I have not given — even though it follows that if I have not given, then he has not received.

S. I see, and I am pleased because I see.

T. Do you have any further doubt that just as the angel who stood steadfast received perseverance because God gave it, so to the angel who did not stand God did not give perseverance because he did not receive it?

S. You have not yet shown me this. You have proved only that the good angel's having received because God gave does not entail that the evil angel did not receive because God did not give. If you wish to maintain that God did not give to him because he did not receive, then I ask why he did not receive: Was it because he could not, or was it because he would not? For if he did not have the ability-to-receive or the will-to-receive, then God did not give it. For if God had given it, he surely would have had it. Therefore, if only by God's giving was [the evil angel] able to have either the ability or the will to receive perseverance, then how did he sin in not receiving what God did not grant him either to be able to receive or to will to receive?

T. God did give him the ability and the will to receive perseverance.

S. Then, he received what God gave, and he had what he received.

T. Yes, he received it and had it.

S. Therefore, he received and had perseverance.

T. No, he did not receive it, and so he did not have it.

S. But did you not say that God gave, and he received, the ability and the will to receive perseverance?

T. I said it. But I did not say that God gave him the receiving of perseverance. I said only that God granted him to be able to, and to will to, receive perseverance.

S. So if he was able [to receive perseverance] and willed [to receive it], then he did receive it.

T. This inference does not necessarily follow.

S. Unless you show me, I fail to see why not.

T. Have you ever begun something with the ability and the will to complete it, but nevertheless failed to complete it because your will was changed before the thing was finished?

S. Often.

T. So you willed to, and were able to, persevere in what you did not persevere.

S. To be sure, I willed [to persevere]; but I did not persevere in willing, and thus I did not persevere in the action.

T. Why did you not persevere in willing?

S. Because I did not will to.

T. Is it not the case that as long as you willed to persevere in the action you willed to persevere in willing?

S. I cannot deny it.

T. Why do you say, then, that you did not will to persevere in willing?

S. I might once again reply that I did will to persevere but that I did not persevere in *this* willing; but then, as I recognize, the argument would continue to infinity, with you always asking the same question and me always giving the same answer.

T. Therefore, you ought not to say: "I did not will to persevere in willing because I did not will to persevere in the willing of this willing." Rather, when you are asked why you did not persevere in an activity in which you willed to persevere and were able to persevere, you can reply that you did not persevere in willing. But if you are then asked why you did not persevere in willing, you must give some other explanation regarding this failure of will than that you did not persevere in the willing of this willing. For your answer simply amounts to [what was granted in] the question, viz., that you did not persevere in willing to persevere in the action.

S. I see that I did not understand what I was saying.

T. Then, tell me in one word what it is to persevere, as far as the matter requires, in doing something.

S. *Perficere* [i.e., to complete it]. For we call persevering in writing something *perscribere* [i.e., to complete writing it]; and

De Casu Diaboli

we call persevering in leading *perducere* [i.e., to lead completely to the destination].

T. So let us likewise say — even though we do not ordinarily use this word — that persevering in willing is *pervelle* [i.e., to will completely].

S. Let it be said.

T. Then, when you did not complete (*perfecisti*) what you willed [to finish] and were able [to finish], why didn't you complete it?

S. Because I did not will it completely (*non pervolui*).

T. So then, say too that the Devil, who received the ability and the will to receive perseverance, and the ability and the will to persevere, did not receive perseverance and did not persevere because he did not will it completely.

S. Once again I ask: Why didn't he will it completely? For when you say that what he willed he did not will completely, it is as if you were saying that what he willed at first, he did not will afterwards. Therefore, when he no longer willed what he willed at first, why did he not will it except that he did not have the will [for it]? I am not talking about the will which he had at first when he did will, but about the will which he did not have when he did not will. Yet, why did he not have this will except because he did not receive it? But why did he not receive it except because God did not give it?

T. Once again I answer: It is not the case that he did not receive it because God did not give it; rather, God did not give it because he did not receive it.

S. Show this.

T. [The Devil] freely lost the will which he had. And just as he received the possession of whatever he had, so he was able to receive the permanent keeping of what he deserted. But because he deserted he did not receive. Therefore, since he did not receive the keeping because he deserted, it is not the case that he did not receive because God did not give; rather, God did not give because he did not receive.

S. He deserted because he did not will to keep — rather than not willing to keep because he deserted. Who does not see this? For to one who is keeping something, not-willing-to-keep always precedes willing-to-desert. For someone wills to desert what he

Anselm of Canterbury

has because he does not will to keep it. Therefore, I ask: Why did [the Devil] not will to keep what he was keeping except because God did not grant him to will [to keep it]?

T. It is not the case that not-willing-to-keep always precedes willing-to-desert.

S. Show me when it is not the case.

T. When you do not will to keep a thing for its own sake but will to desert it for its own sake (for example, a lighted coal placed in your bare hand), then perhaps not-willing-to-keep precedes willing-to-desert, and you will to desert because you do not will to keep. For before you have it you do not will to have it; however, you cannot will to desert it except when you have it. But when you have a thing which only on account of something else you do not will to keep and which only on account of something else you will to desert, and when you prefer this other thing which you cannot have unless you give up what you do have, then willing-to-desert precedes not-willing-to-keep. For example, when a miser wills to keep money but prefers bread, which he cannot have unless he spends money, he wills to spend (i.e., to desert) the money before he does not will to keep it. For it is not the case that he wills to spend money because he does not will to keep it; rather, he does not will to keep it because he must spend it in order to have bread. For before he has money, he wills to have it and to keep it; and when he has it, he does not at all not will to keep it, as long as it is not necessary for him to give it up.

S. That's true.

T. Therefore, it is not always the case that not-willing-to-keep precedes willing-to-desert; sometimes willing-to-desert is prior.

S. I cannot deny it.

T. Therefore, I say that the reason [the Devil] did not will when and what he ought to have willed is not that his will had a deficiency which resulted from God's failure to give; rather, [he did not will when and what he ought to have willed] because by willing what he ought *not* to have willed, he expelled his good will in consequence of a supervening evil will. Accordingly, it is not the case that he did not have, or did not receive, a good persevering will because God did not give it; rather, God did not give it because he deserted it by willing what he ought not to have willed; and by deserting it he did not keep it.

S. I understand what you are saying.

De Casu Diaboli

Chapter Four: How [the Devil] sinned and willed to be like God.

T. Do you still have any doubt about its not being the case that the Devil willed to desert what he had because he did not will to keep it, but its being the case that he did not will to keep it because he willed to desert it?

S. I do not doubt that it can be so; but you have not yet made me certain that it is so. Therefore, first show what [the Devil] did not have but willed to have, so that he willed to desert what he did have — just as you have shown in the case of the miser. Then if nothing is able to be contradicted, I will admit that I do not doubt it to be true.

T. You do not doubt that the Devil sinned, since he was not able to be unjustly damned by a just God; but you are asking how he sinned.

S. That's right.

T. If he had perseveringly kept justice, he would never have sinned or have been unhappy.

S. We believe this.

T. But no one keeps justice except by willing what he ought, and no one deserts justice except by willing what he ought not.

S. No one doubts this.

T. Therefore, by willing something which he was not supposed to will at that time, he deserted justice and thereby sinned.

S. This follows. But I ask: What did he will?

T. Whatever he already had in his possession he was supposed to will.

S. Yes, he was supposed to will what he had received from God, and he did not sin by willing that.

T. Therefore, he willed something which he did not already have and was not supposed to will at that time — just as Eve willed to be like gods[8] before God willed this.

S. I cannot deny that this follows.

T. But [the Devil] was able to will nothing except what is just or beneficial. For happiness, which every rational nature wills, consists of benefits.

S. We can recognize this in ourselves, for we will nothing unless we think it just or beneficial.

T. But [the Devil] was not able to sin by willing justice.

S. That's true.

T. Therefore, he sinned by willing something beneficial which he did not possess and was not supposed to will at that time, even though it was able to increase his happiness.

S. This is clear since [the matter] could not have been otherwise.

T. I think you see that he extended his will beyond justice by inordinately willing something more than he had received.

S. I now see clearly that he sinned both by willing what he ought not to have and by not willing what he ought to have. And, clearly, it is not the case that he willed more than he should have because he did not will to keep justice; rather, he did not keep justice because he willed something else; and by willing this, he deserted justice, as you have shown about the bread and the money in the example of the miser.

T. But when [the Devil] willed what God did not will him to will, he willed inordinately to be like God.

S. If God can be conceived only so uniquely that nothing else can be conceived to be like Him, how was the Devil able to will what he was not able to conceive? For he was not so obtuse as not to know that nothing else can be conceived to be like God.

T. Even if he did not will to be altogether equal to God, but contrary to the will of God willed to be something less than God, then even in this case he willed inordinately to be like God; for he willed something by an autonomous will (*propria voluntate*),[9] which was subject to no one else. For it ought to be the characteristic only of God so to will something by an autonomous will that He is not subordinate to a higher will.

S. That's right.

T. However, not only did [the Devil] will to be equal to God because he presumed to have an autonomous will, but he even willed to be greater [than God] by willing what God did not will him to will, for he placed his will above the will of God.

S. This is clear enough.

T. Therefore, I think that from the foregoing argument it is now evident to you that the Devil both freely departed from willing what he was supposed to will and justly lost what he had *because* he freely and unjustly willed what he did not possess and was not supposed to will.

De Casu Diaboli

S. I think that nothing is more evident.

T. Therefore, although the good angel received perseverance because God gave it, it is not the case that the evil angel did not receive it because God did not give it. Rather, God did not give it because [the evil angel] did not receive it; and he did not receive it because he did not will to receive it.

S. Indeed, you so satisfy me regarding the things about which I ask that neither in what you set forth nor in the outcome of your argument does my mind see any truth to totter.

Chapter Five: Before the fall of the evil angels, the good angels were able to sin.

T. Do you think that the good angels were likewise able to sin before the evil angels fell?

S. Yes, but I would like to understand it rationally.

T. You are certain that if the good angels were not able to sin, then they kept justice not by their own ability but by necessity. It would follow that they no more merited grace from God because they remained standing while the others fell than because they preserved rationality, which they were unable to lose. But if you carefully consider the matter, they would not even [in that case] rightly be called just.

S. So reason shows.

T. Therefore, if the angels who fell had not sinned when they were able [not to sin], then to the degree that they would have been truly just and would have merited grace from God, to that degree they would have been better than the good angels. Thus, it would follow that the men who are elect would eventually be better and greater than the good angels, or else that the [number of] reprobate angels would not be perfectly restored,[10] since the men who would assume their places would not be such as the reprobate angels would have become [viz., better than the good angels].

S. I think that both of these alternatives must be completely denied.

T. Therefore, the good angels were able to sin before the fall of the evil angels; their state was no different from what the state of the angels who sinned was shown to be.

S. I do not see that [the matter] can be otherwise.

Chapter Six: How the good angels were confirmed in their standing and the evil angels in their fallenness.

T. Thus, the angels who preferred the justice which they possessed to the something more which they did not possess received through the reward of justice the good which they lost as if on account of justice (as far as justice in the will was concerned). And they also remained truly secure about that good which they already had. Therefore, they were exalted to the point that they obtained whatever they were able to will, and they no longer see what more they can will.[11] For this reason, they are not able to sin.

But as for the angels who preferred the something more which God did not yet will to give them, and who preferred it to standing in the justice in which they had been created: through the judgment of justice they did not at all obtain that good on account of which they despised justice, and they lost the good which they already had. Therefore, the angels were so separated that (1) those who adhered to justice are able to will no good in which they do not delight and (2) those who deserted justice are able to will no good of which they are not deprived.

S. Nothing is more just or lovely than this separation. But if you are able to say, I would like to hear what kind of benefit it was which the good angels thus gained by justly not willing and the evil angels thus lost by unjustly desiring.

T. I do not know what it was. But whatever it was, it suffices to know that it was something toward which they could grow and which they did not receive when they were created, so that they might attain it by their own merit.

S. And let it now suffice that we have examined the matter this far.

De Casu Diaboli

Chapter Seven: Whether the will and its turning to what it ought not are the very evil which makes [men and angels] evil. Why a rational creature cannot turn himself from evil to good, as he can turn himself from good to evil.

S. I do not know why it is that just when I was hoping to come to the end of our inquiry, I see instead other questions arising, as though sprouting forth from the roots of the questions we have felled. For although I see very clearly that the evil angel could have come to an excessive need of good only because of an immoderate desire, I am quite troubled about the source of his unordered will. For if his will was good, then he fell from such great good into such great evil because of a good will. Likewise, if his will was good, God gave it to him, because from himself he had only nothing. Therefore, if he willed what God gave to will, how is it that he sinned? Or if he had this will from himself, he had something good which he did not receive.

On the other hand, if his will is evil and is something, then it is again the case that this will is only from God, from whom is everything that is something. And we can in like manner ask how he sinned in having a will which God gave, or how God could have given an evil will. But if this evil will was from the Devil himself and is something, then [the evil angel] had something from himself and it is not the case that every being is good. And if, indeed, an evil will is a being, then evil won't be nothing, as we are accustomed to say it is. Or if an evil will is nothing, then [the Devil] was so gravely damned for nothing, and hence was damned without reason.

However, what I am saying about the will can be said about concupiscence or desire, since the will is concupiscence and desire.[12] And just as there is a good and an evil will, so there is a good and an evil concupiscence and a good and an evil desire.

But suppose we say that (1) the will is a kind of being and so is something good, and that (2) when it is turned to what it ought to will, it becomes a good will, but when it is turned to what it ought not to will, it is called an evil will. In this case, I see that whatever I said about the will can be said about the turning of the will. For I am greatly perturbed about from where the Devil had the evil turning of will, and about the other things which I said regarding the will just now.

There is still something else I greatly wonder about when I consider this turning of the will: viz., why did God create that nature, which He had exalted with such great excellence, to be such that it could turn its will away from what it was supposed to will and towards what it was not supposed to will, but could not turn its will away from what it ought not to will towards what it ought to will? For it seems that such a creature from such a creator ought much rather to have received the ability to do the good for which it was created than the ability to do the evil it was created to avoid. We can also ask this same question about our own nature, since we believe that no man can have a good will unless God gives it, but can always have an evil will if God merely permits it.

Chapter Eight: Neither the will nor its turning is the very evil [which makes men and angels evil].

T. We cannot deny, it seems to me, either that the will or that the turning of the will is something. For although the will and its turning are not substances, nevertheless it cannot be proven that they are not beings, since there are many beings besides the ones which are properly called substances. Accordingly, a good will is not anything more than is an evil will; and an evil will is not something evil more than a good will is something good. For a will which wills to bestow mercifully is not anything more than is a will which wills to seize forcibly; and this latter will is no more something evil than the former will is something good. Therefore, if an evil will were the evil in virtue of which someone is called evil, then a good will would be the good in virtue of which someone is made good. But an evil will would be nothing if it were the very evil which we believe to be nothing. Therefore, a good will would be nothing, since a good will is not anything more than is an evil will. Hence, we would be forced to admit that the good which makes [men and angels] good would be nothing, since it would be identical with the good will, which would be nothing. But everyone believes it to be false that a good

De Casu Diaboli

will and this very good are nothing. It follows that an evil will is not the very evil which makes [men and angels] evil — even as a good will is not the very good which makes them good.

What I have just said about the will applies as well to the turning of the will. For the turning which turns the will from seizing [forcefully] to bestowing [mercifully] is not anything more than is the turning which turns that same will from generosity to greed. And the other things which I have just finished mentioning about the will [also apply to the turning of the will].

S. What you say seems true to me too.

T. Therefore, neither the evil will nor the depraved turning of the will is that evil which we call nothing and in virtue of which the angel [Satan] and the man [Adam] became evil. And neither the good will nor the good turning of the will is the good in virtue of which they are made good.

Chapter Nine: Injustice is this very evil and is nothing.

S. Then, what shall we identify as the evil which makes [men and angels] evil, and what shall we name as the good which makes them good?

T. We ought to believe that justice is the good in virtue of which men and angels are good, or just, and in virtue of which the will is called good, or just. But we ought to believe that injustice is the evil which makes both the will and [men and angels] evil and which we call nothing other than the privation of the good; and so we maintain that this very injustice is nothing other than a privation of justice. For when a will was first given to rational nature, it was — at the moment of giving — turned by the Giver towards what it was supposed to will; or better, it was not *turned* but was *created upright*. As long as the will stood fast in this uprightness (which we call truth or justice) in which it was created, it was just. But when it turned itself away from what it was supposed [to will] and turned towards that which it ought not to have [willed], it did not stand fast in the "original" uprightness, so to speak, in which it was created. When [the will] deserted this original uprightness, it lost something great and received nothing in its place except its privation, which has no being and which we call injustice.

Chapter Ten: How evil seems to be something.

S. I concede what you say, viz., that evil is a privation of good. But nonetheless, I regard good as a privation of evil. And just as I perceive that from the deprivation of evil there results something else which we call good, so I notice that from the deprivation of good there results something else which we call evil.

I concede too that there are various arguments which prove that evil is nothing. For example: "Evil is only defect or corruption, which does not at all exist except in some being. And the greater the defect and corruption in this being, the more they reduce it to nothing. Moreover, if this being should become altogether nothing, defect and corruption are also found to be nothing." Although in this or some other way evil is proved to be nothing, my mind cannot give assent (except by faith alone) unless the [following] counterargument which proves to me that evil is only something, is refuted.

For if nothing is signified by the name "evil," then when we hear this name our hearts shudder in vain at what they understand by its signification. Likewise, if the word (*vox*) "evil" is a name (*nomen*), then surely it is significative. However, if it is significative, it signifies. But it signifies only something. Therefore, how is evil nothing if what its name signifies is something?

Finally, while justice is present, there seems to be such great tranquility and peace of mind that in many cases justice (like chastity and patience too) seems to be nothing other than a cessation of evil. But when justice departs, such conflicting and harsh and manifold passion besets the mind that, like a cruel master, it compels the wretched and weak man to be afflicted with worry over so many shameful and oppressive tasks and to labor so grievously at them. It would be astonishing if it could be shown that *nothing* accomplishes all these things.

De Casu Diaboli

Chapter Eleven: By means of their names, evil and nothing cannot be proved to be something but [can be proved to be] as-if-something.

T. I think you are not so mad as to say that nothing is something, even though you cannot deny that "nothing" is a name. Therefore, if by means of the name "nothing" you cannot prove that nothing is something, how do you think that by means of the name "evil" you can prove that evil is something?
S. An example which resolves one difficulty by posing another is useless. For I do not know what this very nothing is. Therefore — since the question before us is about evil, which you say to be nothing — if you wish to teach me what I may understand evil to be, teach me first what I may understand nothing to be. Then reply to the other arguments[13] (besides the argument from the name "evil") by which I said I was troubled about the fact that evil seems to be something.
T. Since to be nothing is exactly the same as not to be anything,[14] how can we say what that which is not anything is?
S. If there is not anything which is signified by the name "nothing," then this name does not signify anything. But if it does not signify anything, it is not a name. But surely it is a name. Therefore, although no one says that nothing is something and although we must always admit that nothing is nothing, nevertheless no one can deny that the name "nothing" is significative. But if this name signifies something rather than nothing, then that which is signified seems unable to be nothing and seems rather to be something. Therefore, if that which is signified is something rather than nothing, how will it be true that by means of this name what is nothing is signified? Indeed, if nothing is spoken of truly, then it is truly nothing, and so it is not anything. Hence, if that which is signified by the name "nothing" is not nothing but something (as this line of reasoning seems to show), then it is falsely and improperly called by this name.

But on the contrary, if as everyone judges, what is named nothing is truly nothing and is not at all anything, does anything at all seem to follow more logically than that the name "nothing" signifies nothing — i.e., does not signify anything?

Thus, how is it that the name "nothing" does not signify nothing but signifies something, and does not signify something but signifies nothing?

T. Perhaps signifying nothing and signifying something are not opposed.

S. If they are not opposed then either the word "nothing" signifies (in different respects) both nothing and something or else a thing must be found which is both something and nothing.

T. What if both alternatives can be discovered to be the case? — viz., that there is an ambiguity of signification in the name "nothing" and that the same thing is both something and nothing?

S. I would like to know of both.

T. It is evident that the word "nothing" does not at all differ, with respect to its signification, from what I term "not-something." Also, nothing is clearer than that the word "not-something" indicates by its signification that absolutely every thing and all that is something should be removed from the understanding, and that no thing whatsoever nor what is at all something should be retained in the understanding. But the removal of a thing cannot at all be signified except together with the signification of that very thing whose removal is signified. (For example, no one understands what "not-man" signifies except by understanding what a man is.) Therefore, it is necessary that the word "not-something" signify something by "destroying" that which is something. But since by removing everything that is something, the word "not-something" signifies no being which it indicates must be retained in the understanding of the hearer, it signifies no thing nor what is something.

Therefore, by means of these different considerations, the word "not-something" does in some respect signify a thing and something, and does not in any respect signify a thing or something. For it signifies by removing and does not signify by establishing.[15] In this manner, the name "nothing," which destroys everything that is something, signifies something rather than nothing by destroying and signifies nothing rather than something by establishing [i.e., by positing]. Therefore, it is not necessary that nothing be something simply because its name somehow or other signifies something. Rather, it is necessary that nothing be nothing, because its name signifies something in the aforemen-

De Casu Diaboli

tioned way. And so in this aforementioned way the fact that evil is nothing is not opposed to the fact that the name "evil" is significative — provided that "evil" signifies something by destroying [i.e., by negating] it, and thus is constitutive of no thing.

S. I cannot deny that in accordance with your reasoning just now the name "nothing" somehow signifies something. But it is well-enough known that the something which in this manner is signified by this name is not named nothing; and when we hear this name ["nothing"], we do not accept it for that thing which it thus signifies. Therefore, I ask about that for which this name stands and about that which we understand when we hear this name. What in the world is it? For this name *properly* signifies that thing; and so it is a name because it is significative of that thing and not because it signifies something in the aforementioned mode of negating. Indeed, it is reckoned to be one name among others because it signifies that thing; and that thing is called nothing. I ask: How is that thing something if it is *properly* called nothing? Or how is it nothing if its significative name signifies something? Or how is the same thing both something and nothing? I ask the same questions about the name "evil" and about that which it signifies and about what is named "evil."

T. You are right in asking, because although by the previous consideration "evil" and "nothing" do signify something, nevertheless what is signified is not evil or nothing. But there is another respect in which they signify something and in which what is signified is something — though not really something but only as-if-something (*quasi aliquid*).

Indeed, many things are said according to form (*secundum formam*) which are not the case according to fact (*secundum rem*).[16] For example, *timere* [to be afraid] is called active according to the form of the word, although it is passive according to fact. So too, blindness is called *something* according to a form of speaking, although it is not something according to fact. For just as we say of someone that he has sight and that sight is in him, so we say that he has blindness and that blindness is in him, although blindness is not something but rather is not-something. Moreover, to have blindness is not to have something but is rather to be deprived of that which is something. For blindness is nothing other than not-seeing, or the absence of sight where sight ought to be. But not-seeing, or the absence of sight, is not anything more where sight ought to be than where it ought not to be. Therefore, blindness is not anything more in the eye because sight ought to be there than not-seeing, or the absence of sight, is in a stone, where sight ought not to be. Also, many other things which are not something are likewise called something according to a form of speaking, since we speak about them as if about existing things.

Therefore, in this way, "evil" and "nothing" signify something; and what is signified is something not according to fact but according to a form of speaking. For "nothing" signifies only not-something, or the absence of things which are something. And evil is only not-good, or the absence of good where good either ought to be or is advantageous to be. But that which is only the absence of what is something is surely not something. Therefore, evil truly is nothing, and nothing is not something. And yet, in a certain sense, evil and nothing *are* something because we speak about them as if they were something, when we say "Nothing caused it" or "Evil caused it" and "What caused it is nothing" or "Evil is what caused it." [These expressions] resemble our saying "Something caused it" or "Good caused it" and "What caused it is something" or "Good is what caused it." Accordingly, when we flatly deny a statement which someone makes, we say: "That which you are saying is nothing." For "that" and "which" are properly said only of that which is something. And when "that" and "which" are said in the manner I have just mentioned, they are not said about that which is something but about that which is called as-if-something.

S. You have satisfied me regarding the argument from the name "evil" — an argument by means of which I used to think I could prove that evil is something.

Chapter Twelve: The angel [Satan] was not able to have his first willing from himself. Many things are said "to be able" by reason of another's ability and "not to be able" by reason of another's inability.

S. It remains now for you to teach me what I can reply to those other arguments[17] which tend to persuade me that evil is something.

De Casu Diaboli

T. In order to elucidate the truth of the matter, we must begin a bit more slowly. But it is necessary that you not be content to understand merely one at a time those things which I shall say; rather, you must gather them all together in your mind as if in one view.

S. To be sure, I shall be as attentive as I can. But if in any respect I am slower than you wish, do not be displeased to wait for me according as you see my slowness to require.

T. Then, let us suppose that God is now creating the angel [Satan], whom He wills to make happy, and is creating him not as a whole at once but in stages. And let us suppose that the angel has been created up to the point of now being adapted for having a will but without as yet willing anything.

S. Suppose what you wish, and explain what I am asking about.

T. Then, do you think that the angel would be able to will something by himself (*per se*)?

S. I do not understand exactly what you mean by "by himself." For because he has nothing which he has not received, he can [do] nothing by himself — just as you said earlier[18] about every creature.

T. By "by himself" I mean "by means of that which he already has." For example, someone who has feet and those features which are sufficient for being able to walk is able to walk by himself. But someone who has feet but does not have feet free of infirmity is not able to walk by himself. Thus, in this sense I am asking whether that angel who is already adapted for willing but does not as yet will anything is able to will something by himself.

S. I think that he is *able* if he ever *wills*.

T. You are not answering my question.

S. In what way am I not?

T. I am asking about a state where there is no willing and about an ability which precedes an occurrence. And you are answering in terms of an actual willing and of an ability which accompanies an occurrence. For by the very fact that anything *is* it is *able to be*. But not everything which is was able to be before it was. Therefore, when I ask whether the angel who is not willing anything is able to will, I am asking about an ability prior to the willing, by which ability he would be able to move himself to willing. But when you reply that if he wills he is able [to will], you are speaking of an ability which accompanies the willing. For if he wills, it is necessary that he is able to will.

S. I know that there are two abilities: one which is not yet operative, and a second which is already operative. But regarding whatever is so able to be that it already is, I cannot fail to know that if at some time it was not, then it was able to be before [it was]. For if it had not been able [to be], it would never have been. Therefore, I think I have given a good answer, for anyone who is able to will because he already wills must have been able before he willed.

T. Do you think that what is nothing has nothing at all and so has no ability, and without any ability is altogether unable?

S. I cannot deny this.

T. I think that the world was nothing before it was created.

S. You speak the truth.

T. Therefore, before it was, it was altogether unable.

S. This follows.

T. Therefore, before it was, it was not able to be.

S. And I say: if [the world] was not able to be, it was impossible that it should ever be.

T. Before the world existed, it was both possible and impossible [to be]. Indeed, it was impossible for that which did not have the ability to make it exist. But it was possible for God, who had the ability to create it. Therefore, the world exists because God was able to create it before it was created, not because the world itself was able to exist before [it did exist].

S. I am unable to contradict your reasoning; but our common way of speaking does not agree [with your statement].

T. It is not surprising. For in our common way of speaking many things are said improperly. But when it is necessary to search out the very core of truth, it is necessary to analyze the troublesome impropriety as far as the subject-matter requires and allows. As a result of this impropriety of speaking we happen very often to say (1) that a thing is able, not because *it* is able but because another thing is able, and to say (2) that a thing which *is* able is not able, since another thing is not able. For example, if I say, "A book is able to be written by me," surely the book is unable; but I am able to write a book. And when we say, "This

De Casu Diaboli

man is not able to be overcome by that man,'' we mean only that the latter is not able to overcome the former.

Hence, we say that God is not able [to do] anything opposed to Himself or anything evil, since He is so powerful in happiness and justice — or better, since He is so all-powerful in simplicity of goodness (for happiness and justice are one good in Him and not different goods) — that nothing is able [to cause] any harm to the Supreme Good. For He is not able to be corrupted or to lie.

So, then, whatever does not exist is not able, before it exists, to exist by its own ability. But if another thing is able to cause this thing to exist, then in this manner this thing is able to exist by means of another's ability.

But although *ability* or *inability* can be divided in many ways, let it suffice for the present [to note] only that many things are said *to be able* not by their own ability but by another's, and many things are said *not to be able* not by their own inability but by another's.[19] Therefore, regarding the angel whom we postulated as newly created and already created up to the point that he is adapted for having a will but is not yet willing anything — when I ask about him whether he is able to will anything by himself, I am speaking about his own ability. Answer me in terms of this ability.

S. If [the angel] is already so adapted for willing that nothing else is lacking to him than to will, I do not see why he cannot [will] by himself. For whoever is adapted for seeing and does not see when he is placed in the light with his eyes closed, is able to see by himself. So, by comparison, in the case of the one who is not willing, why would he not will by himself,[20] just as someone who is not seeing is able to see by himself?

T. Because the one who is not seeing has sight and the will by which he is able to direct his sight. But we are speaking about one who has no will. Therefore, if a certain thing moves itself from not willing to willing, tell me whether it thereby wills to move itself.

S. If I say that the thing is moved without willing, there will follow that it is not moved by itself but by something else — except perhaps in a case where someone blinks at an oncoming blow or is compelled by some disadvantage to will what he was not previously willing. For in these cases I do not know whether he first wills to move himself to this willing.

Anselm of Canterbury

T. No one is compelled by fear or by a sense of any disadvantage, or attracted by the love of any benefit, to will anything, unless he first has a natural will [i.e., inclination] to avoid disadvantage or to possess what is beneficial. By this natural will he moves himself to other willings.

S. I cannot deny it.

T. Then, say that whatever moves itself to willing wills first to move itself to willing.

S. That's right.

T. Therefore, that which does not at all will is not at all able to move itself to willing.

S. I cannot dispute this.

T. It remains, then, that that angel who has been created already-adapted for having a will, but who does not yet will anything, is not able to have his first willing from himself.

S. I must admit that anyone who is not willing anything is not able to will anything by himself.

T. However, he is not able to be happy unless he wills happiness. I here mean by "happiness" not happiness with justice but the happiness which everyone wills — even the unjust. Indeed, all will to be well-off. For leaving aside the fact that every nature is called good, we commonly speak of two goods and of two opposing evils. One good is what is called justice, whose opposing evil is injustice. The other good is what seems to me able to be called benefit (*commodum*), to which the opposing evil is disadvantage (*incommodum*).[21] But, of course, not everyone wills justice, and not everyone flees from injustice. But not only every rational nature but even everything which is able to sense wills benefit and avoids disadvantage. For no one wills anything except what he considers to be in some respect beneficial to himself. In this manner, then, everyone wills to be well-off, and no one wills to be badly-off. I am speaking now about this happiness because no one is able to be happy who does not will happiness. For no one can be happy either in having what he does not will or in not having what he does will.

S. It must not be denied.

T. And someone who does not will justice ought not to be happy.

S. This must equally be conceded.

De Casu Diaboli

Chapter Thirteen: If [Satan] received only the will-for-happiness, he was able to will only happiness and was not able to keep from willing it; and regardless of what he willed, his will was neither just nor unjust.

T. Let us hypothesize, then, that at first God gives him [viz., the angel Satan] only the will-for-happiness, and let us see whether simply by virtue of having received a will, he is now able to move himself to willing something other than what he has received to will.

S. Proceed with what you have begun. For I am ready to understand.

T. It is evident that [the angel] does not yet will anything other than happiness, because he has not received anything else to will.

S. True.

T. Therefore, I ask you whether he is able to move himself to willing anything else.

S. Since he does not will anything else, I am unable to see how he would move himself to willing something other than happiness. For if he wills to move himself to willing something else, he wills something else.

T. Therefore, just as before he was given a will he was not able to will anything by himself, so after he has received only the will-for-happiness he is not able to have any other will from himself.

S. That's right.

T. Isn't it the case that if he thinks something to be conducive to acquiring happiness, he is able to move himself to willing it?

S. I am not sure what to answer. For if he is *not* able to, I do not see how he is willing happiness, for he is not able to will that by means of which he thinks he is able to attain happiness. On the other hand, if he *is* able to, I do not understand how he is unable to will something other than happiness.

T. If someone wills something not for the sake of the thing he is seen to will but rather for the sake of something else, should he be properly judged to will (1) that which he is said to will or (2) that for the sake of which he wills?

S. Assuredly, (2) that for the sake of which he is seen to will.

T. Therefore, someone who wills something for the sake of happiness does not will anything other than happiness. Therefore, he is able both to will what he thinks to be conducive to happiness and to will only happiness.

S. That's plain enough.

T. I ask, further, whether after having received only the will-for-happiness he is able to keep from willing happiness.

S. He is not able at the same time both to will and not to will.

T. True. But I am not asking that. Rather, I am asking whether he is able to desert this willing and to move himself from willing happiness to not willing happiness.

S. Indeed, if he does this unwillingly, he does not do it. But if he does it willingly, he wills something other than happiness. But he does not will anything other than happiness. Therefore, I think it obvious that he is not at all able by himself to keep from willing the only thing he has received to will.

T. You understand correctly. But tell me now whether [this angel], who wills only happiness and is not able to keep from willing happiness, is able to keep from willing a greater happiness in proportion as he understands it to be greater.

S. If his will for happiness did not increase to the degree that he thought there to be a better and a greater happiness, then either he would not be willing happiness at all or else he would be willing something else on account of which he did not will the better happiness. But we are hypothesizing that he wills happiness and not anything else.

T. Therefore, he wills to be happy in proportion to his recognition that a greater happiness is possible.

S. Without doubt, he so wills.

T. Therefore, he wills to be like God.

S. Nothing is clearer.

T. What do you think?: Would his will be unjust if in this manner he willed to be like God?

S. I do not wish to call it just, because he would be willing what was not fitting; nor do I wish to call it unjust, because he would will of necessity.

T. But we posited that someone who wills only happiness wills only benefits.

S. That's right.

De Casu Diaboli

T. Therefore, if that [angel], who willed only benefits, were not able to have greater and truer benefits, would he not will whatever lesser benefits he was able to use?

S. By all means. In fact, he would not be able to keep from willing even the very lowest of benefits if he was not able [to have] greater ones.

T. When he willed unclean and very base benefits in which irrational animals take pleasure, wouldn't this same will be unjust and blameworthy?

S. How would it be unjust and blameworthy, for it would will what it had received not to be able to keep from willing?

T. However, it is evident that this will is the work of God and the gift of God (even as is life or sensibility), whether when it wills the loftiest benefits or when it wills the basest ones. And it is evident that neither justice nor injustice are in this will.

S. No doubt about it.

T. Therefore, insofar as [this will] is a being, it is something good. But as far as justice or injustice is concerned, [this will] is neither good nor evil.

S. Nothing is clearer.

T. But [the angel] ought not to be happy if he does not have a just will. Indeed, he cannot be completely and laudably happy if he wills what neither is able to be nor ought to be.

S. That's quite apparent.

Chapter Fourteen: The case is similar if [Satan] received only the will-for-uprightness. And so he received both wills at the same time in order to be both just and happy.

T. So let us consider the will-for-justice. If this will were given to this same angel to will only what was fitting for him to will, would he be able to will anything other [than what was fitting]? Or would he be able by himself to keep from willing what he had received to will?

S. What we saw in the case of the will-for-happiness must in every respect hold true in the case of this will too.

T. Then, [Satan] would have neither a just nor an unjust will. For even as *there* [in the case of the will-for-happiness] the will would not be unjust if it willed unfitting things, since it would not be able to keep from willing them, so *here* [in the case of the will-for-justice] if the will willed fitting things, it would not thereby be just, since it would have received this capability in such way that it would not have been able to will otherwise.

S. That's right.

T. Then, since [Satan] cannot be called just or unjust merely because he wills happiness or merely because he wills what is fitting (for he would will these of necessity), and since he neither can nor ought to be happy unless he wills to be happy and wills justly, it is necessary for God to make both wills so agree in him that he wills to be happy and wills justly. Accordingly, the addition of justice would so temper the will-for-happiness that its excesses would be checked while its power to transgress would remain unabridged. Thus, although with respect to the fact that he would will to be happy, he would be able to exceed the mean, nevertheless with respect to the fact that he would will justly, he would not will to exceed the mean. And so, thus possessing a just will-for-happiness he could and should be happy. And by not willing what he ought not to will, although able [to will it], he would merit never to be able to will what he ought not to will. And by always keeping justice by means of a tempered will, he would in no way experience need. But if he were to desert justice by means of an immoderate will, he would in every way experience need.

S. Nothing more fitting can be thought.

T. Keep in mind that when we were previously considering only the will-for-happiness — apart from the limit which we added [viz., justice] so that the will would subordinate itself to God — we said that regardless of what it willed, neither justice nor injustice was in it.

S. I remember well.

Chapter Fifteen: Justice is something.

T. Do you think that a thing which when added to this same will[22] tempers it, so that it does not will more than it ought to will or more than is profitable to will, is something?

S. No one with any sense will think it to be nothing.

De Casu Diaboli

T. I believe you are sufficiently aware that this thing is nothing other than justice.
S. It cannot conceivably be anything else.
T. Therefore, it is certain that justice is something.
S. Indeed, it is something exceedingly good.

Chapter Sixteen: Injustice is only the absence of required justice.

T. Before that will received this justice, was it under obligation to will and not to will in accordance with justice?
S. No, it was not under an obligation with respect to what it had not received and therefore did not have.
T. However, you do not doubt that it was under an obligation after it received [justice] — unless it were to lose [justice] as the result of some overpowering force?
S. I think that the will is always bound to this obligation, whether it keeps what it has received or whether it willingly deserts it.
T. You judge correctly. But what if, having no need and being unconstrained by any overpowering force, this same will [for happiness] were to desert the justice which was so usefully and so wisely added to it — to desert by freely using its own power, i.e., by willing [something] more than it ought [to will]? Would anything remain with this will other than what we saw to be there before the addition of justice?
S. Since only justice was added, then when justice is gone, surely there remains only what was first there — except for the fact that having received justice has made the will a debtor, and, so to speak, certain lovely vestiges of justice have remained after justice has been deserted. For by the very fact that [the will] remains a debtor to justice, it is shown to have been adorned with the honor of justice. But even this is sufficiently just, viz., that what once received justice should always be under obligation with respect to justice — unless it were to lose justice as a result of being overpowered. And certainly a nature which is proved once to have had so honorable a good and to be always obliged to have it is proved to be much more worthy than a nature which is known never to have this good and never to be obliged [to have it].

T. You are thinking well. But add to your thought that the more praiseworthy the nature which had this good and ought [to have it] is shown to be, the more blameworthy the person who does not have what he ought [to have] is proven to be.

S. I strongly agree.

T. In the case under consideration, determine for me what shows the nature to be praiseworthy and what makes the person blameworthy.

S. To have had, or to be under obligation with respect to, [justice] manifests a natural dignity; not to have [justice] causes personal dishonor. For owing[23] was caused by the one who gave; but not having was caused by the one who deserted. For he is indebted because he has received; but he does not have because he has deserted.

T. Therefore, what you are blaming in the will which did not stand fast in justice is not that it owes justice but that it does not have justice.

S. What I blame in that will is nothing at all other than the absence of justice, or the not-having of justice. For, as I have already said, to owe [justice] beautifies; but not to have [justice] mars. And the more the debt is becoming, the more the not-having is unseemly. Indeed, the will is marred by the not-having, for which it itself is to blame, only because it is adorned by the obligation-to-have, which results from the goodness of the Giver.

T. Don't you judge this will, which does not have the justice it ought to have, to be unjust and to have injustice in it?

S. Who would not so judge?

T. If [this will] were not unjust and if injustice were not in it, then I think that you would be blaming nothing in it.

S. Absolutely nothing.

T. So you are blaming nothing else in it except injustice and the fact that it is unjust.

S. I cannot blame anything else in it.

T. Then, if you blame nothing in the will other than the absence of justice and its not having justice, as you said a moment ago, and if it is true that you blame nothing else in it except the fact that injustice is in it, or that it is unjust, then it is evident that in the will injustice, or being unjust, is only the absence of justice, or the not having of justice.

S. These can in no respect be different.

De Casu Diaboli

T. Then, even as the absence of justice and the not having of justice have no being, so injustice and being unjust have no being; and thus they are not something, but are nothing.

S. Nothing follows more logically.

T. Also bear in mind that we have already established that when justice departed [from the will], nothing else remained in it except the debt of justice and what [the will] had before it received justice.

S. Assuredly, this has been established.

T. But before [the will] had justice, it was not unjust and did not have injustice.

S. Right.

T. Therefore, when justice departs either injustice is not in the will and the will is not unjust or else injustice and being unjust are nothing.

S. Nothing can appear more necessary.

T. But you have conceded that the will has injustice and is unjust after it has deserted justice.

S. Indeed, I cannot help seeing [this point].

T. Therefore, injustice and being unjust are nothing.

S. What I earlier believed without knowing, you have caused me, still believing, to know.

T. I think that you also now know — since injustice is only the absence of justice, and being unjust is simply not having justice — why after justice has been deserted, rather than before justice has been given, (1) the absence of justice is called injustice, and (2) not to have justice is to be unjust, and (3) the absence of justice and not having justice are blameworthy. The only reason is that it is not unfitting for justice to be absent except where it ought to be present. For even as not having a beard is not unbecoming for a man who ought not yet to have one, though when the time comes for him to have a beard, his not having one is unseemly: so too not having justice does not mar a nature which ought not to have it, though not having justice does disgrace a nature which ought to have it. And the more the fact that one ought to have [a beard] manifests a manly nature, the more not having [a beard] blemishes a manly appearance.

S. I see well enough that injustice is only the absence of justice where justice ought to be.

Chapter Seventeen: Why the renegade angel is unable to return to justice.

T. When we hypothesized[24] that only the will-for-happiness was given to the aforementioned angel [viz., Satan], we saw that he would have been unable to will anything else.
S. We saw clearly what you say.
T. Once justice has been abandoned and there is only the prior will-for-happiness remaining, is this renegade angel able to return by himself to the will-for-justice, to which he could not come before it was given?
S. He is now much less [able to come by himself to justice]. For *then* [i.e., when he at first had only the will-for-happiness] he was unable to have [justice] because of his state of nature; but *now* [i.e., after having received and deserted justice] he ought not to have it also because of his merited fault.
T. Therefore, he is in no respect able to have justice from himself when he does not have justice, because [he is unable to have it from himself] either before he receives it or after he deserts it.
S. He ought not to have anything from himself.

Chapter Eighteen: How the evil angel caused himself to be unjust and the good angel caused himself to be just. The evil angel owes gratitude to God for the goods which he received and deserted, even as the good angel, who kept the goods which he received, [owes gratitude].

T. Isn't it the case that in some way, even when [Satan] had justice, he was able to give it to himself?
S. How could he have?
T. We say "to cause" in many modes. For example, we speak of causing something when we cause a thing to be, and also when we are able to cause it not to be but do not cause it not to be.[25] And so, since the evil angel was able both to remove justice from himself and not to remove it from himself, he was able in this

De Casu Diaboli

manner to give justice to himself — even as the angel who stood steadfast in the truth in which he was created did not (when able to) cause himself not to have justice, and so gave himself justice, and received this entire gift from God. For both angels received from God the possession [of justice] and the ability to keep it and the ability to forsake it. God gave this latter ability so that they would be able in some manner to give justice to themselves. For if they were in no manner able to remove justice from themselves, they would in no manner be able to give justice to themselves. Therefore, he who in this manner gave justice to himself received from God the fact that he gave justice to himself.

S. I see that by not removing justice they were able to give it to themselves. Yet, the one gave it to himself, whereas the other removed it from himself.

T. Do you see, then, that they owe to God equal amounts of gratitude, in proportion to His goodness, and that it is not the case that the Devil, because he removed from himself what God gave and because he was unwilling to accept what God offered, is under a lesser obligation to return to God what is God's?

S. Yes, I see.

T. Therefore, the evil angel ought always to thank God for the happiness which he himself removed from himself, even as the good angel [ought always to thank God] for the happiness which he himself gave to himself.

S. Absolutely true.

T. I think you are aware that God can in no manner cause anyone to be unjust except by not causing someone who is unjust to be just, although able to do so. For before having received justice, no one is just or unjust; and after having received justice, no one becomes unjust except by willingly deserting justice. Therefore, even as the good angel caused himself to be just by not removing justice from himself when able, so God causes the evil angel to be unjust by not returning justice to him, although able to do so.

S. This is easily recognized.

Chapter Nineteen: Insofar as it is, the will is something good.
No thing is an evil.

T. Let us return to considering the will, and let us remember what we have already considered,[26] viz., that before the will-for-happiness receives justice it is not something evil but something good, regardless of what it wills. Hence, it follows that when [the will] deserts the justice it has received, then if it is the same being that it previously was, it is something good with respect to what it is [essentially]. But with respect to the fact that the justice which was in it is no longer there, [the will] is called evil and unjust. For if to will to be like God were an evil, the Son of God would not will to be like the Father. Or if to will the basest of pleasures were an evil, the wills of brute animals would be called evil. But the will of the Son of God is not evil, for it is just; and an irrational will is not called evil, for it is not unjust.

Thus, it follows that no will is an evil thing and that every will, insofar as it is, is a good thing because it is the work of God. And only insofar as it is unjust is it evil. And since no thing is called evil except an evil will or else on account of an evil will (e.g., an evil man and an evil action), nothing is more apparent than that no thing is an evil, and that evil is simply the absence, in the will, of that forsaken justice — or the absence of justice in some other thing, on account of an evil will.

Chapter Twenty: How God causes evil wills and evil actions; and
how they are received from Him.

S. Your argument is so bound together by true, necessary, and clear reasons that I do not in any respect see how what you say can be undone — except that I do see something to be implied which I do not believe ought to be said, but which I do not see how to deny if what you say is true. For if to will to be like God is not nothing or is not an evil but is a good, then this will was able to exist only from Him from whom all existing things come. Therefore, if the angel did not have what he did not receive, then what he had, he received from Him from whom he had it. How-

De Casu Diaboli

ever, what did the angel receive from Him except what He gave? Therefore, if he had the will to be like God, he had it because God gave it.

T. Why is it strange if just as we say that God leads into temptation when He does not deliver from it,²⁷ so we say that He gives an evil will by not preventing it when He can — especially since the ability to will anything at all comes only from Him?

S. Put this way, it does not seem to be inappropriate.

T. Therefore, if there is no giving without a receiving, then just as someone who willingly concedes and also someone who permits, though disapproving, are commonly said to give, so someone who receives what has been conceded and someone who dares to take forbidden things are not incorrectly said to receive.

S. What you say seems to me neither incorrect nor uncommon.

T. Then, what do we say in opposition to the truth if we say that when the Devil willed what he ought not to have [willed] he received this willing from God because God permitted it, and also did not receive it [from God] because God did not consent to it?

S. Nothing here seems to be opposed to the truth.

T. Therefore, when the Devil turned his will to what he ought not to have [willed], that willing and that turning were something. And yet, he had something only from God and [by permission] of God, since he was able to will something or to move his will only by permission of the one who creates all natures — substantial and accidental, universal and individual. For insofar as the will and its turning, or movement, are something, each is a good and is due to God. But insofar as the will lacks the justice which it ought not to lack, it is *something* evil — rather than an absolute evil. And what is evil is not due to God but is due to the one who wills, or who moves his will.

To be sure, injustice is an unqualified evil since it is identical with the evil which is nothing. But a nature in which there is injustice is *something* evil because the nature is something and is something other than injustice, which is an evil and nothing. Therefore, what is something is caused by God and is of God's doing; but what is nothing, or an evil, is caused by someone unjust and is of his doing.

S. Indeed, we must admit that God creates the natures of all things. But who would concede that He causes the particular actions of evil wills — for example, the depraved movement of will by which this evil will moves itself?

T. Why is it strange to say that God causes the particular actions which are done by an evil will?[28] For we say that He causes the particular substances which are made by an unjust will and by dishonorable action.

S. I do not have anything to say against this. Indeed, I am not able to deny that any given action is really something. Nor do I wish to deny that what really has some being is caused by God. Nor does your reasoning in any way accuse God or excuse the Devil; rather, it completely excuses God and accuses the Devil.

Chapter Twenty-one: The evil angel was not able to foreknow that he would fall.

S. But I would like to know whether this renegade angel foreknew these things about himself.

T. When you ask whether the angel who did not stand fast in the truth foreknew that he would fall, we must decide about the kind of knowledge you mean. For if you are talking about the knowledge present only when something is understood with rational certainty, then I answer that what is able not to be is altogether unable to be known. For what is able not to be, cannot at all with rational certainty be inferred to be. Hence, it is evident that [the evil angel] was not at all able to foreknow his fall, the future occurrence of which was not necessary. For let us postulate that this fall had not been going to occur. Then, do you think that it could have been foreknown, if it was not going to occur?

S. It seems that what is able not to happen in the future cannot be foreknown and also that what is foreknown is not able not to happen in the future. Yet, I am reminded now of that very celebrated question about free choice and divine foreknowledge. For although the claim that free choice and divine foreknowledge are compatible is made with such great authority and is held with such great utility that it must not at all be doubted on the basis of any human reasoning, nevertheless they do seem incompatible from the point of view of rational reflection. Thus, with regard to this question, we see some persons inclining so much towards one of the alternatives that they completely desert the other and

De Casu Diaboli

perish under a wave of unbelief; but many others, by holding back [from one side or the other] are endangered as if by contrary winds battering against each other from different directions. Therefore, although it is evident that there is divine foreknowledge of all things done by free choice and that none of these deeds occur of necessity, nevertheless what is foreknown seems to be able not to happen in the future.

T. For the time being, I will give a brief answer to this. God's foreknowledge is not properly called foreknowledge.[29] For the one to whom all things are always present does not have foreknowledge of future things; rather He has knowledge of present things. Therefore, since *foreknowledge of a future event* is a different notion from *knowledge of a present event*, divine "foreknowledge" and the foreknowledge about which we are asking need not have the same consequence.

S. Agreed.

T. Let us return to the question which was at hand.

S. I agree to your proposal — but with the stipulation that when I shall ask about the problem I mentioned, you shall not refuse to tell me what God will deign to reveal to you about it. For a solution to this puzzle is exceedingly necessary — if a solution has already been given by someone, or if one can be given. For, leaving out of consideration what is said by Divine Authority (which I believe without doubting), I confess that as yet I have nowhere read an account which would satisfy me intellectually as a solution to this problem.

T. When we shall come to this problem — if perchance we do come to it — the solution will be as God will give. However, since it is now evident, on the basis of the argument just given, that the apostate angel could not have foreknown his downfall by means of that foreknowledge from which the necessity of the event follows, receive still another argument which excludes his having had any premonition — not only by foreknowledge but by any thought or suspicion whatsoever — of his fall.

S. I await this.

T. If while he was still standing fast with a good will, he foreknew that he would fall, then either he was willing that it happen or else he was unwilling.

S. One of these alternatives must be true.

T. But if together with foreknowledge of his fall he were ever willing to fall, he would *already* be fallen because of this evil will.

S. What you say is clear.

T. Therefore, if he were willing to fall, it would not be the case that he knew he would fall *before* he fell.

S. There can be no objection to your conclusion.

T. On the other hand, if he knew that he would fall but he were unwilling to fall, he would have been wretched with grief to the same degree that he willed to remain upright.

S. It cannot be denied.

T. But the more he willed to stand fast, the more just he was; and the more just he was, the more he ought to have been happy.

S. It cannot be denied.

T. Therefore, if he foreknew that he would fall but he were unwilling to fall, he would have been as wretched as he ought to have been happy — something unfitting.

S. Indeed, I cannot deny that your inference holds. But often this [sort of thing] is known to happen not only fittingly but even laudably and by heavenly grace. For many times — to recall a few things regarding the troubles of the just — the more just someone is, the more he is affected by the pain of sympathy over another's downfall. Often, too, we see that someone who has a greater steadfastness in justice suffers a greater force of persecution by the unjust.

T. The argument is not the same in the case of men and in the case of that angel. For because of the sin of our first parent human nature was made capable of suffering countless troubles; from this passibility grace works incorruptibility in us in many ways. But that angel, having not yet sinned, did not deserve to suffer from any evil.

S. You have met my objection. Clearly, just as this argument removes from the evil angel any foreknowledge of his fall, so it equally removes all thought thereof.

T. There is also something else which seems to me sufficient to show that beforehand he in no way thought of his future transgression. Surely, he would have thought that this transgression would be either compelled or voluntary. But there was no way in which he might suspect that he would ever be compelled; and as long as he willed to persevere in the truth, he was in no way able to think that by his own will alone he would desert the truth. For I

De Casu Diaboli

have already shown[30] that as long as he had an upright will, he willed to persevere in this will. Therefore, I see no way in which while he was willing perseveringly to keep what he had, he could even have suspected that in the absence of any other cause he would willingly desert what he had. I do not deny that he knew he was able to change the will he had. But I say he could not have supposed that in the absence of any other cause he would ever freely change the will he was willing perseveringly to keep.

S. Anyone who closely understands what you are saying sees clearly that the evil angel was in no way able to know, or even to suspect, that he would do what he evilly did.

Chapter Twenty-two: [The evil angel] knew that he ought not to will that which he sinned in willing; and he knew that he ought to be punished if he sinned.

S. But I also want you to show me in equal measure whether [the evil angel] knew that he ought not to will what he willed in transgressing.

T. You ought not to be in doubt with regard to this issue if you consider what was just said. For if he had not known that he ought not to will what he unjustly did will, he would not have known that he ought to keep the will which he deserted. Therefore, he would not have been just by keeping, nor unjust by deserting, the justice which he would not have known. Indeed, if he did not know that he ought to be content with what he had received, then he was not able to keep from willing [something] more than he had. Finally, since he was so rational that nothing prevented him from using his reason, he was not ignorant of what he ought or ought not to have willed.

S. I do not see that your reasoning can be invalidated. But nevertheless, a certain question does seem to me to arise from it. For if [the evil angel] knew that he ought not to desert what he had received, then surely he knew equally that he ought to be punished if he were to desert. So, having received an inseparable will to be happy, how could he freely have willed that which would make him unhappy?

Chapter Twenty-three: [The evil angel] ought not to have known that if he sinned he would be punished.

T. Just as it is certain that he could not have escaped knowing that he *ought to be* punished if he sinned, so he ought not to have known that he *would be* punished if he sinned.

S. How did he fail to know this if he was so rational that his rationality was not prevented from knowing the truth, as ours often is prevented by a burdensome corruptible body?[31]

T. Because he was rational he was able to understand that he could be justly punished if he were to sin. But since "the judgments of God are a great deep,"[32] and "His ways unsearchable,"[33] he was unable to discern whether God would do what he justly could do.

But suppose someone should claim:

> [That angel] was not at all able to believe that God was going to damn, because guilty, His own creature whom He had created by means of such great goodness. [And he] especially [could not have believed it] because [of the following considerations]: No example of justice punishing injustice had previously occurred. Moreover, he would have been certain that the number of those who had been created to enjoy God was fixed by such great wisdom that just as it had no superfluity, so if it were diminished it would be imperfect; but so excellent a work of God would not remain imperfect in any respect. Now, if man had already been created, then [that angel] would not at all have been able to know that God was going to substitute human nature for angelic nature, or angelic nature for human nature, if either were to fall. Rather, he would have believed that God was going to restore each nature to that end for which it had been created — restore each to its own place, not to the other's place. On the other hand, if man had not yet been created, then [the angel] would have been all the less able to suppose that man was going to be created as a substitute for angelic nature.

Now, if someone should make this claim, what unfittingness would there be in it?

S. Indeed, there seems to me to be more fittingness than unfittingness.

T. Let us return to what I said earlier, viz., that [the angel] ought not to have had this knowledge [that he would be punished if he sinned]. For if he had known, then while possessing and willing happiness he would not have been able freely to will what would have caused him to be unhappy. Therefore, he would not

De Casu Diaboli

have been just when he kept from willing what he ought not to have willed, for he would not have been able to will it. But even on the basis of the following argument consider whether he ought to have known what you ask about: Assume that he knew. Then, he either would have sinned or would not have sinned.

S. One of these alternatives would be the case.

T. If having foreseen such great punishment he would have sinned without being in any need and without anything compelling, then he would have been all the more deserving of punishment.

S. That's right.

T. Then, this foreknowledge was not advantageous to him.

S. For one who was going to sin it was truly no advantage to have prior knowledge of punishment.

T. On the other hand, if he had not sinned, then either he would have kept from sinning solely because of a good will, or else because of fear of punishment.

S. Nothing else can be said.

T. But by his very deed he demonstrated that he would not have kept from sinning solely from love of justice.

S. There's no doubt about it.

T. But if he had kept from [sinning] because of fear, then he would not have been just.

S. It is obvious that he ought in no manner to have known that his sinning would result in the punishment which came to be imposed on him.

Chapter Twenty-four: Even the good angel ought not to have known this [viz., that if he sinned he would be punished].

S. But since we believe that both the angel who stood in the truth and the angel who did not stand in the truth were endowed with equal knowledge in their original state, I do not see why this knowledge[34] was denied to the angel whose good will was so resolute that it sufficed to avoid sinning.

T. [If the good angel had foreknown], he neither could have nor ought to have disdained the punishment which he would have foreknown.

S. So it seems.

T. Therefore, just as the love of justice would have sufficed by itself to keep him from sinning, so would the aversion to punishment have sufficed by itself.

S. Nothing is clearer.

T. Therefore, he would have had two inducements (*causas*) for not sinning — the one honorable and useful, the other not honorable and not useful — viz., a love of justice and an aversion to punishment. For it is not honorable to keep from sinning merely because of an aversion to punishment; and where the love of justice is by itself sufficient for not sinning, the aversion to punishment is useless therefor.

S. There is nothing I could object to.

T. What then? When there is seen to be in the good angel only that inducement for persevering which is useful and honorable because uncompelling (*spontanea*), isn't his perseverance much more splendidly pleasing than if at the same time there is seen to be in him that inducement which is understood to be useless and dishonorable because compelling (*necessaria*)?

S. What you say is so clear that I now rejoice that he did not know that which a moment ago I was wishing he knew — except that we cannot deny that he now has this same knowledge, which he cannot fail to have from the example of the angel who sins.

Chapter Twenty-five: Even if the only reason the good angel is said to be now unable to sin were that he now has this knowledge from the Devil's fall, nevertheless [not to be able to sin] would be to his glory.

T. As for the fact that both the good angel and the evil angel are now certain that this kind of punishment follows this kind of guilt: just as each has a different kind of knowledge, so the cause of the knowledge is not the same and the consequence of the knowledge is dissimilar. For what the evil angel knows by his own experience the good angel learned from the evil angel's example. But the former [knows] in his way because he did not persevere; the latter [learned] in his way because he did persevere. Therefore, just as the evil angel's knowledge is to his dis-

De Casu Diaboli

grace since blamably he did not persevere, so the good angel's knowledge is to his glory since laudably he did persevere.

So if the only reason the good angel is said to be now unable to sin were that he has this knowledge, it is clear enough that just as the knowledge which is obtained from laudably persevering is glorious, so the inability to sin which is the result of this glorious knowledge would be to his glory. Therefore, just as the evil angel deserves to be blamed because he is unable to return to justice, so the good angel deserves to be praised because he is unable to depart from justice. For just as the former is now unable to return because he departed solely by an evil will, so the latter is now unable to depart because he remained steadfast solely by a good will. Therefore, it is evident that just as it is the penalty of sin for the evil angel to be unable to recover what he deserted, so it is the reward of justice for the good angel to be unable to desert what he kept.

S. Your reflections upon the good angel's knowledge and inability would be very lovely if, as you maintain, this knowledge and this inability had accrued to him because he persevered. For he seems to have acquired these not because he himself persevered but because the renegade angel did not persevere.

T. If what you say is true, then the good angel would be able to rejoice over the fall of the apostate angel, inasmuch as it would have been to his benefit that the other angel fell; for the knowledge by which he would no longer be able either to sin or to be unhappy would have been acquired not because he himself was well-deserving but because the other angel was ill-deserving. But this entire inference is utterly absurd.

S. The more absurd it seems (as you show) for the fall of the angel who sins to benefit the angel who stands, the greater the need for you to show it not to be the case that the good angel acquired this knowledge[35] because the other angel sinned.

T. You ought not to say that the good angel gained this knowledge *because* the evil angel sinned; rather, you ought to say that the good angel gained this knowledge *by the example of* the falling angel because he sinned. For if neither had sinned, God would surely have given this knowledge in some other way — on account of the merit of perseverance, and without the example of someone's falling. For no one will deny that God was able to give this knowledge to His angels in some other way. Therefore, when the evil angel sinned, God used the example of his fall to teach the good angel what He was going to teach [him in any case]. [God taught in this way] not because of an inability which resulted in His not being able to teach in another way, but because of a greater ability by means of which He was able to make good come from evil, so that not even evil would remain unordered in the kingdom belonging to omnipotent Wisdom.

S. What you say is especially pleasing to me.

T. Clearly, then, were it the case that the good angel is no longer able to sin only because he knows that punishment followed the sin of the evil angel, this inability [to sin] would serve not to diminish his praiseworthiness but to reward him for the justice he kept. But you know (because it was made clear earlier)[36] that the reason he is not able to sin is the following: on account of the merit of perseverance he has been so elevated that he no longer sees anything more that he can will.

S. None of the things learned in the course of our rational investigation has slipped my memory.

Chapter Twenty-six: What we dread when we hear the name "evil"; and what causes the works which injustice is said to cause, since injustice and evil are nothing.

S. But although you have satisfactorily answered all my questions, yet I still await your explaining what it is that we dread when we hear the name "evil," and (since evil is nothing) what causes the works which injustice, itself an evil, seems to cause — e.g., in the case of robbery or of sensuality.

T. I shall give you a brief answer. The evil which is injustice is always nothing; but the evil which is disadvantage (*incommoditas*) is without doubt sometimes nothing (as is blindness) but is sometimes something (as are sadness and pain). And we always regard with aversion the disadvantage which is something. Therefore, when we hear the name "evil," we fear not an evil which is nothing but an evil which is something that follows the absence of good. For injustice and blindness, which are evils and are nothing, are followed by many disadvantages which are evils

De Casu Diaboli

and are something; and these latter are what we dread when we hear the name "evil."

However, when we say that injustice causes robbery or that blindness causes a man to fall into a pit, we should not at all understand that injustice and blindness cause something. Rather, we should understand that if justice were in the will and sight in the eye, then neither the robbery nor the fall into the pit would occur. Such is the case when we say, "The absence of a rudder drives the ship onto the rocks," or "The absence of a bridle causes the horse to run wild."[37] Here we mean only that if the ship had a rudder or the horse a bridle, then the winds would not drive the ship [onto the rocks] nor would the horse run wild. For just as a ship is directed by a rudder and a horse by reins, so a man's will is directed by justice and his feet by sight.

S. You have so satisfied me about the evil which is injustice that every query which used to be in my mind regarding evil has now been settled. For the puzzle concerning this evil seems to arise from the fact that if this evil were some sort of being, it would be from God, from whom must derive all that is something, and from whom cannot possibly derive sin or injustice. But I see nothing to be against right faith if the evil which is disadvantage is sometimes something.

Chapter Twenty-seven: From where evil came to an angel who was good.

S. But let it not weary you to reply briefly to my foolish question, so that I may know how to answer those who ask me about the same thing. (Indeed, it is not always easy to answer wisely one who is asking foolishly.) I ask, then: From where did the first evil that is called injustice or sin come to an angel who was created just?

T. Tell me from where nothing comes to something.

S. Nothing neither comes nor goes.

T. Then, why do you ask from where injustice, which is nothing, comes?

S. Because when justice departs from where it was, we say that injustice approaches.

Anselm of Canterbury

T. Then, express yourself more properly and clearly, and ask about the departure of justice. For, indeed, a suitable question often conduces to an answer, whereas an unsuitable question often produces a greater hindrance.

S. So why did justice depart from the just angel?

T. If you wish to speak properly, justice did not depart from him, but he deserted justice by willing what he ought not to have [willed].

S. Why did he desert it?

T. When I say that he deserted it by willing what he ought not to have [willed], I indicate clearly *why* and *how* he deserted it. For he deserted it *because* he willed what he ought not to have willed; and he deserted it *in this manner*, viz., by willing what he ought not to have [willed].

S. Why did he will what he ought not to have [willed]?

T. There was no cause which preceded this willing — except that he was able to will.[38]

S. Did he will because he was able?

T. No, for the good angel was likewise able to will [what he ought not to have willed]; nevertheless he did not will [it]. For although no one would ever will if he were not able [to will], nonetheless it is not the case that what someone is able to will he wills *because* he is able, and for no other reason (*causa*).

S. Then, why did he will [what he ought not to have willed]?

T. Only because he willed [it]. For this willing had no other cause (*causa*) by which in any respect to be driven or drawn; rather, it was an efficient cause of itself — if this can be said — and an effect.

Chapter Twenty-eight: The ability to will what he ought not to have [willed] was always good; and this willing, with respect to its being, was good.

S. If that ability to will[39] and that willing were something, then they were good and were from God.

T. Each was something. Indeed, that ability was only something good and was a free gift from God. And indeed, with respect to its being, that willing was good; yet, since it was

De Casu Diaboli

unjustly done it was evil; nevertheless it was from God, from whom is everything that is something. Surely, someone has from God not only that which God freely gives but also that which he unjustly seizes with God's permission. And even as God is said to cause what He permits to occur, so He is said to give what He permits to be seized. Therefore, since with God's permission the evil angel, through robbery,[40] used the ability freely given by God, he had the use — which is the same thing as the willing — from God. For to will is nothing other than to use the ability to will (just as to speak and to use the ability to speak are identical).

THE HARMONY OF THE FOREKNOWL-EDGE, THE PREDESTINATION, AND THE GRACE OF GOD WITH FREE CHOICE
(De Concordia Praescientiae et Praedestinationis et Gratiae Dei cum Libero Arbitrio)

THE HARMONY OF THE FOREKNOWL-
EDGE, THE PREDESTINATION,
AND THE GRACE OF GOD
WITH FREE CHOICE.[1]
(De Concordia Praescientiae et Praedestinationis et Gratiae Dei cum Libero Arbitrio)

With the help of God I shall try to set forth in writing what He will deign to reveal to me concerning these three controversies in which free choice seems to be incompatible with (1) the foreknowledge, (2) the predestination, and (3) the grace of God.

First Controversy: Foreknowledge and Free Choice[2]

I

Admittedly, free choice and the foreknowledge of God seem incompatible; for it is necessary that the things foreknown by God be going to occur, whereas the things done by free choice occur without any necessity. Now, if these two are incompatible, then it is impossible that God's all-foreseeing foreknowledge should coexist with something's being done by freedom of choice. In turn, if this impossibility is regarded as not obtaining, then the incompatibility which seems to be present is completely eliminated.

Therefore, let us posit as existing together both God's foreknowledge (from which the necessity of future things seems to follow) and freedom of choice (by which many actions are performed, we believe, without any necessity); and let us see whether it is impossible for these two to coexist. If this coexistence is impossible, then some other impossibility arises from it. For, indeed, an impossible thing is one from which, when posited, some other impossible thing follows. Now, on the assumption that some action is going to occur without necessity, God foreknows this, since he foreknows all future events. And that which is foreknown by God is, necessarily, going to occur, as is foreknown. Therefore, it is necessary that something be going to occur without necessity. Hence, the foreknowledge from which necessity follows and the freedom of choice from which necessity is absent are here seen (for one who rightly understands it) to be not at all incompatible. For, on the one hand, it is necessary that what is foreknown by God be going to occur; and, on the other hand, God foreknows that something is going to occur without any necessity.

But you will say to me: "You still do not remove from me the necessity of sinning or the necessity of not sinning. For God foreknows that I am going to sin or foreknows that I am not going to sin. And so, if I sin, it is necessary that I sin; or if I do not sin, it is necessary that I do not sin." To this claim I reply: You ought to say not merely "God foreknows that I am going to sin" or "God foreknows that I am not going to sin" but "God foreknows that it is without necessity that I am going to sin" or "God foreknows that it is without necessity that I am not going to sin." And thus it follows that whether you sin or do not sin, in either case it will be without necessity; for God foreknows that what will occur will occur without necessity. Do you see, then, that it is not impossible for God's foreknowledge (according to which future things, which God foreknows, are said to occur of necessity) to coexist with freedom of choice (by which many actions are performed without necessity)? For if this coexistence were impossible, then something impossible would follow. But no impossibility arises from this coexistence.

Perhaps you will claim: "You still do not remove the constraint of necessity from my heart when you say that, because of God's foreknowledge, it is necessary for me to be going to sin without necessity or it is necessary for me to be not going to sin without necessity. For *necessity* seems to imply coercion or restraint. Therefore, if it is necessary that I sin willingly, I interpret this as indicating that I am compelled by some hidden power to will to sin; and if I do not sin, [I interpret this as indicating that] I

De Concordia I

am restrained from willing to sin. Therefore, it seems to me that if I sin I sin by necessity, and if I do not sin it is by necessity that I do not sin."

2

And I [reply]: We must realize that we often say "necessary to be" of what is not compelled-to-be by any force, and "necessary not to be" of what is not excluded by any preventing factor. For example, we say "It is necessary for God to be immortal" and "It is necessary for God not to be unjust." [We say this] not because some force compels Him to be immortal or prohibits Him from being unjust, but because nothing can cause Him not to be immortal or can cause Him to be unjust.[3] Similarly, then, I might say: "It is necessary that you are going to sin voluntarily" or "It is necessary that, voluntarily, you are not going to sin" — just as God foreknows. But these statements must not be construed to mean that something prevents the act of will which shall not occur, or compels that act of will which shall occur. For God, who foresees that some action is going to occur voluntarily, foreknows the very fact that the will is neither compelled nor prevented by anything. Hence, what is done voluntarily is done freely. Therefore, if these matters are carefully pondered, I think that no inconsistency prevents freedom of choice and God's foreknowledge from coexisting.

Indeed, (if someone properly considers the meaning of the word), by the very fact that something is said to be *foreknown*, it is declared to be going to occur.[4] For only what is going to occur is foreknown, since knowledge is only of the truth. Therefore, when I say "If God foreknows something, it is necessary that this thing be going to occur," it is as if I were to say: "If this thing will occur, of necessity it will occur." But this necessity neither compels nor prevents a thing's existence or nonexistence. For because the thing is presumed to exist, it is said to exist of necessity; or because it is presumed not to exist, it is said to not-exist of necessity. [But our reason for saying these things is] not that necessity compels or prevents the thing's existence or nonexistence. For when I say "If it will occur, of necessity it will occur," here the necessity follows, rather than precedes, the presumed existence of the thing.[5] The sense is the same if we say "What will be, of necessity will be." For this necessity signifies nothing other than that what will occur will not be able not to occur at the same time.

Likewise, the following statements are equally true: (1) that some thing did exist and does exist and will exist, but not out of necessity, and (2) that all that was, necessarily was, all that is, necessarily is, and all that will be, necessarily will be. Indeed, for a thing to be past is not the same as for a past thing to be past; and for a thing to be present is not the same as for a present thing to be present; and for a thing to be future is not the same as for a future thing to be future. By comparison, for a thing to be white is not the same as for a white thing to be white. For example, a staff is not always necessarily white, because at some time before it became white it was able not to become white; and after it has become white, it is able to become not-white. But it is necessary that a white staff always be white. For neither before a white thing was white nor after it has become white can it happen that a white thing is not-white at the same time. Similarly, it is not by necessity that a thing is temporally present. For before the thing was present, it was able to happen that it would not be present; and after it has become present, it can happen that it not remain present. But it is necessary that a present thing always be present, because neither before it is present nor after it has become present is a present thing able to be not-present at the same time. In the same way, some event — e.g., an action — is going to occur without necessity, because before the action occurs, it can happen that it not be going to occur.[6] On the other hand, it is necessary that a future event be future, because what is future is not able at the same time to be not-future. Of the past it is similarly true (1) that some event is not necessarily past, because before it occurred, there was the possibility of its not occurring, and (2) that, necessarily, what is past is always past, since it is not able at the same time not to be past. Now, a past event has a characteristic which a present event or a future event does not have. For it is never possible for a past event to become not-past, as a present event is able to become not-present, and as an event which is not necessarily going to happen has the possibility of not happening in the future. Thus, when we say of what is going to happen that it is going to happen, this statement must be true, because it is never the case that what is going to happen is not going to happen.

(Similarly, whenever we predicate something of itself, [the statement is true]. For when we say "Every man is a man," or "If he is a man, he is a man," or "Every white thing is white," or "If it is a white thing, it is white": these statements must be true because something cannot both be and not be the case at the same time.) Indeed, if it were not necessary that everything which is going to happen were going to happen, then something which is going to happen would not be going to happen — a contradiction. Therefore, *necessarily*, everything which is going to happen is going to happen; and if it is going to happen, it is going to happen. (For we are saying of what is going to happen that it is going to happen.) But ["necessarily" here signifies] subsequent necessity, which does not compel anything to be.

3

However, when an event is said to be going to occur, it is not always the case that the event occurs by necessity, even though it is going to occur. For example, if I say "Tomorrow there will be an insurrection among the people," it is not the case that the insurrection will occur by necessity. For before it occurs, it is *possible* that it not occur even if it *is* going to occur. On the other hand, it is sometimes the case that the thing which is said to be going to occur does occur by necessity — for example, if I say that tomorrow there will be a sunrise. Therefore, if of an event which is going to occur I state that it must be going to occur, [I do so] either in the way that the insurrection which is going to occur tomorrow is, necessarily, going to occur, or else in the way that the sunrise which is going to occur tomorrow is going to occur by necessity. Indeed, the insurrection (which will occur but not by necessity) is said necessarily to be going to occur — but only in the sense of subsequent necessity. For we are saying of what is going to happen that it is going to happen. For if the insurrection is going to occur tomorrow, then — necessarily — it is going to occur. On the other hand, the sunrise is understood to be going to occur with two necessities: (1) with a preceding necessity, which causes the event to occur (for the event will occur because it is necessary that it occur), and (2) with a subsequent necessity, which does not compel anything to occur (for because the sunrise is going to occur, it is — necessarily — going to occur).

Therefore, when of what God foreknows to be going to occur we say that it is necessary that it be going to occur, we are not in every case asserting that the event is going to occur by necessity; rather, we are asserting that an event which is going to occur is, necessarily, going to occur. For something which is going to occur cannot at the same time be not going to occur. The meaning is the same when we say "If God foreknows such-and-such an event" — without adding "which is going to occur." For in the verb "to foreknow" the notion of future occurrence is included, since to foreknow is nothing other than to know the future; and so if God foreknows some event, it is necessary that this event be going to occur. Therefore, from the fact of God's foreknowledge it does not in every case follow that an event is going to occur by necessity. For although God foreknows all future events, He does not foreknow that all of them are going to occur by necessity. Rather, He foreknows that some of them will occur as the result of the free will of a rational creature.

Indeed, we must note that just as it is not necessary for God to will what He does will, so in many cases it is not necessary for a man to will what he does will. And just as whatever God wills must occur, so what a man wills must occur — in the case, that is, of the things which God so subordinates to the human will that if it wills them they occur and if it does not will them they do not occur. For since what God wills is not able not to occur: when He wills for no necessity either to compel the human will to will or to prevent it from willing, and when He wills that the effect follow from the act of human willing, it is necessary that the human will be free and that there occur what it wills. In this respect, then, it is true that the sinful deed which a man wills to do occurs by necessity, even though the man does not will it by necessity. Now, with respect to the human will's sin when it wills to sin: if someone asks whether this sin occurs by necessity, then he must be told that just as the will does not will by necessity, so the will's sin does not occur by necessity. Nor does the human will act by necessity; for if it did not will freely, it would not act — even though what it wills must come to pass, as I have just said. For since, in the present case, to sin is nothing other than to will what ought not [to be willed]: just as willing is not necessary, so sinful willing is not necessary. Nevertheless, it is true that if a man wills to sin, it is

De Concordia I

necessary that he sin — in terms, that is, of that necessity which (as I have said)[7] neither compels nor prevents anything.

Thus, on the one hand, free will is able to keep from willing what it wills; and, on the other hand, it is not able to keep from willing what it wills — rather, it is necessary for free will to will what it wills. For, indeed, before it wills, it is able to keep from willing, because it is free. And while it wills, it is not able not to will; rather, it is necessary that it will, since it is impossible for it to will and not to will the same thing at the same time. Now, it is the will's prerogative that what it wills occurs and that what it does not will does not occur. And the will's deeds are voluntary and free because they are done by a free will. But these deeds are necessary in two respects: (1) because the will compels them to be done, and (2) because what is being done cannot at the same time not be done. But these two necessities are produced by freedom-of-will; and the free will is able to avoid them before they occur. Now, God (who knows all truth and only truth) sees all these things as they are — whether they be free or necessary; and as He sees them, so they are. In this way, then, and without any inconsistency, it is evident both that God foreknows all things and that many things are done by free will. And before these things occur it is possible that they never occur. Nevertheless, in a certain sense they occur necessarily; and this necessity (as I said)[8] derives from free will.

4

Moreover, that not everything foreknown by God occurs of necessity but that some events occur as the result of freedom-of-will can be recognized from the following consideration. When God wills or causes something, He cannot be denied to know what He wills and causes, and to foreknow what He shall will and shall cause. ([It makes no difference here] whether we speak in accordance with eternity's immutable present, in which there is nothing past or future, but in which all things exist at once without any change (e.g., if we say only that He wills and causes something, and deny that He has willed or has caused and shall will or shall cause something), or whether we speak in accordance with temporality (as when we state that He shall will or shall cause that which we know has not yet occurred).) Therefore, if

God's knowledge or foreknowledge imposes necessity on everything He knows or foreknows, then He does not freely will or cause anything (either in accordance with eternity or in accordance with a temporal mode); rather, He wills and causes everything by necessity. Now, if this conclusion is absurd even to suppose, then it is not the case that everything known or foreknown to be or not to be occurs or fails to occur by necessity. Therefore, nothing prevents God's knowing or foreknowing that in our wills and actions something occurs or will occur by free choice. Thus, although it is necessary that what He knows or foreknows, occur, nevertheless many events occur not by necessity but by free will — as I have shown above.[9]

Indeed, why is it strange if in this way something occurs both freely and necessarily? For there are many things which admit of opposite characteristics in different respects.[10] Indeed, what is more opposed than coming and going? Nevertheless, when someone moves from one place to another, we see that his movement is both a coming and a going. For he goes away from one place and comes toward another. Likewise, if we consider the sun at some point in the heavens, as it is hastening toward this same point while always illuminating the heavens: we see that the point to which it is coming is the same point from which it is going away; and it is constantly and simultaneously approaching the point from which it is departing. Moreover, to those who know the sun's course, it is evident that in relation to the heavens, the sun always moves from the western sector to the eastern sector; but in relation to the earth, it always moves only from east to west. Thus, the sun always moves both counter to the firmament and — although more slowly [than the firmament] — with the firmament.[11] This same phenomenon is witnessed in the case of all the planets. So then, no inconsistency arises if (in accordance with the considerations just presented) we assert of one and the same event (1) that, necessarily, it is going to occur (simply because it *is* going to occur) and (2) that it is not compelled to be going to occur by any necessity — except for the necessity which (as I said above)[12] derives from free will.

5

Now, Job says to God with reference to man: "You have established his end, which cannot be escaped."[13] On the basis of this verse someone might want to prove — in spite of the fact that sometimes someone does seem to us to cause his own death by his own free will — that no one has been able to hasten or delay the day of his death. But his objection would not tell against that which I have argued above. For since God is not deceived and sees only the truth — whether it issues from freedom or from necessity — He is said to have established immutably with respect to Himself something which, with respect to man, can be altered before it is done. This is also what the Apostle Paul says about those who, in accordance with [God's] purpose, are called to be saints: "Whom He foreknew He predestined to become conformed to the image of His Son, so that His Son would be the firstborn among many brethren. And whom He predestined, these He also called. And whom He called, these He also justified. And whom He justified, these He also glorified."[14] Indeed, within eternity (in which there is no past or future but is only a present) this purpose, in accordance with which they have been called to be saints, is immutable. But in these men this purpose is at some time mutable because of freedom of choice. For within eternity a thing has no past or future but only a present; and yet, without inconsistency, in the dimension of time this thing was and will be. Similarly, that which within eternity is not able to be changed is proved to be, without inconsistency, changeable by free will at some point in time before it occurs. However, although within eternity there is only a present, nonetheless it is not the temporal present, as is ours, but is an eternal present in which the whole of time is contained. For, indeed, just as present time encompasses every place and whatever is in any place, so in the eternal present the whole of time is encompassed at once, as well as whatever occurs at any time.[15] Therefore, when the apostle says that God foreknew, predestined, called, justified, and glorified His saints, none of these actions is earlier or later for God; rather everything must be understood to exist at once in an eternal present. For eternity has its own "simultaneity" wherein exist all things that occur at the same time and place and that occur at different times and places.

But in order to show that he was not using these verbs in their temporal sense, the same apostle spoke in the past tense of even those events which are future. For, temporally speaking, God had not already called, justified, and glorified those who He foreknew were still to be born. Thus, we can recognize that for lack of a verb [properly] signifying the eternal present, the apostle used verbs of past tense; for things which are temporally past are altogether immutable, after the fashion of the eternal present. Indeed, in this respect, things which are temporally past resemble the eternal present more than do things which are temporally present. For eternally present things are never able not to be present, just as temporally past things are never able not to be past. But all temporally present things which pass away do become not-present.

In this manner, then, whenever Sacred Scripture speaks as if things done by free choice were necessary, it speaks in accordance with eternity,[16] in which is present immutably all truth and only truth. Scripture is not speaking in accordance with the temporal order, wherein our volitions and actions do not exist forever. Moreover, just as when our volitions and actions do not exist, it is not necessary that they exist, so it is often not necessary that they ever exist. For example, it is not the case that I am always writing or that I always will to write. And just as when I am not writing or do not will to write, it is not necessary that I write or will to write, so it is not at all necessary that I ever write or will to write.

A thing is known to exist in time so differently from the way it exists in eternity that at some point the following statements are true: (1) in time something is not present which is present in eternity; (2) in time something is past which is not past in eternity; (3) in time something is future which is not future in eternity. Similarly, then, it is seen to be impossible to be denied, in any respect, that in the temporal order something is mutable which is immutable in eternity. Indeed, being mutable in time and being immutable in eternity are no more opposed than are not existing at some time and always existing in eternity — or than are existing in the past or future according to the temporal order and not existing in the past or future in eternity.

For, indeed, the point I am making is not that something which always exists in eternity never exists in time, but is only that there is some time or other at which it does not exist. For example, I am not saying that my action of tomorrow at no time exists; I am merely denying that it exists today, even though it always exists in eternity. And when we deny that something which is past or

De Concordia I

future in the temporal order is past or future in eternity, we do not maintain that that which is past or future does not in any way exist in eternity; instead, we are simply saying that what exists there unceasingly in its eternal-present mode does not exist there in the past or future mode. In these cases no contradiction is seen to raise an obstruction. Thus, without doubt and without any contradiction, a thing is said to be mutable in time, prior to its occurrence, although it exists immutably in eternity. [In eternity] there is no time before it exists or after it exists; instead, it exists unceasingly, because in eternity nothing exists temporally. For there exists there, eternally, the fact that temporally something both exists and — before it exists — is able not to exist (as I have said).[17] It seems to me to be sufficiently clear from what has been said that free choice and God's foreknowledge are not at all inconsistent with each other. Their consistency results from the nature of eternity, which encompasses the whole of time and whatever occurs at any time.

6

But since we do not in all respects have free choice, we must consider where and what that *freedom* of choice is which we believe a man always to have, and what that choice itself is. For choice and the freedom in terms of which the choice is called free are not identical. We speak of freedom and of choice in many cases — as, for example, when we say that someone has the freedom to speak or not to speak and that whichever of these he wills lies within his choice. Likewise, in many other instances we speak of a freedom and of a choice which are not always present or else are not necessary to us for the salvation of our souls. However, the present investigation is being conducted only with respect to that choice and that freedom without which a man, after once being able to use them, cannot be saved. For many people lament because they believe that free choice is of no avail for salvation or condemnation, but that as a result of God's foreknowledge only necessity [determines salvation or condemntion]. Therefore, since after a human being has reached the age of understanding,[18] he is not saved apart from being just: the choice and the freedom which are under discussion must be dealt with in terms of where the seat of justice is. Accordingly, first justice must be exhibited, and next this freedom and this choice.

Indeed, any justice whatever (whether great or small) is uprightness-of-will kept for its own sake. And the freedom [which is under discussion] is the ability to keep uprightness-of-will for its own sake. I regard myself as already having set forth these definitions with clear reasoning — the first one in the treatise which I wrote *On Truth*,[19] and the second in the treatise which I composed *On* this very *Freedom*.[20] In the latter, I also showed how this freedom is present in a man inseparably and naturally, even though he does not always use it. Moreover, [I showed] that it is so powerful that as long as a man wills to use it nothing is able to remove from him the aforementioned uprightness (i.e., justice) which he has. By contrast, justice is not a natural possession; in the beginning it was separable from the angels in Heaven and from men in Paradise. And even now in this life [it is separable], not by necessity but by the autonomous[21] willing of those who possess it. Now, since it is evident that the justice by which someone is just is uprightness-of-will, which (as I have said) is present in someone only when he wills what God wills for him to will: it is evident that God is not able to remove this uprightness from him against his will; for God cannot will this removal.[22] Moreover, neither can God will for one who possesses uprightness to desert it unwillingly as the result of some compelling force. (Indeed, [were that the case] God would will for him not to will that which He wills for him to will — which is impossible). Therefore, it follows that in this manner God wills that an upright will be free for willing rightly and for keeping this uprightness. And when the upright will is able [to do] what it wills, it does freely what it does. Hence, we can also recognize very clearly that both a will and its action are free — without its being the case that God's foreknowledge is incompatible therewith, as was demonstrated above.[23]

Let us now posit an example in which there appears an upright (i.e., a just) will, freedom of choice, and an actual choice. And [let us consider] both how the upright will is attacked so that it deserts uprightness, and how the upright will keeps uprightness by means of free choice. [Let us suppose that] someone desires to cling to the truth because he discerns that it is right to love the truth. Surely, he already has an upright will and uprightness-of-will. But the will is distinguishable from the uprightness by which it is upright. Now, [suppose that] another man approaches and threatens the first man with death unless he tells a lie.[24] We see that it is now within this man's choice whether to relinquish his life for the sake of uprightness-of-will or to relinquish uprightness for the sake of his life. This choice — which can be called a judgment — is free; for reason, by means of which uprightness is understood, teaches that this uprightness ought always to be cherished for its own sake, and that whatever is extended in order [to induce] the forsaking of uprightness ought to be despised. Moreover, it is the prerogative of the will to reject and to elect in accordance with what rational discernment teaches. For to this end, especially, will and reason have been given to rational creatures. Therefore, the will's choice to desert uprightness is not compelled by any necessity, even though the man is beset by the obstacle of death. For although it is necessary either to relinquish his life or his uprightness, no necessity determines which one of these he keeps or relinquishes. Assuredly, the will alone here determines what he keeps; and where only the will's choosing is operative, there the force of necessity accomplishes nothing. Now, someone who is not under the necessity of deserting the uprightness-of-will which he possesses is obviously not lacking in the ability, or freedom, to keep uprightness. For this ability is always free. For this is the freedom which I have defined as the ability to keep uprightness-of-will for its own sake. In terms of this freedom both the choice and the will of a rational nature are called free.

7

Since God is believed to foreknow or know all things, we are now left to consider whether His knowledge derives from things or whether things derive their existence from His knowledge. For if God derives His knowledge from things, it follows that they exist prior to His knowledge and hence do not derive their existence from Him; for they can only exist from Him in accordance with His knowledge. On the other hand, if all existing things derive their existence from God's knowledge, God is the creator and the author of evil works and hence is unjust in punishing evil creatures — a view we do not accept.

Now, this issue can easily be resolved provided we first recognize that the good which is identical with justice is really something, whereas the evil which is identical with injustice lacks all being. (I have presented this solution very clearly in the treatise on *The Fall of the Devil*[25] and in the short work which I entitled *The Virgin Conception and Original Sin*.)[26] For injustice is neither a quality nor an action nor a being but is only the absence of required justice and is present only in the will, where justice ought to be. And every rational nature as well as any of its actions is called just or unjust in accordance with a just or an unjust will. Indeed, every quality and every action and whatever has any being comes from God, from whom all justice and no injustice is derived. Therefore, God causes all the things which are done by a just or an unjust will, viz., all good and evil deeds. Indeed, in the case of good deeds He causes what they are [essentially] and the fact that they are good; but in the case of evil deeds He causes what they are [essentially] but not the fact that they are evil. Now, for anything to be just or good is for it to be something; but it is not the case that for a thing to be unjust or evil is for it to be something. For, indeed, to be good or just is to have justice, and having this is something; but to be evil or unjust is to lack the justice which one ought to have, and it is not the case that this lack is something. For justice is something, but injustice is nothing, as I have said.

But there is another kind of good, which is called benefit; and its opposite is the evil which is detriment. In some cases (e.g., blindness) this evil is nothing; in other cases (e.g., pain) it is something.[27] When this evil is something, we do not deny that God causes it, because (as is read) He is the one who "causes peace and creates evil."[28] For He creates detriments by means of which He tries and purifies the just as well as punishing the unjust. Therefore, with regard only to that evil which is identical with injustice and by virtue of which a man is called unjust: assuredly, this evil is never something. And it is not the case that for a thing to be unjust is for it to be something. And even as God does not cause injustice, so He does not cause something to be unjust. Nevertheless, He does cause all actions and movements, because He causes the things by which, from which, through which, and in which they are produced; and, unless God grants it, nothing has any power to will or to do anything. Moreover, the act of willing — which is sometimes just, sometimes unjust, and which is nothing other than using the will and the power-to-will which God bestows — is, with respect to the fact that it is,[29] something good and is derivative from God. Indeed, when willing exists rightly, it is something good and just; but when it does not exist rightly, then solely in virtue of the fact that it does not exist rightly, it is evil and unjust. However, existing rightly is something, and it is from God; but not existing rightly is not something and is not from God. Now, when someone uses his sword or his tongue or his ability-to-speak, the sword or the tongue or the ability-to-speak is not one thing when its use is correct and something different when its use is incorrect. Similarly, the will, which we use for willing (even as we use reason for reasoning), is not one thing when someone uses it rightly and something different when he uses it wrongly. Now, the will is that in virtue of which a substance or an action is called just or unjust; and when the will is just, it is not any more or any less that which it is essentially than when it is unjust. Thus, then, in the case of all good wills and deeds God causes both what they are essentially and the fact that they are good; but in the case of all evil wills and deeds, He does not cause the fact that they are evil but causes only what they are essentially.[30] For even as the being of things comes only from God, so their rightness comes only from Him.

Now, the absence of this uprightness about which I am speaking — an absence which is identical with injustice — is found only in the will of a rational creature, who ought always to have justice. But why does a creature not have the justice which he always ought to have, and how is it that God causes good things only by means of His goodness and causes evil things only through the fault of man and the Devil? And how does a man, under the guidance of grace, do good works by free choice and do evil by the working only of an autonomous will?[31] And what part does God have, blamelessly, in evil works, and does man have, laudably, in good works, so that nevertheless the good deeds of man are clearly seen to be imputed to God and the evil works to man? By the gift of God [the answers] will become more evident, it seems to me, when we shall take up [the topic of] grace and free choice. But for now I will say only that an evil angel does not have justice because he abandoned it and did not subsequently receive it again. On the other hand, man is deprived of justice because in his first parents he cast it away and subsequently either did not receive it again or else, having received it again, rejected it anew.

I think that by the assistance of God's grace I have shown — provided the points I have made are weighed carefully — that the coexistence of free choice and God's foreknowledge is not impossible, and that there can be no objection which is not answerable.

Second Controversy: Predestination and Free Choice

I

Therefore, trusting in God, who has led us thus far, let us now undertake to resolve the conflict which seems to exist between predestination and free choice. By means of our preceding discussion we have already made no little progress toward this goal — as will become apparent in what follows.

Predestination is seen to be the same thing as foreordination or predetermination. And so, that which God is said to predestine, He is recognized to foreordain — i.e., to determine to be going to occur. But what God determines to be going to occur must, it seems, be going to occur. Therefore, it is necessary that whatever God predestines is going to occur. Hence, if God predestines the good and the evil actions which are done, nothing is done by free choice but everything occurs of necessity. On the other hand, if He predestines only good actions, only good actions occur of necessity, and there is free choice only with respect to evil actions — a consequence which is utterly absurd. Therefore, it is not the case that God predestines only good actions. But if free choice does any good works through which men are justified apart from predestination, then God does not predestine all the good works which justify men. Accordingly, He did not [predestine] those men who are justified by virtue of the works of free choice. Therefore, it would not be the case that God foreknew these men, since "whom He foreknew, these He also predestined."[32] But it is false that there are some good works or just men that God does not foreknow. Therefore, it is not the case that some good works of free choice alone are justificatory; instead, only those good works which God predestines are justificatory. Hence, if God predestines all things, and if things predestined occur of necessity: since nothing done by free choice is done by necessity, it seems to follow that as long as there is predestination there is no free choice, or — if we establish that in some cases there is free choice — that in these cases there is no predestination.

2

At the outset, then, and before settling the main issue, we must notice that predestination can be said [to apply] not only to good men but also to evil men — even as God is said to cause (because He permits)[33] evils which He does not cause. For He is said to harden a man when He does not soften him, and to lead him into temptation when He does not deliver him.[34] Hence, it is not inappropriate if in this manner we say that God predestines evil men and their evil works when He does not correct them and their evil works. But He is more properly said to foreknow and to predestine good works, because in them He causes both what they are [essentially] and the fact that they are good. But in evil deeds He causes only what they are essentially; He does not cause the fact that they are evil — as I have already said above.[35] We must also realize that just as *fore*knowledge is not properly said to be found in God, so *pre*destination is not either. For nothing is present to God either earlier or later, but all things are present to Him at once.

3

Let us now consider whether some things which are going to occur as a result of free choice can be predestined. Surely, we ought not to doubt that God's foreknowledge and predestination do not conflict. Instead, just as He foreknows, so also He predestines. In the discussion about foreknowledge we saw[36] clearly that, without any inconsistency, some actions which are going to occur as a result of free choice, are foreknown. Therefore, reason and plain truth also teach that, without any inconsistency, some actions which are going to occur by means of free choice, are likewise predestined. For God neither foreknows nor predestines that anyone will be *just* by necessity. For he who does not keep justice by means of his free will is not just. Therefore, although things foreknown and predestined must occur, it is nonetheless equally true that some things foreknown and predestined occur not by the necessity which precedes a thing and causes it, but by the necessity which succeeds a thing — as I have said above.[37] For although God predestines these things, He causes them not by constraining or restraining the will but by leaving the will to its own power. But although the will uses its own power, it does nothing which God does not cause — in good works by His grace, in evil works not through any fault of His but through the will's fault. (As I promised,[38] this shall become clearer when I shall speak about grace.) And just as foreknowledge, which is not mistaken, foreknows only the real thing as it will occur — either necessarily or freely — so predestination, which is not altered, predestines only as the thing exists in foreknowledge. And although what is foreknown is immutable in eternity, it can nevertheless be changed in the temporal order at some point before it occurs. Similarly, the case is in every respect the same for predestination.

Therefore, if these statements which have been made are examined closely, it is evident from them that predestination does not exclude free choice and that free choice is not opposed to predestination. For, indeed, all the considerations by which I have shown above that free choice is not incompatible with foreknowledge show equally that it is compatible with predestination. Therefore, whenever something happens by the agency of free will (e.g., when one man wrongs another man and as a result is killed by this other), it is unreasonable for certain people to give vent loudly to the words: "Thus it was foreknown and predestined by God; and hence it was done by necessity and could not have been done otherwise." Indeed, neither the man who provoked the other by a wrong nor the other who avenged himself did this by necessity. Rather, [each acted] voluntarily, because if each had not freely willed to, neither one would have done what he did.

Third Controversy: Grace and Free Choice

I

It remains now for us to consider grace and free choice — doing so with the assistance of this grace. This controversy arises from

De Concordia III

the fact that Divine Scripture sometimes speaks in such a way that only grace — and not at all free choice — seems to avail to salvation. On the other hand, it sometimes speaks as if our entire salvation were dependent upon our free will. For, indeed, the Lord says concerning grace: "Without me you can do nothing,"[39] and "No one comes to me unless my father draws him."[40] And the Apostle Paul [asks]: "What do you have that you have not received?"[41] And concerning God [he says]: "He has mercy on whom He wills to, and He hardens whom He wills to."[42] [He says] also: "It is not of him who wills nor of him who runs but of God, who shows mercy."[43] We also read many other texts which seem to ascribe our good works and our salvation to grace alone apart from free choice. Furthermore, there are many people who profess to prove by experience that a man is never at all supported by any free choice. For they feel that countless individuals put forth an enormous effort of mind and body. But because these individuals are burdened by some obstacle — indeed, by some impossibility — they either make no headway, or else after having made much headway they suddenly and irretrievably fail.

But in the following manner Scripture teaches that we do have free choice. God declares through Isaiah: "If you are willing and shall hearken unto me, you shall eat the good things of the land."[44] And David [says]: "Who is the man who wants life, who loves to behold good days? Keep your tongue from evil; and let not your lips speak guile. Turn away from evil and do good."[45] And the Lord [says] in the Gospel: "Come unto me all of you who are laboring and are heavily laden, and I will give you rest. Take my yoke upon you and learn from me, for I am meek and lowly in heart, and you shall find rest for your souls."[46] Moreover, there are countless other passages which are seen (1) to urge free choice to do good and (2) to reprove it because it spurns their admonitions. Divine Authority would never do this if it knew that there were no freedom-of-will in man. And if no one were to do good or evil by free choice, there would not be any way for God justly to reward good men and evil men according to their respective merits.

Therefore, since we find in Sacred Scripture certain passages which seem to favor grace alone and certain passages which are believed to establish free choice alone, apart from grace: there have been certain arrogant individuals who have thought that the whole efficacy of the virtues depends only upon freedom of choice; and in our day there are many who have completely given up on the idea that there is any freedom of choice. Therefore, in regard to this dispute, my intention will be to show that free choice coexists with grace and cooperates with it in many respects — just as we found it to be compatible with foreknowledge and with predestination.

2

We must recognize that just as this controversy (as I have said above)[47] concerns no other free choice than that without which no one (after he has reached the age of understanding) merits salvation, so it concerns no other grace than that without which no man is saved. For every creature exists by grace, because by grace he was created; moreover, by grace God gives in this life many goods without which a human being can still be saved. Indeed, in the case of infants who die, baptized, before they are able to use their free choice, the harmony which we are seeking does not appear. For in their case grace alone accomplishes salvation apart from their free choice. For the following fact occurs by grace: viz., that to others is given the will to assist, by their faith, these infants. Therefore, the solution we are seeking must be exhibited with regard to those who have reached the age of understanding,[48] because the controversy concerns them alone.

There is no doubt that whoever of these are saved are saved because of justice. For eternal life is promised to the just, because "the just shall live forever, and their reward is with the Lord."[49] Now, Sacred Authority often teaches that justice is uprightness-of-will. It suffices to cite one example of this fact. David said: "The Lord will not cast off His people nor forsake His inheritance until justice is turned into judgment."[50] And after he had said this, then in order to teach us what justice is, he asked: "And who is conformed to justice?" To this he replies, answering himself: "All who are upright in heart" — i.e., all who are upright in will. For although we both believe and understand in our heart,[51] even as we will in our heart, nevertheless the Holy Spirit does not deem to have an upright heart a man who believes

De Concordia III

rightly or understands rightly but does not will rightly. For this man does not use the uprightness of faith and of understanding for rightly willing; and rightly believing and rightly understanding are given to a rational creature for the sake of rightly willing. For he who does not rightly will in accordance with right understanding ought not to be said to have right understanding. And he who does not rightly will to act in accordance with faith — for this is the reason for which faith is given — is not said to have any faith except a dead faith.[52] Therefore, we correctly understand David to have meant by "the upright in heart" the upright in will. But lest someone think that Divine Authority calls just or upright a man who keeps uprightness-of-will only for the sake of something else, we say that justice is uprightness-of-will kept for its own sake.[53] For he who keeps uprightness only for the sake of something else does not cherish uprightness but cherishes that thing for whose sake he keeps uprightness. And so he must not be called just, and such uprightness must not be called justice.

When I dealt with foreknowledge and free choice, I showed by an example[54] that uprightness-of-will, which I am calling justice, can coexist with free choice. (By means of this one example it is easy to discern that the same thing holds true in many other instances.) Therefore, if we can show that no creature can obtain uprightness-of-will except by means of grace, the harmony between grace and free choice will be manifest. This is the harmony which we are seeking and whose purpose is man's salvation.

3

Assuredly, there is no doubt that the will wills rightly only because it is upright. For just as sight is not acute because it sees acutely but sees acutely because it is acute, so the will is not upright because it wills rightly but wills rightly because it is upright. Now, when it wills uprightness-of-will, then without doubt it wills rightly. Therefore, it wills uprightness only because it is upright. But for the will to be upright is the same as for it to have uprightness. Therefore, it is evident that it wills uprightness only because it has uprightness. I do not deny that an upright will wills an uprightness which it does not have when it wills more uprightness than it already has. But I maintain that the will is not able to will any uprightness unless it has the uprightness by which to will uprightness.

Let us now consider whether someone who does not have uprightness-of-will can in some way have it from himself. Surely, he could have it from himself only by willing it or without willing it. But, indeed, it is not the case that by willing it someone is able to obtain it by his own efforts, because he is able to will it only if he has it. On the other hand, no one's mind accepts the view that someone who does not have uprightness-of-will can acquire it by himself without willing it. Therefore, a creature can in no way have uprightness from himself. But neither can one creature have it from another creature. For just as one creature cannot save another creature, so one creature cannot give to another creature the necessary means for salvation. Thus, it follows that only by the grace of God does a creature have the uprightness which I have called uprightness-of-will. Now, I have shown that uprightness-of-will can be kept by free choice (as I stated above).[55] Therefore, by the gift of God we have found that His grace harmonizes with free choice in order to save human beings. Thus, as happens in the case of infants, grace alone can save a human being when his free choice can do nothing; and in the case of those with understanding, grace always assists the natural free choice (which apart from grace is of no avail to salvation) by giving to the will the uprightness which it can keep by free choice.

Now, God does not give to everyone; for "He shows mercy to whom He wills to, and He hardens whom He wills to."[56] Nevertheless, He does not give to anyone on the basis of any antecedent merit; for "who has first given to God and it shall be recompensed to him?"[57] But if by free choice the will keeps what it has received and thereby merits either an increment of received justice, or, as well, the power for a good will, or some kind of reward: all of these are the fruits of the first grace, and are "grace for grace."[58] And so, everything must be imputed to grace because "it is not of him who wills" that he wills, "nor of him who runs" that he runs, but, instead, "is of God, who shows mercy."[59] For to all except God alone it is said: "What do you have that you have not received? And if you have received it, why do you glory as if you had not received it?"[60]

4

I deem myself to have shown[61] in my treatise on *Freedom of Choice* how a free will which is keeping its received uprightness is not beset by any necessity to abandon it but is beset by difficulty and yields to this difficulty willingly rather than unwillingly. Since grace assists in many ways, I cannot list all the ways in which grace aids free choice (after free choice has received this uprightness) to keep what it has received. Nonetheless, it will not be useless to say something about this matter. Assuredly, no one keeps this received uprightness except by willing it. But no one can will it unless he possesses it. And he cannot at all possess it except by means of grace. Therefore, just as no one receives uprightness except by means of grace preceding, so no one keeps uprightness except by means of this same grace following. Assuredly, even though uprightness is kept by free choice, still its being kept must be imputed not so much to free choice as to grace; for free choice possesses and keeps uprightness only by means of prevenient and of subsequent grace.

However, grace so follows its own gift that the only time grace ever fails to bestow this gift — whether it is something large or something small — is when free choice by willing something else forsakes the uprightness it has received. For this uprightness is never separated from the will except when the will wills something else which is incompatible with this uprightness — as when someone receives the uprightness of willing sobriety and rejects it by willing the immoderate pleasure of drinking. When a man does this, it is by his own will; and so, through his own fault he loses the grace which he received. For when free choice is under attack to abandon the uprightness it has received, grace even assists free choice — either by mitigating the assailing temptation's appeal, or by completely eliminating its appeal, or by increasing free choice's affection for uprightness. In fact, since everything is subject to the ordinance of God, all of what happens to a man which assists free choice to receive or to keep this uprightness of which I am speaking must be imputed to grace.

I have said[62] that all justice is uprightness-of-will kept for its own sake. Hence, it follows that everyone who has uprightness-of-will has justice and is just (since everyone who has justice is just). But it seems to me that eternal life is promised not to all who are just, but only to those who are just without any injustice. For these are properly and unqualifiedly called just in heart and upright in heart. For [there is a case where] someone is just in some respect and unjust in another respect (for example, a man who is both chaste and envious). The happiness of the just is not promised to such individuals, since even as true happiness exists without any deficiency, so it is given only to him who is just without being at all unjust.[63] The happiness which is promised to the just shall be like unto that of God's angels. Therefore, even as in the good angels there is no injustice, so no one with any injustice will be admitted into their company. But it is not my purpose to show how a man becomes free of all injustice. Nevertheless, we do know that for a Christian this state is attainable by means of holy endeavors and the grace of God.

5

If the points which have been made are considered carefully, one recognizes clearly that when Sacred Scripture says something in favor of grace it does not completely do away with free choice; and when it speaks in favor of free choice, it does not exclude grace. The case is not as if grace alone or free choice alone sufficed to save a man (as it seems to those who are the cause of the present controversy). Indeed, the divine sayings ought to be construed in such way that, with the exception of what I said about infants,[64] neither grace alone nor free choice alone accomplishes man's salvation.

Indeed, when the Lord says: "Without me you can do nothing,"[65] what He means is not "Your free choice is of no avail to you," but "It is of no avail without my grace." And when we read "It is not of him who wills nor of him who runs, but of God, who shows mercy,"[66] Scripture is not denying that free choice is of some use in the case of one who wills or runs; rather, it is indicating that the fact that he wills and the fact that he runs have to be credited to grace rather than to free choice. For when Scripture says "It is not of him who wills nor of him who runs," we must supply: "The fact that he wills and the fact that he runs." The case is like someone's giving clothes to a naked person to whom he owes nothing and who by himself is unable to obtain a garment. Although the naked person has the ability to use and not to use the clothing he has received, still if he does use it, the fact that he is clothed must be credited not to him but to the one who gave him clothes. Therefore, we can speak as follows: "The fact that he is clothed is not of the one who is clothed but is of the one who shows mercy — i.e., of the one who gives the clothing." Much more would this be said if the one who gave the clothing had also given the ability to keep it and to use it — as when God gives to a man the oft-mentioned uprightness, He also gives the ability to keep and to use it, because He first gave the free choice for keeping and using uprightness. Now, if clothing were not given to this naked person to whom nothing is owed, or if this person were to throw it away after having received it, his state of nakedness would be credited to no one but himself. Similarly, when God gives willing and running to someone conceived and born in sin,[67] to whom He owes nothing except punishment, "it is not of him who wills nor of him who runs but is of God, who shows mercy." And as for one who does not receive this grace, or one who rejects it after having received it: the fact that he remains in his obduracy and iniquity is due to him rather than to God.

The same interpretation — viz., that free choice is not ruled out — must be held to in the other passages in which Scripture speaks in favor of grace.

Likewise, when the divine sayings are expressed in such way that they seem to attribute man's salvation to free choice alone, grace ought in no respect to be excluded. Therefore, grace and free choice are not incompatible but cooperate in order to justify and to save a man — even as, although natural functioning procreates an offspring only by means of a mother and not without a father, nevertheless no accurate account excludes either a father or a mother from an offspring's generation.

6

Yet, in regard to those passages in which Scripture is seen to invite free choice to right-willing and right-working, people wonder why it invites a man to will rightly and why it condemns him if he is disobedient, seeing that no one can have or receive uprightness unless grace bestows it. We must note [the following comparison]: Without any cultivation on man's part the earth produces countless herbs and trees by which human beings are not nourished or by which they are even killed. But those herbs and trees which are especially necessary to us for nourishing our lives are not produced by the earth apart from seeds and great labor and a farmer. Similarly, without learning and endeavor human hearts freely germinate, so to speak, thoughts and volitions which are not conducive to salvation or which are even harmful thereto. But without their own kind of seed and without laborious cultivation human hearts do not at all conceive and germinate those thoughts and volitions without which we do not make progress toward our soul's salvation. Hence, those men upon whom such caretaking is bestowed the apostle calls "God's husbandry."[68] Now, the word of God constitutes the seed of this husbandry — or, better, not the word but the meaning which is discerned by means of the word. (For, indeed, without meaning, a word forms[69] nothing in the mind.)[70] And not only does the meaning of the word [of God] constitute a seed of willing rightly but so also does the entire meaning or signification of "uprightness" — which signification the human mind conceives either as a result of hearing or of reading or of reasoning or in whatever other way. For no one is able to will what he does not first conceive in his mind.[71] Now, to will to believe what ought to be believed is to will rightly. Therefore, no one can will this if he does not know what ought to be believed. For after the apostle had first stated "Whoever shall call upon the name of the Lord shall be saved," he added: "How, then, shall they call upon Him in whom they have not believed? Or how shall they believe Him whom they shall not hear? And how shall they hear without a preacher? And how shall they preach unless they are sent?"[72] And a little later [he said]: "Therefore, faith [comes] by hearing; and hearing [comes] by the word of Christ."

Now, the apostle's statement that faith is derived from hearing must be interpreted to mean that faith is derived from that which the mind conceives as a result of hearing — derived not in such way that the mere mental concept produces faith in a man, but in such way that the concept is a necessary condition of faith. For, indeed, when uprightness-of-willing is added to the concept, faith

De Concordia III

is produced by grace, because the man believes what he hears. "And hearing comes by the word of Christ" — i.e., by the word of those who preach Christ. But there are no preachers unless they are sent. But the fact that they are sent is a grace. Therefore, preaching is a grace, because what derives from grace is a grace; and hearing is a grace, and the understanding which comes from hearing is a grace, and uprightness-of-willing is a grace. But sending, preaching, hearing, and understanding are worthless unless the will wills what the mind understands. But the will can do this only if it has received uprightness. For, indeed, it wills rightly when it wills what it ought. Thus, what the mind conceives as a result of hearing the word constitutes the seed of the preacher; and uprightness constitutes the growth which God gives — without which growth "neither he who plants nor he who waters is anything, but only God, who gives the growth." [73]

Therefore, just as in the beginning God miraculously — without seeds and without a cultivator — created wheat and other things which grow from the earth for the nourishment of men, so He miraculously — without human teaching — made the Gospels and the hearts of the prophets and apostles to be rich in salutary seeds. From these seeds we receive whatever we beneficially sow, in God's husbandry, for the nourishment of our souls — just as that which we cultivate for the nourishment of our bodies comes to us only from the first seeds of the earth. For, indeed, in our preaching, nothing which Sacred Scripture — made fruitful by the miracle of the Holy Spirit — has not set forth or does not contain is conducive to spiritual salvation. Now, if on the basis of rational considerations we sometimes make a statement which we cannot clearly exhibit in the words of Scripture, or cannot prove by reference to these words, nonetheless in the following way we know by means of Scripture whether the statement ought to be accepted or rejected. If the statement is arrived at by clear reasoning and if Scripture in no respect contradicts it, then (since even as Scripture opposes no truth, so it favors no falsity) by the very fact that Scripture does not deny that which is affirmed on the basis of rational considerations, this affirmation is supported by the authority of Scripture. But if Scripture unquestionably opposes a view of ours, then even though our reasoning seems to us unassailable, this reasoning should not be believed to be supported by any truth. So, then, Sacred Scripture — in that it either clearly affirms them or else does not at all deny them — contains the authority for all rationally derived truths.[74]

Let us now see in terms of examples how the word is the seed. When those to whom it is addressed hear the phrase "If you are willing and will hearken unto me . . ." they understand and conceive of what is called willing and obedience, or hearing. (For he who hears and does not obey is said not to hear.) Now, they cannot obey unless they will to. But to will to obey is to will rightly. And no one can will rightly unless he has uprightness-of-will, which a man has only by grace. But uprightness-of-willing something is given to no one except to one who understands willing and what he ought to will. Thus, we see (1) that unless uprightness is added, the words "If you are willing and will hearken unto me . . ." are not at all a seed which bears fruit by itself, and (2) that uprightness-of-will is given only by means of seeds.

Likewise, when God says "Be converted to me,"[75] the seed is without germination as long as God does not turn a man's will to willing the conversion which this man thinks when he hears the words "Be converted"; but without this seed no one can will to be converted. Even to those who are already converted the command "Be converted" is addressed — either so that they become still further converted or so that they maintain the fact of their conversion. Now, those who say "Convert us, O God"[76] are already to some extent converted, because in willing to be converted they have an upright will. But because of the fact that they have already received conversion they are praying that their conversion be increased — even as those who were already believers requested: "Increase our faith."[77] It is as if both the former and the latter were saying: "Increase in us what You have given; complete what You have begun."

What I have shown with respect to these cases must be understood [to hold true] in similar cases as well.

So it is not the case that without seeds the earth naturally brings forth those plants which are especially necessary for the health of our bodies. And although God does not give growth to every seed, nevertheless our farmers do not cease to sow in the hope of some small harvest. Similarly, the soil of the human heart does not bring forth the fruit of faith and of justice without the appropriate seeds. And although God does not cause all seeds of this kind to grow, nevertheless He commands His husbandmen to sow His word earnestly and in hope. I have shown, it seems to me, how it is not superfluous to invite men to faith in Christ and to those things which this faith demands, even though they do not all accept this invitation.

7

I said [78] that we can also ask why those who do not accept the word of God are blamed, seeing that they cannot do this unless grace directs their wills. For the Lord says, with reference to the Holy Spirit: "He will accuse the world of sin because they do not believe in me." [79] Although it may be difficult to reply to this question, I ought not to keep to myself what I am able to answer with God's help. We must note that the inability which results from [someone's] guilt does not, as long as the guilt remains, excuse the one who has the inability.[80] Hence, in the case of infants,[81] in whom God demands from human nature the justice which it received in our first parents, together with its receiving the ability to keep justice in all its offspring: the inability to possess justice does not excuse human nature, since human nature fell into this inability blamably. For, indeed, the very fact that human nature does not possess that which it is unable by itself to reacquire [viz., justice] constitutes its inability to have [justice]. Human nature fell into this [condition of] inability because it freely abandoned that which it was able to keep. Therefore, since human nature abandoned justice by sinning, the inability which it brought upon itself by sinning is reckoned to it as sin. And in those who are not baptized, not only the inability to have justice but also the inability to understand it is likewise reckoned as sin, for this latter inability also results from sin.

We can also reasonably maintain the following point: the fact that human nature was corrupted and diminished in relation to the original dignity and strength and beauty of the human condition is reckoned to it as sin. For human nature thereby diminished, as much as it could, the honor and the praise of God. Indeed, the wisdom of an artisan is praised and proclaimed in accordance with the excellence of his work. Therefore, the more human nature diminished and marred in itself the precious work of God, from which God was supposed to receive glory, the more it dishonored God by its own fault.[82] And this dishonoring is reckoned to it as such a grave sin that it is blotted out only by the death of God.[83]

Indeed, Sacred Authority shows very [clearly] that the following are reckoned as sin: viz., the impulses or appetites to which (as are brute animals) we are subject as a consequence of Adam's sin. The apostle calls these appetites flesh and concupiscence.[84] And when he says[85] "What I hate, that I do" (i.e., "against my will I inordinately desire"), he evidences that against his will he experiences concupiscence. Indeed, the Lord says of merely the impulse to anger, unexpressed in deed or word: "He who is angry with his brother will be held accountable for it at the judgment."[86] When He says this, He shows clearly that this guilt is not light — a guilt from which such grave condemnation (viz., the condemnation to death) follows. It is as if He were to say: "He who does what a man ought not to do, and who would not have done it if he had not sinned, ought to be removed from among men." And Paul says regarding those who against their will experience the flesh, i.e., carnal desires: "There is no condemnation to those who are in Christ Jesus, who do not walk after the flesh" — i.e., who do not freely consent [to the flesh].[87] When he says this, without question he signifies that those who are not in Christ are followed by condemnation as often as they feel carnal desire, even if they do not walk in accordance with it. For man was made in such way that he ought not to feel carnal desire, just as I said regarding anger. Therefore, if anyone considers carefully what I have said, he does not at all doubt that those who cannot — by their own fault — receive the word of God are rightly to be blamed.

8

But as regards those to whom the grace of Christian faith is given: just as in baptism the original injustice with which they are born is forgiven them, so [in baptism] there is forgiven all guilt of inability and of all the corruption which they incurred because of the sin of our first parent — corruption through which God is dishonored. For after baptism they are not blamed for any of the guilt which was in them before baptism,[88] even though the corruption and the appetites which are the penalty for sin are not immediately blotted out in baptism. Moreover, after baptism no transgression is charged to them except that which they commit of their own volition. Hence, it appears that the corruption and the evils which were the penalty for sin and which remain after baptism are not in themselves sins. For, indeed, only injustice is in itself a sin; and until injustice is forgiven, these evil consequences which follow from injustice are, due to their cause, *deemed* to be sins. For if they were [properly] sins, they would be blotted out in baptism, in which all sins are washed away by the blood of Christ. Likewise, if they were properly called sins they would be sins in the case of brute animals, after whose likeness our nature undergoes these evil consequences as a result of sin.

There is something else which can be discerned in human nature's first sin and which must be greatly feared. Since man is a "wind which goes out and does not return":[89] after he freely falls — to speak now only of voluntary sins — he can in no way rise up again unless he is raised up by grace. And unless he is held back by mercy, he is plunged by his own doing from one sin into another, down into the bottomless abyss (i.e., the measureless depth) of sins, in such way that even the good becomes something hateful to him and is for him unto death. Hence, the Lord says to the apostles: "If the world hates you, know that it hated me before hating you."[90] And the apostle [says]: "We are a good odor to God — among some the odor of death unto death, but among others the odor of life unto life."[91] For this reason Scripture says concerning God: "He shows mercy to whom He wills to, and He hardens whom He wills to."[92] But He is not equally merciful to all to whom He is merciful; and He does not equally harden all whom He hardens.

9

Another question is why in this life the penalty for sin remains in us after the sin has been blotted out. Although I did not plan to deal with this question now, I will say briefly that if the faithful were immediately transformed at baptism or at martyrdom into the state of incorruption, then merit would perish and men would be saved without any merit (except for those first men who would believe without any precedent). Surely [in that case, then,] faith and hope — without which no man who has understanding[93] can merit the Kingdom of God — would vanish. (For faith and hope are directed toward those things which are unseen.) For since men would see those who would be converted to Christ pass over immediately into the state of incorruptibility,[94] there would be no one who would be able even to will to turn away from this very great happiness which he would behold. Therefore, in order that through the merit of faith and of hope we may more gloriously obtain the happiness we desire, we remain — for as long as we are in this life — in this state which is no longer reckoned unto us as sin, even though it has resulted because of sin.

In fact, it is not the case that through baptism and the Christian faith we are assured of the happiness which Adam had in Paradise before sinning. Rather, we are assured of the happiness which he was going to have when the number of men who were to be added to fill up the Heavenly City[95] would be complete. This city is to be filled with angels and men; but in it men will not procreate,[96] as they would have done in Paradise. Therefore, if converts to Christ were immediately to pass over into that state of incorruptibility, there would not remain men from whom this number could be gathered, because no one would be able to keep from rushing toward the happiness he would behold. I think that this is what the apostle means when he says regarding those who through faith have worked justice: "And all of these, approved by the witness of their faith, did not receive the promise, since God is providing something better for us, so that they are not made complete without us."[97] Now, if one asks what better thing God has provided for us from their not having received the promise, I do not see that anything can be replied more suitably than what I said above, viz., the following: If the happiness promised to the just were not delayed for those who have been approved, merit would perish in those who would learn of this fact by experience rather than by faith. Also the process of human procreation from which we are begotten would stop, since all men would run after that incorruptibility which they would see to be present. Therefore, God provided a great good for us when for the saints who have been approved by the witness of their faith He delayed the reception of the promise. [He caused this delay] in order that we would continue to be propagated and that faith would remain — by which faith we would together with them merit the promise and would be made perfect at the same time as they.

De Concordia III

There is also another reason why the baptized and the martyrs do not immediately become incorruptible. Suppose that a master severely scourges his servant, whom he had planned to enrich some day with great honors, for a wrong for which the servant is not at all able by himself to make satisfaction. And suppose that after this scourging the master is going to thrust his servant, at a fixed time, into a dreadful prison where he will be afflicted with grievous punishments. Suppose, further, that someone influential with his master makes satisfaction for him and reconciles him. Surely, the stripes which the guilty servant deservedly received prior to the satisfaction and while he was at fault, are not removed; but the graver torments into which he was not yet thrust are averted by the prevening reconciliation. Moreover, as for the honors which, had he not sinned, he was going to receive in due time and of which, had he not been reconciled, he was going to be deprived after his wrongdoing: because of the complete satisfaction these honors are given to him without any alteration, as was originally determined. Indeed, if he had been disinherited of these honors before his reconciliation (just as, had he not been reconciled, he would deservedly and irrecoverably have been disinherited of them after his wrongdoing), there would have been no way for any reconciliation to assist [in their recovery]. But since he could not be disinherited of an honor which he did not yet have and was not required to have, the reconciliation can intervene prior to this disinheritance and can avert it — provided that while lying in the soreness of his stripes until such time as this soreness passes away, the servant pledges in heart and in word fidelity to his master and self-reform, and provided he fulfills his pledge.

The relationship between God and man is analogous to this one. Indeed, when human nature first sinned, it was scourged with the following penalty: (1) it would never by natural means beget offspring except in that state in which we observe infants to be born; (2) after this life it would be forever banished into Hell — banished from the Kingdom of God, for which it was created. [This was to happen] unless someone reconciled human nature — something which human nature was unable to do by itself. But Christ is the only one by whom human nature is able to be reconciled. Therefore, in all infants who are begotten by natural means human nature is born with sin and its penalty. When human nature enters the state of reconciliation, this penalty which it received before reconciliation deservedly remains. But those torments which human nature was going to suffer in Hell are remitted for those whom Christ redeems. And human nature is presented with the Kingdom of God which in due time it was going to receive after its sojourn in the earthly paradise — provided that the redeemed persevere unto the end in the faith which they promise at baptism.

10

Certain individuals think that free choice is proved by experience to be able [to accomplish] nothing; for many people make an enormous effort to live rightly, and yet because of some impossibility (as they call it) which stands in their way, they either make no headway or else after having made some progress they fail irreparably. But the fact [that they think this] does not destroy the point which has been rationally demonstrated: viz., that free choice can [accomplish something] cooperatively with grace. But in my opinion the fact that when they make an effort they either do not make any headway or else after having made some progress they fail, occurs not because of an impossibility but because of an obstacle which is sometimes serious, sometimes easily surmountable.[98] Indeed, we are accustomed to say that something which we are unable to accomplish without difficulty is impossible for us. For if each of us carefully examines his own acts of willing, he will discern that he never abandons uprightness-of-will (which he has received by grace) except by willing something else which he cannot will compatibly [with willing uprightness].[99] Surely, he abandons uprightness-of-will not because the *ability* to keep it fails him (which ability constitutes freedom of choice) but because the *will* to keep it fails him. The will-to-keep-uprightness is not deficient in itself but ceases because another willing expels it (as I said).

11

But since this last consideration concerns the will, I deem it necessary to say in more detail about the will something which shall not be useless, it seems to me. In our bodies we have five senses and [various] members, each of which, distinctly, is adapted for its own special function. We use these members and

De Concordia III

senses as instruments. For example, the hands are suited for grasping, the feet for walking, the tongue for speaking, and sight for seeing. Similarly, the soul too has in itself certain powers which it uses as instruments for appropriate functions. For in the soul there is reason, which the soul uses (as its instrument) for reasoning; and there is will, which the soul uses for willing. Neither reason nor will is the whole of the soul; rather, each of them is something within the soul. Therefore, since the distinct instruments have their essence, their aptitudes, and their uses, let us distinguish in the will — in regard to which we are discussing these matters — the instrument, its aptitudes, and its uses.[100] In regard to the will we can call these aptitudes *inclinations* (*affectiones*). Indeed, the instrument-for-willing is modified by its own inclinations. Hence, when a man's soul strongly wills something, it is said to be inclined to will that thing, or to will it affectionally.

Assuredly, the will is seen to be spoken of equivocally — in three senses. For (a) the instrument-for-willing, (b) the inclination of this instrument, and (c) the use of this instrument, are distinguishable. The instrument-for-willing is that power-of-the-soul[101] which we use for willing — just as reason is the instrument-for-reasoning, which we use when we reason, and just as sight is the instrument-for-seeing, which we use when we see. The inclination (*affectio*) of the instrument-for-willing is that by which the instrument is so inclined to will some given thing (even when a man is not thinking of that which he wills) that if this thing comes to mind, then the will wills [to have] it either immediately or at the appropriate time. For example, the instrument-for-willing is so inclined to will health (even when a man is not thinking of it) that as soon as health comes to mind, the will wills [to have] it immediately. And the instrument-for-willing is so inclined to will sleep (even when a man is not thinking of this) that when it comes to mind, the will wills [to have] it at the appropriate time. For the will is never inclined in such way that it ever wills sickness or that it wills never to sleep. Likewise, in a just man the instrument-for-willing is so inclined to will justice (even when a man is asleep) that when he thinks of justice he wills [to have] it immediately.

On the other hand, the use of this instrument is something which we have only when we are thinking of the thing which we will.

Now, the word "will" applies to the instrument-for-willing, to the inclination of this instrument, and to the use of this instrument. (1) Indeed, we call the instrument *will* when we say that we direct the will toward various things (e.g., now toward willing to walk, now toward willing to sit, now toward willing something else). A man always possesses this instrument even though he does not always use it. The case is similar to his having sight, in the sense of the instrument-for-seeing, even when he does not use it (e.g., when he is asleep). But when he does use it, he directs it now toward seeing the sky, now toward seeing the earth, now toward seeing something else. Moreover, the case is similar to our always possessing the instrument-for-reasoning, viz., reason, which we do not always use and which, in reasoning, we direct toward various things. (2) But the inclination of the instrument-for-willing is called *will* when we say that a man always possesses the will for his own well-being. For in this case we label as *will* that inclination (of the instrument) by which a man wills his own well-being. [The same thing is true] when in this way we say that a saint — even when he is sleeping and is not thinking about living justly — continually has the will to live justly. Moreover, when we say that one person has more of the will to live justly than another person, the only thing we are calling *will* is the instrument's inclination, by which a man wills to live justly. For the instrument itself is not greater in one person and less in another. (3) But the use of the instrument-for-willing is called *will* when someone says "I now have the will to read" (that is, "I now will to read") — or says, "I now have the will to write" (that is, "I now will to write"). Indeed, seeing is using sight, i.e., using the instrument-for-seeing; and the use of sight is seeing, or sight (in cases, that is, where "sight" signifies the same thing as "seeing," for "sight" also signifies the instrument-for-seeing). Similarly, willing is using the will, i.e., using the instrument-for-willing; and the use of the will is the willing which occurs only when we are thinking of that thing which we will.

Therefore, there is only one will in the sense of the instrument; that is, there is in a man only one instrument-for-willing (even as there is only one reason, i.e., only one instrument-for-reasoning). But the will by which the instrument is modified is twofold. For just as sight has several aptitudes (viz., an aptitude for seeing light, and an aptitude for seeing figures by means of light, and

De Concordia III

an aptitude for seeing colors by means of figures), so the instrument-for-willing has two aptitudes, which I am calling inclinations. One of these is the inclination to will what is beneficial; the other is the inclination to will what is right.[102] To be sure, the will which is the instrument wills nothing except either a benefit or uprightness. For whatever else it wills, it wills either for the sake of a benefit or for the sake of uprightness; and even if it is mistaken, it regards itself as referring what it wills to these two ends. Indeed, because of the inclination to will what is beneficial, a man always wills happiness and to be happy. On the other hand, because of the inclination to will uprightness, he wills uprightness and to be upright (i.e., to be just). Now, he wills something for the sake of a benefit when, for instance, he wills to plow and to labor in order to have the wherewithal to preserve his life and health, both of which he deems to be benefits. And [he wills something] for the sake of uprightness when, for example, he wills to work at learning in order to know rightly, i.e., to live justly. But the will which is the use of this oft-mentioned instrument is present only when someone is thinking of that thing which he wills, as was already said. The distinctions of this will are multiple; I shall not discuss them now, though perhaps elsewhere I shall.[103]

Indeed, "to will" has equivocal senses, just as does "to see." For just as "to see" is predicated both of the one who uses his sight and of the one who does not use it even though he has the aptitude to see, so "to will" is predicated both of the one who (while he is thinking of the thing he wills) uses the instrument-for-willing and — since he has the inclination (i.e., the aptitude) to will — of the one who does not use it.

From the consideration which follows, we can also recognize that the instrument-for-willing, the inclination of this instrument, and the use of this instrument are different "wills": A just man is said to have — even while he is asleep and is not thinking of anything — the will to live justly. And an unjust man is denied to possess — when he is sleeping — the will to live justly. Now, the same will which is being affirmed of the just man is being denied of the unjust man. But obviously when we deny that the will to live justly is in the unjust man who is sleeping, we are not denying that the will which I have called the instrument is in him; for every man, both while asleep and awake, always has this will.

Therefore, since no other will than that will which is absent from the evil man is said thus to be present in the good man: it is not the will-as-instrument which is being signified to be present in the good man; rather [what is being signified is] that will by means of which the instrument is modified. Now, there is no doubt that the will-as-use is not present in a sleeping man (unless he is dreaming). Hence, when the will to live justly is said to be present in a just man who is asleep, the will-as-use is not meant. Therefore, the will-as-inclination is not identical with the will-as-instrument or with the will-as-use. Moreover, everyone knows that the will-as-instrument is not identical with the will-as-use; for when I say that I do not have the will to write, no one interprets this to mean that I do not have the instrument-for-willing. Consequently, the will-as-instrument, the will-as-inclination, and the will-as-use are not identical.[104]

Indeed, the will-as-instrument moves all the other instruments which we freely use — both those instruments which are a part of us (such as our hands, our tongue, our sight) and those that are independent of us (such as a pen and an ax). Furthermore, it causes all of our voluntary movements; but it moves itself by means of its inclinations. Hence, it can be called an instrument that moves itself. I am saying that the will-as-instrument causes all our voluntary movements. Yet — if we consider the matter carefully — God is more truly said to cause everything that our nature or our will causes, for He causes the nature and the instrument-for-willing, together with the instrument's inclinations, without which the instrument does nothing.

12

A man's every merit, whether good or evil, derives from these two inclinations which I am also calling wills. These two wills also differ in that the one for willing what is beneficial is inseparable, but the one for willing what is upright was (as I have said above)[105] separable, originally, in angels and in our first parents; and it is still separable in those who remain in this life. These two wills also differ in that the one for willing benefit is not this thing which it wills; but the one for willing uprightness is uprightness. Indeed, no one wills uprightness except someone who has uprightness; and no one is able to will uprightness except by means of uprightness. But it is clear that this uprightness belongs to the will considered as instrument. This is the uprightness I am speaking of when I define "justice" as uprightness-of-will kept for its own sake.[106] This uprightness is also the truth of the will wherein the Lord charges the Devil with not having remained steadfastly, as I have stated in the treatise *On Truth*.[107]

We must now consider how men's merits (as I was saying) — whether merits unto salvation or unto condemnation — proceed from the two wills which I am calling aptitudes or inclinations. In itself, to be sure, uprightness is a cause of no evil merit but is the mother of every good merit. For uprightness favors the spirit as it strives against the flesh; and uprightness "delights in the law of God in accordance with the inner man,"[108] i.e., in accordance with the spirit [which strives against the flesh]. However, [even] if evil sometimes seems to follow from uprightness, it does not proceed from uprightness but proceeds from something else. Indeed, because of their uprightness the apostles were a good odor unto God.[109] But the fact that unto certain men the apostles were "the odor of death unto death"[110] did not proceed from their justice but from evil men's wickedness. Now, the will for willing what is beneficial is not always evil, but is evil when it consents to the flesh as it strives against the spirit.[111]

13

But in order to understand this matter more clearly, we must investigate how the will [for what is beneficial] became so corrupt and so prone to evil. For we must not believe that in our first parents God created it prone to evil. Now, when I stated[112] that because of sin human nature became corrupt and acquired appetites similar to those of brute animals, I did not explain how such a will arose in man. Indeed, base appetites are one thing; a corrupt will that assents to these appetites is another thing. Therefore, it seems to me, we must ask about how such a will became the lot of man.

The cause of such a will as this shall readily become apparent to us if we consider the original condition of rational nature. The intention of God was to create rational nature just and happy in order that it would enjoy Him.[113] Now, it was able to be neither just nor happy without the will-for-justice and the will-for-happiness. Assuredly, the will-for-justice is itself justice; but the will-for-happiness is not happiness because not everyone who has the will-for-happiness has happiness. However, everyone believes that happiness — whether angelic happiness is meant or the happiness which Adam had in Paradise — includes a sufficiency of suitable benefits and excludes all need. For although the happiness of angels is greater than the happiness of man in Paradise, still Adam cannot be denied to have had happiness. For, indeed, nothing prevents Adam from having been happy in Paradise and free of all need, in spite of the fact that angelic happiness was greater than his. (By comparison, an intense heat is free of all cold; and, nevertheless, there can be another more intense heat. And cold is free of all heat, even though there can be a more intense cold.) To be sure, having less of a thing than does another is not always identical with being in need; to be in need is to be deprived of something when it ought to be possessed — a condition which was not true of Adam. Where there is need there is unhappiness. God created rational nature for knowing and loving Him; but it is not the case that He created it unhappy when it had no antecedent guilt. Therefore, God created man happy and in need of nothing. Hence, at one and the same time rational nature received (1) the will-for-happiness, (2) happiness, (3) the will-for-justice (i.e., uprightness which is justice itself), and (4) free choice, without which rational nature could not have kept justice.

Now, God so ordained these two "wills," or inclinations, that (1) the will-as-instrument would use the will-which-is-justice for commanding and governing (though being itself instructed by the spirit, which is also called mind and reason), and that (2) without any detriment it would use the other will to the end of obedience. Indeed, God gave happiness to man — not to speak of the angels — for man's benefit. But He gave man justice for His own honor. [He gave] justice in such way that man was able to abandon it, so that if he did not abandon it but kept it perseveringly, he would merit being elevated to fellowship with the angels. But if man did abandon justice, he would not thereafter be able to regain it by himself; nor would he attain to the happiness of the angels. Rather, he would be deprived of that happiness which he possessed; and falling into the likeness of brute animals, he would be subjected with them to corruption and to the appetites I have often mentioned. Nevertheless, the will-for-happiness would remain in order that by means of man's need for the goods which he had lost he would be justly punished with deep unhappiness. Therefore, since he abandoned justice, he lost happiness. And the will which he received as being good and as being for his own good is fervent with desire for benefits which it is unable to keep from willing. And because it is unable to have the true benefits which are suitable for rational nature but which rational nature has lost, it turns itself to benefits which are false and which pertain to brute animals and which bestial appetites suggest. And thus when the will inordinately wills these benefits it either (1) shuns uprightness, so that it does not accept uprightness when uprightness is offered, or else (2) it casts uprightness away after having received it. But when the will wills these benefits within proper bounds, it neither shuns nor casts away uprightness.

So the will-as-instrument was created good, with respect to the fact that it has being; moreover, it was created just and having the power to keep the justice it received. And in the above manner it was made evil by free choice. [It was made evil] not insofar as it exists but insofar as it was made unjust as a result of the absence of justice, which was freely abandoned and which it was always supposed to have. Moreover, it now became powerless to will the justice it had deserted. For it is not the case that by free choice the will can will justice when it does not have justice — as it is the case that by free choice the will can keep justice when it has justice. Furthermore, the will-for-the-beneficial, a will which was created good insofar as it is something, became evil (i.e., unjust) because it was not subordinate to justice, without which it ought to will nothing. Therefore, since the will-as-instrument freely became unjust: after having abandoned justice, it remains (as regards its own power) a servant of injustice and unjust by necessity. For it is unable by itself to return to justice; and without justice the will is never free, because without justice the natural freedom of choice is idle. The will was also made the servant of its own inclination for the beneficial, because once justice has been removed, the will is able to will only what this inclination wills.

I predicate "to will" of both the instrument and its inclination; for the instrument is *will*, and the inclination is *will*. And without impropriety "to will" is predicated of both these wills. For the instrument, which wills by means of its inclination, does indeed will; and the inclination, by means of which the instrument wills, also wills. (Similarly, "to see" is predicated both of the man who sees by means of sight and of the sight by which the man sees.) Hence, we can without absurdity say that the inclinations of this will which I have called the soul's instrument are, so to speak, "instruments" of this instrument, because it does something only by means of them. Therefore, when the "instrument"-for-willing-justice (i.e., when uprightness) has been lost, the will-as-instrument cannot at all will justice, unless justice is restored by grace. Therefore, since the will-as-instrument ought to will nothing except justly, whatever it wills without uprightness, it wills unjustly. None of the appetites which the apostle calls the flesh and concupiscence are evil or unjust with respect to the fact that they exist; rather they are called unjust because they are present in a rational nature, where they ought not to be found. For, indeed, they are not evil or unjust in brute animals, because they ought to be present there.

14

From what has already been said above, one can recognize that the reason a man does not always possess justice (which he ought always to have) is that he cannot at all acquire or regain it by himself. It is also clear that God causes good works only by His goodness, since He creates the will with free choice and gives it the justice in accordance with which it is acting. But God causes evil deeds only because of man's fault; for God would not cause these deeds if man did not will to do them.[114] Nevertheless, God causes that which they are [essentially], since He has placed in man the will which man uses without justice. And so, the evil deeds which God causes occur only by man's fault. For it is not the case [that they occur] by the fault of God, who created in man a will with freedom of choice and who conferred justice on it so that it would will nothing except justly. Rather, [they occur] by the fault of man, who abandoned the justice which he could have kept. Therefore, in the case of good works God causes both the fact that they are good with respect to their being and that they are good with respect to their justice. But in the case of evil works God causes only the fact that they are good with respect to their being; He does not cause the fact that they are evil with respect to the

De Concordia III

absence of required justice — an absence which is not anything. Man, however, in the case of good deeds, causes the fact that they are not evil, because although he was able to abandon justice and to do evil deeds, he did not abandon it but kept it by means of free choice — [justice] being given and followed up by grace.[115] Now, in the case of evil deeds [man causes] only the fact that they are evil, because he does them by an autonomous will (i.e., by an unjust will).[116]

I think that I can now fittingly conclude this treatise which has dealt with three difficult controversies — a treatise which I undertook in the expectation that God would help me. If I have herein said something which ought to suffice any inquirer, I do not impute it to myself, for it is not my [doing] but is [the work of] God's grace in me. However, I do make the following claim: Had someone given me — when I was asking about these issues and when my mind, perplexed, was seeking in them a rationale — the answers which I have written, I would have been grateful, because he would have satisfied me. Therefore, since what I know about this topic, by God's revelation, was especially pleasing to me: knowing that it would likewise please certain others if I recorded it, I wanted freely to bestow, on those who are seeking, that which I have freely received.

ABBREVIATIONS

M	*Monologion*
P	*Proslogion*
DV	*De Veritate*
DL	*De Libertate Arbitrii*
DIV	*Epistola de Incarnatione Verbi*
CDH	*Cur Deus Homo*
DCV	*De Conceptu Virginali et de Originali Peccato*
DP	*De Processione Spiritus Sancti*
DC	*De Concordia Praescientiae et Praedestinationis et Gratiae Dei cum Libero Arbitrio*
PF	*Ein neues unvollendetes Werk des hl. Anselm von Canterbury* (Philosophical Fragments)
DT	*De Trinitate* (Augustine)
PL	*Patrologia Latina* (ed. J. P. Migne)
S	*Sancti Anselmi Opera Omnia* (ed. F. S. Schmitt). E.g., S I, 237:7 indicates Volume I, page 237, line 7.

VOLUME II: NOTES

PHILOSOPHICAL FRAGMENTS

1. These fragments are translated from *Ein neues unvollendetes Werk des hl. Anselm von Canterbury*, edited by F. S. Schmitt (*Beiträge zur Geschichte der Philosophie und Theologie des Mittelalters*, 33/3). Münster (Westfalen): Aschendorff Press, 1936.
   Numbers in the margin of the translation indicate the page and line of the Latin text. For the most part, we have eliminated the numbers used by Schmitt to show grouping.
   For a philosophical analysis of the fragments see D. P. Henry, *The Logic of Saint Anselm* (Oxford University Press, 1967).

2. Dating of the fragments is uncertain — except for the fact that at least the Exordium was written after CDH (i.e., after 1097).

3. Cf. CDH I, 1 (S II, 49:7-10). *"Potestas"* and *"impotentia"* are also used as opposites at CDH II, 17 (S II, 123:19-20); DL 12 (S I, 224:2-3); DCD 12 (S I, 254:5). Note the use of *"possibilitas"* for *"potestas"* in the Monologion Preface (S I, 7:7) and in DIV 16 (S II, 35:14).

4. Cf. CDH II, 10 (S II, 106:17-18); the title of CDH II, 17 (S II, 122:23-24); and DCD 12 (S I, 253:32).

5. Cf. CDH II, 10 (S II, 107:11-13). See also CDH II, 16 (S II, 120:15-19).

6. Cf. CDH II, 17 (S II, 123:11-12).

7. Cf. CDH II, 18 (S II, 128:4-6). See also CDH II, 16 (S II, 122:19-21) and DV 2 (S I, 178:28-29).

8. Cf. CDH I, 14 (S II, 72:14-15). Note PF 37:1, where *"suum alicuius"* recurs.

9. The Latin verb *"facere"* means both "to do" and "to cause." In the following sections both translations have been used, depending upon the context and the sound in English. At places, the choice becomes arbitrary. In some of these places we have used parentheses to indicate that both readings contribute to the sense of the passage. E.g., PF 26:7-9: "Therefore, everything of which a verb is predicated does (causes) what is signified by that verb."

10. Note Boethius on infinite terms: PL 64:520. Cf. Aristotle, *On Interpretation* 19^{b}5ff.

11. Note DV 5 (S I, 182:10-17).

12. Cf. M 8 (S I, 22:13-15).

13. Note P 7 and DV 5 (S I, 182:18-19). *"Pati"* means "to endure," "to undergo," "to experience," "to suffer."

14. PF 26:23-27:26 is an almost exact repetition of PF 25:14-26:22. We have therefore omitted it in the translation. The non-repetitive lines are the

Notes

following: "Often 'to do' is used in place of negative verbs too — even in place of 'not to do.' For example, he who does not love the virtues and does not hate the vices does evilly; and he who does not do what he ought not to do does rightly. Thus, 'to do' is used in place of every verb, whether positive or negative; and every verb is a doing" (PF 27:10–14).

15. Cf. DG 8 (S I, 152:33) and 21 (S I, 166:26–27). Note also M 17 (S I, 31:27–30).
16. Anselm uses "*sanus*" interchangeably with "*salus.*" Note PF 38:3.
17. John 3:20.
18. John 3:21. Cf. DV 5 (S I, 182:10–12).
19. Cf. *Liber de Voluntate* (PL 158:488C). Note also DV 5 (S I, 181:24–25; 182:12–14).
20. Cf. M 6 (S I, 19:1–3).
21. These modes are modes both of causing and of discourse about causing. Note, e.g., PF 33:6–8, 22–23; 34:10–12; 35:22–23.
22. See Diagram I, table A, appended to PF.
23. In the texts which follow, "*per se*" has been translated both as "directly" and as "through itself (himself, themselves)." For Anselm contrasts it both with "*per medium*" and with "*per aliud.*"
24. Cf. CDH II, 10 (S II, 107:29–31).
25. Cf. CDH I, 9 (S II, 62:9–10).
26. Note PF 41:1–2.
27. Cf. CDH I, 9 (S II, 64:3–8).
28. See Diagram I, table B, in the Appendix. N.B. The example of the armed man is also found in Augustine's discussion of Aristotle's categories. *Confessions* 4.16.28. DT 5.7.8.
29. The Latin text begins anew the discussion of *facere non esse*.
30. The Latin text repeats "*Haec quidem exempla de causis efficientibus assumpsi, quoniam in his clarius apparet, quod volo ostendere,*" which is found in the text at the beginning of note 2.

The teacher's speech reverses modes 4 and 5, as presented in the earlier ordering.

31. For example, in Diagram II, table C, the first mode is simply the negation "A does *not* directly *cause* C *to be dead.*" In the five subsequent modes we say "A does *not cause* C *to be dead*" for the five respective reasons cited in the examples. Anselm's point is: If we form the contrary of this negative statement, and if we then transform this contrary into an affirmation, we shall have "A *causes* C *not to be dead.*" And this statement is substitutable for the original negation — as the examples in modes 2–6 illustrate. For instance, we say in mode 3 "A does not cause C to be dead" because A causes C to be armed. But we might equally well say "A causes C not to be dead" because A causes C to be armed. A similar point can be made with regard to table D. In last analysis, then, in Diagram II, modes 2–6 of table B are substitutable for modes 2–6 of table C; and modes 2–6 of table A are substitutable for modes 2–6 of table D.
32. The examples which follow are illustrated in Diagram II, appended to PF.
33. Exodus 32:6.

Notes

34. Job 29:15.
35. *"Figura."* Boethius uses *"forma"* and *"figura"* to translate Aristotle's fourth kind of quality. See PL 64:250D (Aristotle, *Categories* 10^{a}11).
36. Cf. CDH II, 18 (S II, 128:27–30). See also DCD 12 (S I, 253:22–27); DV 8 (S I, 188:9–18).
37. Cf. CDH II, 18 (S II, 128:30–129:1).
38. We take part of this Latin sentence as ". . . *sed sint aliud hoc* [*est*] *indigentes. . . .*"
39. Cf. CDH II, 18 (S II, 128:23–26).
40. Cf. CDH II, 18 (S II, 129:1–2).
41. Cf. CDH II, 18 (S II, 128:13–22).
42. Matt. 6:12.
43. Luke 6:38.
44. Cf. *Liber de Voluntate* (PL 158:487C).
45. Cf. CDH I, 10 (S II, 65:21–25).
46. Cf. CDH I, 10 (S II, 65:26–27).
47. Ps. 113B:3 (115:3).
48. Rom. 9:18.
49. *Loc. cit.*
50. Cf. CDH I, 9 (S II, 64:3–5).
51. I Tim. 2:4.
52. Anselm does not return to this topic.
53. Cf. DCD 26 (S I, 274:16–24).
54. Ps. 108:24 (109:24).
55. Cf. DCV 5 (S II, 147:1–3). Note also DCD 9, 11, and 16.
56. Note DCD 11.
57. *"Constituere intellectum"* means "to signify." Note DG 14 (S I, 160:31).
58. *Aptitudo scribendi* encompasses:
    1. *aptitudo ad scribendum*
        a. *praecedit ipsam scriptionem*
        b. *idem est ac potestas scribendi*
    2. *aptitudo in scribendo*
        a. *non praecedit ipsam scriptionem*
        b. *effectum aptitudinis ad scribendum*
        c. *secundum quam dicimus quia "apte scribit"*

DE GRAMMATICO

1. (1) The translators have chosen to render *"grammaticus"* as "expert-in-grammar" and *"grammatica"* as "expertise-in-grammar." "Grammar" may be construed in either the narrow contemporary sense (illustrated by the end of section 18) or in the broader sense of history, literature, and the interpretation of poetry. Either construal is compatible with Anselm's argument; and for this reason it is unprofitable to debate the issue of how broadly or narrowly he was using the term *"grammatica."*

(2) "Expert-in-grammar" and "expertise-in-grammar" are regarded throughout as single words. Whereas the conventions of the German language

Notes

allow for making single words out of compounds, English relies mainly upon hyphenation.

(3) Parentheses around the article "an" in "(an) expert-in-grammar" (and in other expressions) indicate that the insertion of "an" into the translation, or its deletion therefrom, may make a difference to the argument. (For instance, to speak of being an expert-in-grammar suggests a substance, whereas to speak of being expert-in-grammar suggests a quality.) The same rationale accounts for the use of "Every/Everything," "No/Nothing" as quantifiers.

(4) Italics are employed where Anselm both mentions and uses a word in the same sentence. For example, near the beginning of section 19 the translation reads: "If *expert-in-grammar* is a quality because it signifies a quality, then *armed* is a substance because it signifies a substance."

(5) Italics are also employed to indicate a genus or a species or a concept (e.g., in section 8, proposition (*ii*), and in section 10).

(6) Finally, italics are NOT employed for emphasis. Nor are they utilized where Anselm is only mentioning a word. Rather, such words are put into quotation marks.

2. Although the mss. contain no divisions, F. S. Schmitt's edition of the text — in accordance with previous editions — retains the twenty-one divisions which follow. However, Schmitt uses Roman numerals and places them in brackets. See S I, 145n.

This dialogue was probably written between 1080 and 1085.

3. For an analysis of the argument of this dialogue see D. P. Henry's *The De Grammatico of St. Anselm* (South Bend, Indiana: University of Notre Dame Press, 1964).

Aristotle speaks of naming something derivatively (or paronymously) when its name is derived from another name which differs only in case-termination. For instance, γραμματικός (*grammaticus*) is derived from γραμματική (*grammatica*). See Aristotle, *Categories*, Ch. 1; Boethius, *On Aristotle's Categories*, Bk. I (PL 64, 167).

4. Indented propositions are numbered consecutively in each section by the translators as a simple means of reference.

5. See Aristotle, *Categories*, Ch. 8 (10[a]); Boethius, *On Aristotle's Categories*, Bk. III (PL 64, 252).

6. This proposition is equivalent to its converse, which therefore may also be said to follow from the foregoing premises.

7. Cf. Dan. 13:22.

8. Viz., in section 2.

9. Viz., propositions (*i*) and (*ii*) at the beginning of this section.

10. That is: (*ix*) No man is (an) expert-in-grammar.

11. That is: from (*vii*) (*x*) and from (*viii*) (*xi*) of this section.

12. (*xiii*) is equivalent to (*iii*).

13. Viz., from propositions (*i*) and (*ii*), taken in the sense of (*vii*) and (*viii*).

14. In section 2.

15. That is, the Student now thinks that his original conclusion (viz., proposition (*viii*) of this section, which is equivalent to proposition (*v*) of section 2) is correct.

16. In section 5.

Notes

17. Section 5, proposition (v).
18. Proposition (v) of this section.
19. Sections 2–5 eliminate this conclusion.
20. Viz., from the proposition "Being a man is not identical with being an animal."
21. Section 5.
22. *Categories*, Ch. 2; Boethius, *On Aristotle's Categories*, Bk. I (PL 64, 169).
23. *Categories*, Ch. 5 (3^a); Boethius, *On Aristotle's Categories*, Bk. I (PL 64, 189).
24. *Loc. cit.*
25. Section 9.
26. Cf. section 2.
27. See the end of section 9.
28. Statements (i) and (ii) deal with expert-in-grammar as if it were a quality — as is expertise-in-grammar.
29. A term's signifying of and by itself (*significare per se*) is contrasted with a term's signifying on the basis of something else (*significare per aliud*). Anselm explains this distinction in section 14.
30. For a clarification of "*significare ut unum*," see section 19.
31. Signification properly so called is signification of and by itself (*significatio per se*).
32. Or: ". . . would be a part of its essence." See M 4, n. 12.
33. Or: ". . . of this very object" (viz., (an) expert-in-grammar).
34. It is not appropriate because it is redundant.
35. For Aristotle's definition of "verb" see his *De Interpretatione*, Ch. 3; Boethius, *On Aristotle's De Interpretatione* (PL 64, 306). Boethius: "A verb is an expression which signifies a time, along with signifying something else, and no part of which, by itself, signifies anything."
36. For Aristotle's definition of "name" see his *De Interpretatione*, Ch. 2; Boethius, *On Aristotle's De Interpretatione* (PL 64, 301). Boethius: "A name is a verbal expression which is significative by convention, which contains no reference to time, and no part of which is significative by itself."
37. For Aristotle's definition of "λόγος ("*oratio*") see his *De Interpretatione*, Ch. 4; Boethius, *On Aristotle's De Interpretatione* (PL 64:311). Boethius: "An *oratio* is a significative verbal expression, some part of which is significative by itself."
38. In section 13.
39. See the end of section 13.
40. In section 13.
41. "Things" ("*res*") is here used in the broadest sense, so that qualities and Aristotle's other accidents can be called things. As *Reply to Gaunilo* 8 makes clear: when Anselm says that words signify things, he does not assume that a word can be significative only if the "thing" signified really exists.
42. *Categories*, Ch. 4 (1^b25); Boethius, *On Aristotle's Categories*, Bk. I (PL 64:180). Note especially PL 64:162B.
43. Or translated more simply: "Each non-complex expression signifies

Notes

either a substance or a quantity, [(etc.)]." Note the second speech of the Teacher in section 18.

44. *Categories*, Ch. 5 (3^{b}10); Boethius, *On Aristotle's Categories*, Bk. I (PL 64:194).
45. See the end of section 17.
46. Cf. DCD 11 (S I, 250:21-24).
47. ἔχειν (*habere*, having) is one of Aristotle's categories.
48. Note sections 8, 12, and 13.
49. Section 12.
50. Note DIV 11, where Anselm also uses the expression "*collectio proprietatum.*"
51. The Teacher rejects this comparison between "man" and "white."

PREFACE TO THREE DIALOGUES

1. That is, it does not pertain to the study of Scripture.
2. See DL 3.
3. This topic is dealt with in DC.

ON TRUTH

1. This dialogue was probably written between 1080 and 1085.
2. Cf. John 14:6.
3. M 18.
4. Literally: "For what [end] is an affirmation made?"
5. Anselm will attempt to show that every instance of truth is an instance of rightness. He investigates correct statements, right thoughts, upright willing, righteous action, correct perception, the straightness of a material object, and the rightness of all natures. The continuity of his argument depends upon the presence in Latin of a single term, "*rectitudo*," which he applies to this range of cases. English has no single word applicable to all these different cases; and thus the one Latin word will be translated by a number of English expressions.
6. Ch. 5.
7. E.g., by conjecture.
8. John 8:44.
9. John 3:20, 21.
10. It has received this from the Supreme Truth, viz., God. Cf. DV 7 (S I, 185:11-13). Also cf. S I, 186:30; 222:22; and 235:4. In these passages the expressions "*ab eo, quo,*" "*ab eo a quo,*" and "*ab illo, a quo*" obviously indicate God. Note also Augustine's "*ab illo a quo sunt omnia bona, hoc est Deo* (*De Libero Arbitrio*, Bk. 2, Ch. 19 = PL 32:1267-1268). Finally, cf. S I, 265:2-3 (DCD 20) with S I, 244:21 (DCD 7).
11. John 3:21.
12. Note PF 25:14ff.
13. Cf. Matt. 5:10.
14. II Cor. 5:10.
15. Note PF 26:13-14.
16. John 8:44.

Notes

17. Ch. 2.
18. Literally: "(for example, through glass not of its own color [i.e., not of the natural color of glass] but to which another color is added) . . . ."
19. Literally: "which report what they are able to since they have received thus to be able."
20. On Anselm's use of "*essentia*" see M 4, n. 12.
21. Note DC I, 4 (S II, 253:1-15).
22. Cf. CDH I, 7 (S II, 57:17ff.).
23. Cf. PF 35:14ff.; CDH II, 18 (S II, 128:27-32).
24. Note DL 5 (S I, 217:1-6); DCD 12 (S I, 253:22-27); CDH II, 10 (S II, 107:5-6); CDH II, 17 (S II, 123:15-22); CDH II, 18 (S II, 128:27-30).
25. I.e., the truth which is in thoughts and the truth which is in statements.
26. M 18.
27. Ps. 31:11 (32:11).
28. Ps. 106:42 (107:42).
29. Viz., that what is is or that what-is-not is not.
30. I.e., it will be no less right for what-ought-to-be-signified to be signified.
31. Viz., will demand that what-ought-to-be-signified be signified.

FREEDOM OF CHOICE

1. This dialogue was probably written between 1080 and 1085.
2. Cf. Aristotle, *Categories*, Ch. 1 (1^{a}6ff.); Boethius, *On Aristotle's Categories*, Bk. 1 (PL 64:167).
3. Viz., the ability to sin.
4. John 8:34.
5. "*Potestas*" means both ability and power.
6. Anselm regards faith as in some cases propaedeutic to understanding. Note especially DIV 1 (S I, 7:5-8:6).
7. See DV 12.
8. By "keeping uprightness-of-will for its own sake" Anselm means always willing what is right only because it is right (i.e., always willing it for no other reason than that it is right).
9. E.g., free choice.
10. I.e., from neither angels nor the first man.
11. I.e., in accordance with these two respects of willing.
12. Note DV 8 (S I, 188:18-22); DCD 12 (S I, 253:22-27); CDH II, 10 (S II, 107:5-6); CDH II, 17 (S II, 123:15-22); CDH II, 18 (S II, 128:27-30).
13. Cf. DC III, 10.
14. In DC III, 11 Anselm distinguishes three wills (or three senses of the word "will"): the instrument-for-willing, the inclinations of the instrument, and the use of the instrument.
15. Cf. DC III, 9.
16. Ps. 77:39 (78:39).
17. John 8:34.

THE FALL OF THE DEVIL

1. This dialogue was probably written between 1085 and 1090.
2. I Cor. 4:7.

Notes

3. Cf. DCD 18 (S I, 263:7-12). Note PF 29:20-30; CDH II, 10 (S II, 107:29-31).
4. On Anselm's use of *"essentia"* see M 4, n. 12.
5. Isa. 45:7.
6. John 8:44.
7. Literally: "I see it to be a necessary cause that not-receiving follow." Freely: "I see that it logically entails not-receiving."
8. Gen. 3:5.
9. Cf. DIV 10 (S II, 27:1-16); CDH II, 9 (S II, 105:22-24). Note especially DC III, 14 (S II, 288:10). And see DC I, 6 (S II, 256:22-24).
10. Cf. DCD 23 and CDH I, 16-18, where Anselm also discusses the elevation of human beings to the places of the angels who fell.
11. I.e., they no longer see anything to will which exceeds what they already have.
12. Note CDH I, 9 (S II, 63:27-29).
13. In Ch. 7.
14. Note M 8.
15. Note PF 42-43.
16. Cf. DG 18 (S I, 164:9-14).
17. These other arguments are found in Ch. 7.
18. In Ch. 1.
19. Note DL 5 (S I, 217:1-6); DV 8 (S I, 188:18-22); CDH II, 10 (S II, 107:5-6); CDH II, 17 (S II, 123:15-22); CDH II, 18 (S II, 128:27-30).
20. I.e., why wouldn't he be able to will by himself . . .?
21. Cf. DC III, 11 (S II, 281:5-7).
22. I.e., added to the will-for-happiness.
23. One *owes* justice when he *ought* to have it but does not. *"Debeo"* means both "I owe" and "I ought." Cf. CDH II, 18 (S II, 128:27-129:13).
24. In Ch. 13.
25. Note DCD 1 (S I, 234:6-9), PF 29:20-30, and CDH II, 10 (S II, 107:29-31).
26. In Ch. 13.
27. Note DCD 1 (S I, 234:15-16).
28. Cf. DC III, 14.
29. Cf. DC I, 5; M 63 (S I, 73:8-10).
30. Ch. 3.
31. Cf. DCV 2 (S II, 141:9-16).
32. Ps. 35:7 (36:6).
33. Rom. 11:33.
34. Viz., the knowledge that he would be punished if he sinned.
35. Literally: "acquired the knowledge about which it is discussed. . . ."
36. Ch. 6.
37. Cf. PF 42:9-13.
38. I.e., being able to will x is a *necessary* causal condition of willing x, but it is not a *sufficient* condition.
39. I.e., Satan's ability to will what he ought not to have willed.
40. Cf. Phil. 2:6. In willing to be like God Satan "robbed" God of honor. Note DIV 10 (S II, 27:1-3) and CDH II, 9 (S II, 105:22-24).

Notes

THE HARMONY OF THE FOREKNOWLEDGE, THE PREDESTINATION, AND THE GRACE OF GOD WITH FREE CHOICE

1. This treatise was written about 1107–1108.
2. This caption is not found in the mss. but is supplied by F. S. Schmitt.

In the mss. the text is divided into three parts, corresponding to the three different controversies. For convenience of reference Schmitt retains the further divisions found in the Gerberon edition. He indicates these divisions with Roman numerals (at the places where we have used arabic numerals). And he incloses them in brackets to show that they are not contained in the mss. See S II, 245 n.

3. Note CDH II, 17 (S II, 123:31–124:2) and PF 24:16–25.
4. Note DCD 21 (S I, 266:16–22).
5. On the distinction between antecedent and subsequent necessity, see CDH II, 17.
6. Anselm continues to use the word *"res"* (i.e., "thing"), which we now translate as *event*.
7. DC I, 2 (S II, 249:2–3).
8. A few lines earlier.
9. Note the last portion of DC I, 3.
10. Note DV 8 (S I, 187:2–17).
11. Anselm is referring to the fact that the sun appears to revolve around the earth from *east to west* (i.e., "with the firmament") once every day. At the same time, the sun actually moves among the stars from *west to east* (i.e., "counter to the firmament"), making one complete circuit of the heavens in a year. Because the sun changes its position in the heavens constantly at a uniform rate, it requires a few more minutes than do the stars to complete its daily apparent revolution about the earth. A similar effect is generally true for the planets as well.
12. DC I, 3 (S II, 251:27).
13. Job 14:5.
14. Rom. 8:28–29.
15. Note P 21.
16. Literally: "In this manner, then, whatever Sacred Scripture states as necessary regarding those things which are done by free choice, it states in accordance with eternity. . . ."
17. Earlier in this section (S II, 254:4–6).
18. Cf. the phrase used here (*"ad intelligibilem pervenit aetatem"*) with the phrase used at DCV 8 (S II, 150:3): *"in aetate perfecta."*
19. DV 12.
20. DL 3 (S I, 212:19–20).
21. Note DC III, 14 (S II, 288:9–10); DCD 4 (S I, 242:3–10); DIV 10 (S II, 27:1–16); CDH II, 9 (S II, 105:22–24). Also note DC I, 7 (S II, 259:26).
22. Note the full argument in DL 8.
23. DC I, 1–2.
24. Cf. the example in the first part of DL 5.
25. E.g., in DCD 9 and 16.

Notes

26. DCV 5.
27. Note the first section of DCD 26. See also the last paragraph of DCV 5.
28. Isa. 45:7.
29. I.e., with respect to its essential being.
30. Cf. DC III, 14. See also DCD 19–20.
31. See n. 21.
32. Rom. 8:29.
33. Note DCD 28 (S I, 276:10–11); DCD 1 (S I, 234:6–9).
34. See Rom. 9:18; Matt. 6:13.
35. DC I, 7 (S II, 259:17–19).
36. DC I, 1–2.
37. DC I, 2–3.
38. DC I, 7 (S II, 259:23–29).
39. John 15:5.
40. John 6:44.
41. I Cor. 4:7.
42. Rom. 9:18.
43. Rom. 9:16.
44. Isa. 1:19.
45. Ps. 33:13–15 (34:12–14).
46. Matt. 11:28–29.
47. DC I, 6 (S II, 256:5–7, 9–10).
48. See n. 18.
49. Wisd. of Sol. 5:16.
50. Ps. 93:14–15 (94:14–15).
51. *"Cor"* is broader than the English word "heart" — even in the figurative sense of "heart," viz., the seat of all affections. Indeed, in its figurative sense, *"cor"* signifies the seat of all affections and of all mental activity. Accordingly, it can in some instances — as in the above instance — also be translated as *mind*. N.B. CDH II, 4 (S II, 99:8).
52. Regarding dead faith see M 78.
53. Note DV 12.
54. DC I, 6 (S II, 257:5–24).
55. *Loc. cit.*
56. Rom. 9:18.
57. Rom. 11:35.
58. John 1:16.
59. Rom. 9:16.
60. I Cor. 4:7.
61. DL 5–7.
62. DC III, 2 (S II, 265:14–15).
63. See CDH I, 24 (S II, 93:7–9).
64. In the first part of DC III, 2.
65. John 15:5.
66. Rom. 9:16.
67. Ps. 50:7 (51:5).
68. I Cor. 3:9.
69. Cf. M 10; P 4; *On Behalf of the Fool* 4; PF 43:5–11.

Notes

70. "In the mind," i.e., *in corde*. See n. 51.
71. See n. 51.
72. See Rom. 10:13–15.
73. I Cor. 3:7.
74. Cf. the last paragraph of DP 14.
75. Isa. 45:22.
76. Ps. 84:5 (85:4).
77. Luke 17:5.
78. At the beginning of DC III, 6.
79. John 16:8–9.
80. See the first portion of CDH I, 24. Note DCV 29.
81. See DCV 2 (S II, 142:1–4).
82. Cf. CDH I, 15.
83. I.e., by the death of Jesus, who was God.
84. Rom. 7:7–8.
85. Rom. 7:15.
86. Matt. 5:22.
87. Rom. 8:1.
88. Cf. DCV 29.
89. Ps. 77:39 (78:39).
90. John 15:18.
91. II Cor. 2:15–16.
92. Rom. 9:18.
93. I.e., no one who has passed beyond infancy and reached the age of understanding. See n. 18.
94. Cf. the last part of the Teacher's speech in DL 9.
95. Note CDH I, 16–18.
96. Note CDH I, 18 (S II, 83:12–16). Also see DCD 5 and 23.
97. Heb. 11:33, 39, 40.
98. Cf. DL 6.
99. See DCD 3 for Anselm's fuller argument.
100. In DL 7 Anselm distinguishes only two wills (or two senses of "will"): the instrument-for-willing and the uses of this instrument.
101. The instrument-for-willing is thus the power-of-willing. Cf. DCV 4 (S II, 143:27–28).
102. Note DCD 4 (S I, 241:13–16).
103. See PF 37ff., where various distinctions occur. We are not required, however, to infer that this section of PF was written *later* than DC. Anselm is suggesting that he may publish another work; but portions of it may have been written prior to DC.
104. In DL 7 Anselm distinguishes only between will-as-instrument and will-as-use. DCD 13–14 discusses the will-as-inclination without designating it by this label. The present treatment is an explicit refinement of the view put forth in DCD.
105. DC I, 6 (S II, 256:22–23).
106. DC III, 2 (S II, 265:14–15). Note DV 12.
107. DV 4.
108. Gal. 5:17.

Notes

109. Cf. II Cor. 2:15.
110. II Cor. 2:16.
111. Gal. 5:17.
112. DC III, 7 (S II, 274:3–7). Note DCD 23 (S I, 270:1–3); DCV 2 (S II, 141:12–16).
113. See CDH II, 1.
114. Note DCD 20.
115. Note the first part of DC III, 4.
116. Note DC I, 6 (S II, 256:24); DC I, 7 (S II, 259:26); DCD 4 (S I, 242:3–10); DIV 10 (S II, 27:1–6); CDH II, 9 (S II, 105:22–24).

WITHDRAWN
SAINT PETER'S COLLEGE LIBRARY